Teaching English

D1149177

The Open University Postgraduate Certificate of Education

The readers in the PGCE series are:

Thinking Through Primary Practice
Teaching and Learning in the Primary School
Teaching and Learning in the Secondary School
Teaching English
Teaching Mathematics
Teaching Science
Teaching Technology
Teaching Modern Languages
Teaching History

All of these readers are part of an integrated teaching system; the selection is therefore related to other material available to students and is designed to evoke critical understanding. Opinions expressed are not necessarily those of the course team or of the University.

If you would like to study this course and receive a PGCE prospectus and other information about programmes of professional development in education, please write to the Central Enquiry Service, PO Box 200, The Open University, Walton Hall, Milton Keynes, MK7 6YZ. A copy of *Studying with the Open University* is available from the same address.

Teaching English

Edited by Susan Brindley
at The Open University

London and New York
in association with
The Open University

First published 1994
by Routledge
11 New Fetter Lane, London EC4P 4EE

Simultaneously published in the USA and Canada
by Routledge
29 West 35th Street, New York, NY 10001

Selection and editorial material: © 1994 The Open University

Typeset in Garamond by Florencetype Ltd, Kewstoke, Avon
Printed and bound in Great Britain by
Biddles Ltd, Guildford and King's Lynn

British Library Cataloguing in Publication Data
A catalogue record for this book is available from the British Library.

Library of Congress Cataloging in Publication Data
Teaching English / edited by Susan Brindley.
    p.   cm.
Includes bibliographical references (p.) and index.
1. English language–Study and teaching (Secondary)–England.
2. Language arts (Secondary)–England.   3. English language–Study
and teaching (Secondary)–Wales.   4. Language arts (Secondary)
–Wales.   I. Brindley, Susan, 1951–   .
LB1631.T275   1993
428'.0071'241–dc20   93-23077
                                                               CIP

ISBN 0–415–10251–0

Contents

Foreword

The form of teacher education is one of the most debated educational issues of the day. How is the curriculum of teacher education, particularly initial, pre-service education to be defined? What is the appropriate balance between practical school experience and the academic study to support such practice? What skills and competence can be expected of a newly qualified teacher? How are these skills formulated and assessed and in what ways are they integrated into an ongoing programme of professional development?

These issues have been at the heart of the development and planning of the Open University's programme of initial teacher training and education – the Postgraduate Certificate of Education (PGCE). Each course within the programme uses a combination of technologies, some of which are well tried and tested, while others, on information technology for example, may represent new and innovatory approaches to teaching. All, however, contribute in an integrated way towards fulfilling the aims and purposes of the course and programme.

All of the PGCE courses have readers which bring together a range of articles, extracts from books, and reports that discuss key ideas and issues, including specially commissioned chapters. The readers also provide a resource that can be used to support a range of teaching and learning in other types and structures of course.

This series from Routledge, in supporting the Open University PGCE programme, provides a contemporary view of developments in primary and secondary education and across a range of specialist subject areas. Its primary aim is to provide insights and analysis for those participating in initial education and training. Much of its content, however, will also be relevant to ongoing programmes of personal and institutional professional development. Each book is designed to provide an integral part of that basis of knowledge that we would expect of both new and experienced teachers.

Bob Moon
Professor of Education, The Open University

Introduction

Susan Brindley

> A good English teacher has to know about the subject . . . . You need to feel confident that if you don't understand, you can go to the teacher and she will get down to the point and sort you out. There's no point in having a confused pupil.

This observation was made by a markedly unconfused pupil in a recent conversation with a group of 16-year-olds about what makes a 'good' English teacher, and was met with approbation by the other members of the group. There were of course other contributions to the debate about what makes a 'good' English teacher (one pupil observed: 'it's important to have a teacher who's passionate about the work because if they really love teaching English then they inspire you'), but 'knowing the subject' was clearly a major criterion in the definition of good English teachers by those on the receiving end: the pupils in the classroom. *Teaching English* sets out to support the student teacher in that part of becoming a 'good' English teacher – 'knowing the subject' – by bringing together some of the thinking on key areas in English, and relating that thinking to effective classroom practice. The chapters, over half of which are newly commissioned, are written by people with substantial experience and expertise in their field. Existing articles have been selected for chapters as already having proved valuable to teachers of English. These chapters and their authors form part of the debate on English teaching and PGCE students will find that they will encounter the ideas and names elsewhere in their exploration of the subject. In areas of rapid change, such as assessment, the chapters chosen address the principles involved rather than discussing any current practices which may quickly become out of date.

Inevitably, word-length constraints also meant it was not possible to include all the articles which an ideal world would have allowed. However, each part of this reader was designed to tell at least part of the story of English teaching, so the chapters chosen had to play a double role: as valid in their own right, but also having a particular part to play in the telling of that story.

Teaching English offers an opportunity to engage with the debates in English teaching, and to explore the viewpoints of writers who have contributed to those debates. The notion of exploration is critical here. In reading *Teaching English* you, as reader, are being asked to take part in a dialogue: a dialogue which exists between yourself as reader and teacher of English, and the ideas on English teaching presented in this book. Indeed, your professional life as an English teacher will be characterised by such interaction with ideas and opinions; conversations about English with a variety of people including colleagues, parents and pupils are part of the life of an English teacher. This reader is intended to stimulate and inform these discussions.

ORGANISATION OF THE READER

The reader is divided into five parts which cover the development of English as a subject, the three major areas of speaking and listening, reading and writing, and the contribution research has made to the thinking about English teaching.

Part I

An historical perspective

The historical perspective approaches the evolution of English and English teaching through three chapters. The first, 'Shaping the image of an English teacher' by Robert Protherough and Judith Atkinson, traces significant developments since the beginning of the century and links these to the ways in which teachers of English have been formed. Their interviews with teachers of English lead them to conclude that, as far as a definition of English teaching is concerned, 'There is clearly no consensus here about what is to count as English' (p. 14). The second chapter, taken from *English Our English* by John Marenbon, takes quite the opposite point of view. John Marenbon challenges what he calls the 'new orthodoxy' of English teaching, which, he says, 'finds little value in grammatical correctness and has no place for literature as a heritage' (p. 16). In this chapter Marenbon describes his view of what should constitute effective English teaching. First published in 1987 by the Centre for Policy Studies, this chapter predates the writing of the National Curriculum which in itself began to define English in particular ways. In 1992, the NCC (now part of the School Curriculum and Assessment Authority) recommended a revision of the National Curriculum. In his letter of 15 July 1992 to the Secretary of State, John Patten, David Pascall, chair of NCC, wrote:

> We have discussed the issues involved at great length and have concluded that there is a case for change to ensure that the Order provides the best basis for meeting the objectives of the Education Reform Act.

The NCC was commissioned in September 1992 by the Secretary of State John Patten to undertake that revision. David Pascall continued in his letter:

> We intend . . . to develop the strengths of the current Order and we think

that teachers will recognise that our advice is designed to secure the objectives which they rightly consider to be important.

Professor Brian Cox, chair of the English Working Party whose report formed the basis of the National Curriculum, replies to this statement in the third chapter, 'The National Curriculum in English'. Brian Cox's chapter represents an important perspective, since the NCC recommendations were not met with the response by teachers anticipated in David Pascall's letter. Brian Cox argues that both the timing and the political dimension of the Orders give cause for concern. He foresees that 'These conflicts will continue through the 1990s'.

Chapter 1

Shaping the image of an English teacher

Robert Protherough and Judith Atkinson

THE PRE-HISTORY OF ENGLISH TEACHING

For how long has there been a separate, identifiable group that could be called English teachers? Not very long, certainly. Before the turn of the century, there was no subject 'English' (in the sense of an acknowledged, unified field of study) for them to teach.[1] The regulations of the 1890s treated 'English' as concerned solely with parsing and analysis, quite separate from reading, composition and literature, which might all be in the hands of different teachers.[2] Years later in London's elementary schools what we should consider English was still being divided and timetabled as nine separate 'subjects'.[3] Even while the subject was gaining wider acceptance in the early years of this century (made compulsory in state schools by the 1904 Regulations; its 'claim to a definite place in the curriculum of every secondary school' asserted by the Board of Education report of 1910) it is clear that the various English activities were not seen as the responsibility of one teacher. Indeed, that report had to argue strongly that literature and composition were not *really* separate subjects, and that it was 'eminently desirable' that the same teacher should be responsible for both.[4]

A decade later, the Historical Retrospect of the Newbolt Report opens by remarking that the subject has 'scarcely any history': 'Of conscious and direct teaching of English the past affords little sign'.[5] In the public and grammar schools, 'English was not seriously considered as an educational subject' (para. 105) and further up the educational hierarchy, 'it is not too much to say that, till quite lately, English had no position at all in the Universities' (191) and 'the serious study of English Language and Literature is a comparatively new one' (193).

Looking back, we can detect three overlapping phases resulting from universal compulsory education and the development of an increasingly specialised curriculum at secondary level. A concern for the discrete skills of English was slowly followed by the gradual establishing of English as a separate subject in the curriculum, and later still by the appointment of English teachers specifically responsible for it. As one significant study concluded, before the twentieth century 'there were certainly very few teachers who could be called or would have called themselves teachers of English'.[6]

Even for the next twenty years, circumstances were such that very few would have chosen to describe themselves in such a way. 'English' activities had a low social status because over the centuries the teaching of functional literacy to the working class had been seen as unskilled labour, and the reading of English literature was only for girls (while their brothers studied the classics). More profoundly, though, who could have been given the title of English teacher? Teachers in elementary schools would not have thought of themselves in such a way, for they were to work as generalists across the whole curriculum. (In the same way today, although some primary teachers will have specialised in English and may have responsibility for curriculum leadership in that subject, few refer to themselves as English teachers.) The certificated teachers, who in any case made up less than a third of those in elementary schools,[7] were trained in English grammar, reading, recitation, handwriting and English literature among the many other subjects to be 'covered' and examined, but there is no suggestion either of English as a single field of study or of teachers being specially trained for it. As late as 1929, English was just one of ten subjects to be included in training and when subject specialism did begin to appear, it was in other areas like physical education, music, art, woodwork and metalwork.[8]

At secondary level also, when the training of teachers began to expand after the 1902 Act, English was seen as a necessary qualification for entrants, but not as a subject for specialist training. Because the university degree was thought an adequate preparation, and training was regarded as socially demeaning, the absence of degree courses in English ensured both the low status of that subject in schools and the lack of qualified teachers to teach it. Such an inevitable correlation between English literature as a university subject and the training of teachers had been pointed out in the 1880s. Arguing for the establishment of the subject at Oxford as a way of disseminating it more widely, John Churton Collins wrote that its ability to fulfil that function 'depends obviously on the training of its teachers, and the training of its teachers depends as obviously on the willingness or the unwillingness of the Universities to provide that training'.[9]

Because of the relative unwillingness of the universities to contemplate either English or education as academic subjects,[10] it was not until the 1920s and later that graduate English teachers began to emerge in any numbers, and the subject was not regarded as a desirable or even necessary specialism in the public and grammar schools to which most graduates went. According to one headmaster, in 1918 English was viewed with 'belittlement', 'distrust' and 'contempt'.[11] The same author (lamenting the 'few and fumbling' attempts of classics teachers to work with English literature) anticipated a future in which English graduates might take their place in schools, developing new methods, linking reading with writing 'as the importance of their subject becomes more and more recognised'.[12] But that still lay ahead.

THE SIGNIFICANCE OF THE NEWBOLT REPORT

We owe the modern concept of an English teacher, symbolically at least, to the publication of the Newbolt Report, *The Teaching of English in England*, in 1921. By defining English in a quite new way, it created a climate in which English teaching as a specialised profession became inevitable. One simple way of suggesting its influence is to examine the number of texts published on English teaching at different periods. Whereas very few volumes with *Teaching of English* in their titles appeared in the first twenty years of this century, at least thirteen significant books so named were issued between 1921 and 1932.

In the report, 'English' was no longer used to describe a conglomerate of separate skills or a group of 'English subjects', but as a single, organic, all-embracing term for a unique, central school subject, requiring – by implication – special men and women to teach it. The particular concepts that animated the committee were by no means new,[13] but the novelty lay in bringing together under the title of English, 'taught as a fine art', four separate concepts: the universal need for literacy as the core of the curriculum, the developmental importance of children's self-expression, a belief in the power of English literature for moral and social improvement, and a concern for 'the full development of mind and character'. The frontiers of the subject were thus pushed out to cover a whole range of mental, emotional, imaginative, moral and spiritual goals: 'almost convertible with thought', 'a method' as well as 'a subject' that 'must have entry everywhere' (para. 57).

This largely expedient and perhaps deliberately ambiguous map of the subject, colonising areas that had previously lain within other disciplines, has been enormously influential. After the sufferings and doubts of the First World War, English as a newly minted subject was invested with the resonance of 'Englishness', defined through the English language and supremely through the heritage of English literature. It was through a shared experience of English, said the report, drawing on Matthew Arnold, that the social class divisions of the country could be healed and a 'national culture' be established.[14] The committee could hardly have foreseen that a series of debates and divisions lasting into the 1990s would centre on these interconnected definitions of English culture, of the literary heritage and of the teaching and learning of English. Henry Widdowson could justifiably complain in his note of reservation to the Kingman Report that 'what English is on the curriculum *for*, is not really explored here with any rigour'.[15]

The Newbolt Report is thin on practical details about the kinds of teaching that might achieve its aims, or about the kinds of English teacher that might be needed. In proposing a quite new curricular framework, the committee had no existing tradition to draw on. A new sort of subject would demand new kinds of teachers to remedy the failings of the past and present and to bring about the aspirations for the future. The section headings repeatedly use words like neglect, problem, lack, difficulties, and misapprehensions. English *should* be 'the only basis possible for a national education' (para. 9), 'the one indispensable preliminary and foundation of all the rest' which must 'take precedence of all other branches of learning' (6), 'the essential basis of a liberal education for all English people' (13). By contrast with this ideal, however, the members of the committee said that what they found in actuality was 'an altogether inadequate recognition of the place of English in an Englishman's education' (para. 191, echoing 1), caused by a failure to establish the subject as important in schools and universities and by the parallel failure to attract and train teachers for it.

The laudable ambitions for English as a subject depended – as the committee realised – on the provision of appropriately qualified teachers, but the report reveals a basic uncertainty about what those appropriate qualifications are, and indeed about what good English teaching might actually look like. The report admits that 'the methods of teaching English have yet to be explored' (para. 101), and adds that at secondary level, 'probably the greatest obstacle to improvement hitherto has been the absence of a good tradition in the teaching of English' (109). It quotes an Inspectors' Memorandum on the 'unfortunate' truth that 'methods of teaching English are so far little developed. They have been far less thought out than the methods of teaching some other subjects' (117). Three years later, making the best of a bad job and referring vaguely to 'the many difficult questions of method involved in the teaching of English', the Board of Education remarked hopefully that at least 'in developing his [*sic*] method the teacher of English has the advantage of being bound by no tradition'.[16]

Looking back, with the benefit of hindsight, it is possible to see how several distinct but powerful strands of thinking came together in the 1920s to create a model of English teaching that was formative. In bold oversimplification we can detect three of these. First there was the missionary role of English, called on to confront the forces of industrialism and to counter the growing influence of the media. The recurrent images in the report were of people being starved while weeds flourished in the fields; of the power of literature to feed, to purify, to unify, to redeem. Margaret Mathieson has argued that in a time of crisis the functions traditionally attributed to religious faith were attached to a new and idealistic view of English teaching.[17] This idea ran through the Newbolt Report, and was given celebrated expression in George Sampson's claim that the purpose of education is 'not to prepare children for their occupations, but to prepare children against their occupations'.[18] Second, there was the Dewey-inspired emphasis on learning by doing, the notion that English should develop creativity, foreshadowed in the 1910 recommendations about the importance of oral work and by the influence of men like Caldwell Cook.[19] Third, in an age when the influence of the classics was waning, English was seen as the chief way of conveying a cultural tradition, developing sensitivity and moral awareness. For most children, literature would mean English literature. Such a view was pushed to its logical conclusion by F.R. Leavis, who in 1930 argued that teachers of English were ultimately responsible for the health of the language, for the growth of moral values and eventually for the whole quality of life itself.[20] At Cambridge in particular the 'missionary' emphasis of the Newbolt Report was reframed with specific attention to what should be taught and how. This, as Francis Mulhern has argued, emphasised the notion of a professional career in English centring on talent rather than on establishment values of birth and breeding.[21] By contrast with an academic English hierarchy that had become inward looking in its obsession with establishing professional status, the *Scrutiny* group looked out to society, and particularly to the wider education system.

These three trends combined to give a seductively important role to English teachers. They were called to be the elite of the profession, concerned not simply with teaching a subject, but with the total personal and social development of pupils and with the health of society. By 1930 English was becoming a dominant university discipline. 'In terms of its eventually achieved overall influence, at both institutional and symbolic levels, the success of English proved to be more dramatic than that of any other subject.'[22]

WHAT SORT OF ANIMAL IS AN ENGLISH TEACHER?

The emergence of English as a coherent subject demanded the creation of a quite new kind of teacher, shaped in ways that had not previously been considered. The recommendations of the Newbolt Report implied that such a person would require a literary training (though hardly of the kind then offered by English degree courses), a range of personal qualities (sensitivity, understanding), an ability to unlock the creative potential of children (then the province of educational psychology), a social concern for all kinds of children, and some (largely undefined) expertise in language. English teachers were not to be concerned with vocational or utilitarian training ('commercial English is objectionable' because 'the needs of business are best met by a liberal education' – recommendation 30). Nor was their chief concern the imparting of knowledge, but the changing of lives. This depended on establishing a special relationship between teacher and taught ('there is no lesson like the poetry lesson for producing that intimacy between teacher and class which makes school a happy place' – para. 92).

In this crucial respect George Sampson was at one with the official report: both were clear that English was unlike many other school subjects, in that it required essential personal qualities that could not be guaranteed by formal academic qualifications. Sampson said that the English teacher's chief concern was 'not the minds he [sic] can measure but the souls he can save'.[23] This concern for personal qualities was to become a recurrent note from 1921 onwards. Quotations above have indicated the committee's desire to ground an English teacher's abilities in 'necessary insight and enthusiasm' (para. 11), 'knowledge, interest, and the gift of communicating their own enthusiasm' (130), rather than in any particular specialism. Indeed they quote the celebrated (or notorious) judgement that 'the ideal teacher is born, not made' (129). Sampson made the comparison with other subjects specific: 'University qualifications are a safe enough guide when you are looking for acquirements – when you want a science master or a history master; but not when you are choosing someone to be a medium for the transmission of the spirit.'[24] In his conclusion he laments that: 'We have never insisted that the chief and crowning qualification of an English teacher is ability to teach English' – an early expression of the idea that pedagogic not academic qualities are of most importance. (He does, of course, agree that the two may coexist; they are not alternatives.) His view, which must have seemed insanely idealistic at the time, has turned out to be true and prophetic. The only reason that the right sort of English teachers did not exist, he writes, is that society had never asked for them. 'Let the paramount claim of English be admitted and teachers will shape themselves and be shaped for the task of teaching it.'

To teach a subject that in many ways is more than a subject and that has major repercussions outside the classroom walls, has imposed a special responsibility on English teachers, and helps to explain why they are so vulnerable to criticism. Administrators are more comfortable with subjects that have clearly defined specialist knowledge with firm academic boundaries and that are remote from what is learned within the home and the community. A head of department told us of an occasion when she was seeking an additional member of staff. The Head produced a recent advertisement, and suggested that this would do, with another word substituted for 'historian'. 'What word do you use for someone who teaches English?' he asked, and was not satisfied with the answer, 'English teacher'. Proper subjects are taught by people called historians, geographers, physicists and modern linguists, he implied; knowledge of the subject rather than the teaching of it is primary. By contrast, new definitions of English, new ranking of objectives, new styles of teaching, take on additional significance that is not limited to the subject classroom, because 'changing English is changing schooling'[25] – and potentially even more than that. What James Donald has called 'the intractable problem' of English teaching is that 'it remains trapped within its sense of being called to a social and cultural mission – whether healing the State or empowering people to escape its oppressions'.[26] Arguments about what should, or should not, be read in school, about 'correctness' in talk or writing, about assessment and so on, are actually arguments about shaping young people's views of the world. Reflecting on his Working Group's report, Professor Brian Cox has said that 'a National Curriculum in English is intimately involved with questions about our national identity, indeed with the whole future ethos of British society. The teaching of English . . . affects the individual and social identity of us all.'[27]

English has a special power to challenge conventions, institutions, governments, business interests – any established system. This resides in the fact that English is concerned with the uncontrollable power of a shared language that we all speak and the uncontrollable responses to what we read. The work of English teaching involves continual pressing for the expression of alternative ideas, inviting challenge to received opinions, seeking strong personal responses, establishing debate. The teacher's special relationship with students depends on democratie openness, not on knowing the answers. The subject matter of English lessons is likely to draw on the actual interests and experiences of pupils, where they may be more informed than those who teach them. It is often said that English teachers are more in tune with youth culture than those who work in other subjects.

WHAT DOES AN ENGLISH TEACHER TEACH?

One recent book, from the first page onwards, repeatedly uses words like 'unique', 'distinctive', and 'special' to describe English studies.[28] In curricular terms, it is easy to list reasons why this should be so: the subject is uniquely poised between school and the wider life. Only a small part of the teaching of English is carried out by English teachers; children arrive at school with a wealth of existing language experience; the goals of English are not simply subject-specific ones, but are concerned with all aspects of learning and living. English teaches the abilities that underlie the learning of all other subjects. English lessons are concerned with all aspects of the individual; thoughts and feelings are inseparable; students' responses are an essential element of what is being studied; individual differences are often more significant than universal truths. Because there is no generally agreed body of subject matter, the boundaries of the subject are notoriously unclear and cannot be neatly defined.

It is significant that during the upheavals of the 1980s there has been such a flood of books posing basic theoretical questions about what English is or should be. Simply to consider the many titles is enough, with their emphasis on rereading, rewriting or reordering the tradition, on changes, new directions or perspectives, on widening, extending or even exploding the subject.[29] People have talked so much of the 'crisis' in English studies that the prophecy has become self-fulfilling. As different models (or paradigms) of English teaching have successively come under attack, it has become plain both that there is no return to some 'innocent' English and also that there is little prospect of replacing English with some agreed alternative, whatever it might be called (Cultural Studies or Textual Studies, according to some). As Francis Mulhern has argued, 'we face a situation in which a maximum of intellectual attack, a maximum of desire to reconstruct the subject, coincide with a near-minimum of institutional opportunity'.[30]

It is hardly surprising, then, in a survey we conducted of over 110 English teachers, younger teachers expressed uncertainty about the nature of their subject: 'English has emerged as a much wider subject than I had anticipated'. Even the most experienced are still tentative, saying 'there are no certainties' or 'I think it is more complex now than I thought (and I thought it "the hardest subject to teach" then)'. Examining the terminology, the underlying images, used by our sample of English teachers helps to define their sense of subject identity, to establish the hidden curriculum which affects the way in which they make sense of the world, or initiate students and new teachers into the community. Their comments illustrate the validity of the Cox Report's judgement about different, coexisting models of the subject:

> It is possible to identify within the English teaching profession a number of different views of the subject . . . . We stress that they are not the only possible views, they are not sharply distinguishable, and they are certainly not mutually exclusive . . . . Teachers of English will differ in the weight they give to each of these views of the subject.[31]

Many teachers offered views of the subject that fit neatly enough into one or another of the five generalized models put forward in the report.

1 *A personal growth view.* 'The basis of our work is (or should be) human growth and development'; 'nurturing individual development'; 'aware of the centrality of the pupil'; 'our "subject" is so close to the learner – *is* the learner and the process of learning'; 'growth of the whole person through expressive explorations'.
2 *A cross-curricular view.* 'I see it now as being part of the whole curriculum, and see much more how things should link'; 'English will have to become less introverted and accept the cross-curricular development'; 'language is central to all learning so English teachers have a great responsibility'; 'they bear a significant responsibility for the development of language skills and thus help to determine how "accessible" the school curriculum is for pupils in all areas'.
3 *An adult needs view.* 'I see English more as a tool to develop social skills and preparation for the world of work'; 'our subject is a service subject'; 'more need to justify its value in a vocation-orientated curriculum'; 'inner resources and an external structure to deal with the world outside school'.
4 *A cultural heritage view.* 'It consists in maximum exposure to literature';

'saving literature from being marginalised'; 'I believed in bringing great literature to children'; 'as a product of *Use of English* teachers and taught by Leavis sympathisers at university, I went into teaching with those assumptions'.

5 *A cultural analysis view.* 'I've realised its situation within cultural and political frameworks'; 'I see English . . . in terms of developing autonomy and critical awareness – skills and attitudes'; 'cultural development model'; 'a need to assimilate the conceptual revolution of post-structuralist thought'; 'root English in a social view of language'; 'need to reflect multi-racial society'.

Possibly more striking are the comments which implicitly establish a comparison between different models, rejecting some or claiming to have abandoned one in favour of another. Teachers write, for example, of resisting the pressures to cater for the 'needs of technology and form-filling' or 'the further rise of instrumental rationality via TVEI, etc.'; they say that English 'must not be seen as a service medium' or talk of their 'refusal to see the subject English simply as a garage servicing the needs and demands of other subject areas'; they fear that 'the experience of literature of many children will be diminished' or defend 'cultural activities and their importance to survival'. In a number of cases they reveal a change of perception ('I now see . . .') and of practice, a paradigm shift. 'I no longer have a passionate commitment to Great Literature', says one; another now sees pupils as 'human beings in complex social interactions rather than spirits to be nurtured'; a third records that teaching is 'now less (a) literary (b) personal/affective, and more sociologically, politically informed'; a fourth says 'originally I placed too much emphasis on "lit." (having come through school then university) instead of language skills'.

Such a range of views and such evidence of rethinking bear witness to two points raised in the Cox Report: the scale and uncertain boundaries of the subject ('such broadness poses problems' – 2.2) and the impossibility of establishing fixed, permanent principles ('views about English teaching have developed and changed over the past twenty years and will continue to do so' – 2.4).

When English teachers in our survey were asked, 'What do you see as the most urgent problems facing English teachers at this time?', 30 per cent referred to problems concerning the definition or modelling of the subject itself. They mentioned, for example, 'confusion about what "English" is and does', 'maintaining and promoting the special "Englishness" of English', 'the need to reaffirm the type of model of English teaching just described', 'developing a coherent rationale for the subject', 'insecurity regarding the nature of English as a discipline', 'how to maintain an English identity', or – more specifically – 'to fight an over-simplified view of language study as the centre of English studies', 'to establish English among the Arts', 'maintenance of the "progressive" ideal' or 'thinking clearly about what would happen to pedagogy if we accepted the Eagleton camp-followers as gurus'. There is clearly no consensus here about what is to count as English.

NOTES AND REFERENCES

1 For a fuller account, see Protherough, R. (1989). 'English as a subject', in *Students of English*. London, Routledge.
2 Board of Education (1921). *The Teaching of English in England* (the Newbolt Report). London, HMSO, para. 51.
3 Sampson, G. (1921). *English for the English*. Cambridge, Cambridge University Press, p. 20.
4 Board of Education (1910). *The Teaching of English in Secondary Schools*. London, HMSO, para. 10.
5 *The Teaching of English in England,* para. 18.
6 Ball, S.J. (1982). 'Competition and conflict in the teaching of English; a socio-historical analysis', *Journal of Curriculum Studies* 14(1):1.
7 Lawson, J. (1965). 'The historical background', *Aspects of Education* 3: 14–28.
8 Dent, H.C. (1977). *The Training of Teachers in England and Wales 1800–1975*. Sevenoaks, Hodder and Stoughton, ch. 7.
9 Collins, J.C. (1887). 'Can English Literature be taught?', *The Nineteenth Century* 22: 658.
10 See *Students of English*, ch. 1 and works referred to there.
11 Smith, N. (1918). 'The place of literature in education', in A.C. Benson (ed.), *Cambridge Essays on Education*. Cambridge, Cambridge University Press, pp. 107–8.
12 *Ibid.*, pp. 118–19.
13 See, for example, Doyle, B. (1989). *English and Englishness*. London, Routledge, ch. 1.
14 Such ideas still animated the *Spens Report* of 1938, with its view that English teaching could 'soften the distinctions which separate men and classes in later life' (para. 222).
15 DES (1988). *Report of the Committee of Inquiry into the Teaching of English Language*. London, HMSO, p. 7. Compare this with George Sampson's (1921) comment nearly 70 years earlier that 'it cannot be said that the place of English in education is clearly seen', *English for the English*. Cambridge, Cambridge University Press, p. 15.
16 Board of Education (1924). *Some Suggestions for the Teaching of English in Secondary Schools in England*. London, HMSO, paras 1 and 10.
17 Mathieson, M. (1975). *The Preachers of Culture*. London, Allen and Unwin.
18 *English for the English*, p. 11.
19 Cook, C. (1917). *The Play Way*. London, Heinemann.
20 Leavis, F.R. (1930). *Mass Civilization and Minority Culture*. Cambridge, Gordon Fraser.
21 Mulhern, F. (1979). *The Moment of 'Scrutiny'*. London, New Left Books.
22 *English and Englishness*, p. 4.
23 *English for the English*, p. 2.
24 *Ibid.*, p. 79.
25 Goodson, I. and Medway, P. (1990). *Bringing English to Order*. London, Falmer Press, p. vii.

26 Donald, J. (1989). In P. Brooker and P. Humm (eds). *Dialogue and Difference*. London, Routledge, p. 28.
27 Cox, B. (1990). Editorial, *Critical Quarterly* 32(4): 2.
28 *Bringing English to Order, op. cit.*
29 For example, *Re-reading English* (1982), *New Directions in English Teaching* (1982), *Changing English* (1984), *Rewriting English* (1985), *Broadening the Context: English and Cultural Studies* (1987), *Dialogue and Difference: English into the Nineties* (1989), *Bringing English to Order* (1990), *Thinking through English* (1990), *Exploding English* (1990).
30 Mulhern, F. (1987). 'Prospects for English', *The English Magazine* 19:32.
31 DES (1989). *English for Ages 5 to 16*. London, HMSO, paras 2.20 and 2.27.

Chapter 2

The new orthodoxy examined

John Marenbon

THE 'NEW ORTHODOXY'

Grammatical and literary failings among young people are evidence that, in most schools today, English is badly taught, and that it used to be taught better. But English teachers themselves would not agree. Nor would the official body responsible for assessing their activities – HMI (Her Majesty's Inspectorate). To HMI, English is flourishing; in many a school it singles out English teachers for special praise, and its criticisms are reserved for those who persist in traditional ways of teaching grammar and comprehension. HMI does not blame schools for producing pupils unable to write standard English grammatically and ignorant of the literary classics, because it subscribes to a set of views about English teaching which developed in the 1960s and have now gained the status of an orthodoxy. This new orthodoxy finds little value in grammatical correctness and has no place for literature as a heritage. It is shared, not only by many English teachers and HMI, but by educationalists, boards of examination and the authors of textbooks. Seven tenets characterise the new orthodoxy about teaching the English language:

- English is not just a subject;
- English teaching should be child centred;
- It is as important to teach the spoken as the written language;
- Assessment should not concentrate on the pupil's errors;
- Grammar is descriptive not prescriptive;
- No language or dialect is inherently superior to any other;
- Language use should be judged by its appropriateness.

THE SPREAD OF THE NEW ORTHODOXY

The new orthodoxy was the invention of educational theorists. But it did not long remain confined to their narrow circle. It was given official sanction in the Bullock Report of 1975. It has come to dominate the judgements of HMI and to regulate the assessments of the unit at the DES employed to monitor standards in schools. And the thinking behind the new GCSE examinations is based on it.

The new orthodoxy in the Bullock Report

Even by the title of its report, *A Language for Life*, Sir Alan Bullock's Committee indicated how fully it had absorbed the new orthodoxy. A brief chapter (remarkable for its confusion, vagueness and ignorant mishandling of the philosophical concepts it employs) offers a 'theoretical foundation' for the report, which is summarised in its concluding sentence: 'to exploit the process of discovery through language in all its uses is the surest means of enabling a child to master his mother tongue'.[1] Noting the close links between the acquisition of language and any sort of learning, the report rejects any notion of English as a distinctive subject, with a body of knowledge and a set of techniques which its teachers should transmit. The teacher's function is, rather, to help children in their 'process of discovery'. The report rejects 'correctness' as a concept to be used in judging speech, preferring 'appropriateness' as the criterion. Linguists, it comments, have long held the view 'that an utterance may be "correct" in one linguistic situation but not in another'. By using the criterion of appropriateness, it suggests, teachers will be operating 'positively rather than negatively': 'the aim is not to alienate the child from a form of language with which he has grown up and which serves him efficiently in the speech community of his neighbourhood'. Although the child should be enabled to 'use standard forms when they are needed . . . the teacher should start where the child is and should accept the language he brings to school'.[2] In written language too the children should begin from the forms most natural to the child: 'the first task of the teacher is one of encouraging vitality and fluency in the expressive writing that is nearest to speech'.[3]

The Bullock Report draws from these more abstract discussions a number of specific recommendations about teaching methods:

- teachers should not dominate the class but rather encourage the active participation of all the pupils;
- great attention should be paid to 'oracy';
- traditional language exercises, designed to teach correct grammar, should in general be avoided;
- in correcting work, teachers should not pay too much attention to 'surface features' (such as spelling and grammar).

The new orthodoxy and Her Majesty's Inspectorate

HMI's most explicit discussion of the English curriculum, *English from 5 to 16*, is unusual in considering that English teachers should, among other things, aim 'to teach pupils *about* language, so that they achieve a working knowledge of its structure'.[4] This idea was misinterpreted by newspaper reports, which viewed the document as an attempt to reintroduce 'traditional lessons on grammar, spelling and punctuation'.[5] But in fact, in *English from 5 to 16* as elsewhere, HMI shares the new orthodoxy's hostility to old-fashioned *prescriptive* grammar; what the booklet suggests – and that only tentatively – is that more *descriptive* grammar should be taught in schools. In general, *English from 5 to 16* advocates the new orthodoxy. Teaching English is not, it explains, just a matter of imparting skills or knowledge: 'in teaching English we are teaching pupils to think clearly, to be self aware, and to be responsible to their experience of the world of people and things about them'.[6] 'Oracy' receives as much emphasis as literacy; and the teacher is to make his or her start with what children 'want or need to say': 'the language children bring with them from their home backgrounds should not be criticised, belittled or proscribed. The aim should be to *extend* their language repertoires.'[7]

Nevertheless, the original version of this booklet *did* place an emphasis on teaching standard English which is not to be found in HMI's other pronouncements, although it attributed this importance merely to the fact that standard English happens to be 'appropriate' in many contexts. This feature of the booklet, along with the rigour and specificity of the objectives it proposed for pupils at different ages, provoked widespread criticism from teachers. In response, HMI produced a second edition of the booklet, with revised recommendations more clearly in line with the new orthodoxy. For instance, in the revised edition the author stresses that non-standard forms are not 'inherently inferior, or limited in their capacity to convey meaning; in some respects indeed they may be "superior" ';[8] he acknowledges that 'the case for recognising ethnic diversity in English within the framework of commonly agreed objectives has been strengthened by the responses';[9] he removes the rigorous and precise specifications of the original version and replaces them with mere examples of 'the qualities, attitudes and skills which pupils should be seen to be acquiring at the age points given'.[10]

WHAT IS WRONG WITH THE NEW ORTHODOXY

No part of the new orthodoxy, now so widespread among theorists, officials and teachers, stands up to scrutiny. Its tenets express, at best, half truths, in which a point of common sense is exaggerated and distorted; and sometimes not even that.

'English is not just a subject'

This view has a positive aspect (English is more than a subject) and a negative one (English has no specific, definable subject matter). The positive aspect is misguided, and the negative unnecessary. It is doubtless valuable that children should grow emotionally, that they should learn to tolerate the views of others and to engage in critical thinking. But these – and many of the other ambitious aims often proposed for English – are virtues which are slowly acquired in the course of acquiring particular intellectual skills and areas of knowledge. Time given to a vague and generalised attempt to gain such virtues is time lost to the specific and rigorous studies which alone will foster them. English could be one of these studies, were it to pursue the simple and well-defined aims of teaching children to write and speak standard English correctly, and of initiating their acquaintance with the literary heritage of the language.

'English teaching should be child centred'

Good teachers have always recognised that effective instruction requires the active participation of the pupil: unless the pupil's attention and efforts are engaged, the pupil will learn nothing. But the pupil's interest is merely a necessary condition for learning: there is no good reason why it should determine *what* he or she learns. Few would contest this view with regard, for instance, to mathematics. The good mathematics teacher may well gain the pupils' interest by showing how numbers and their relations are relevant to their everyday concerns; but he or she will base his or her teaching not on the pupils' view of their needs, but on his or her own, informed, view of what they need to know in order gradually to achieve a mastery of mathematical techniques. So long as English, too, is recognised as a subject, with definite aims, the same principles should guide its teachers. The grammar of English, its range of vocabulary and styles and its literary heritage exist independently of the child who is learning to use them.

'It is as important to teach the spoken as the written language'

Spoken language is as important – in some respects more important – than written language. But, whereas writing and reading are skills that require specific instruction, children learn to speak and listen just by being present at these activities. The child learns to speak and listen *better* in three main ways: first, by practice in the course of everyday life; second, by coming to understand more about all the various particular activities which can be the subjects of conversation (the more the child knows about – for instance – woodwork, the more easily he or she can be taught to discuss it); third, by mastering the standard written language and thereby increasing his or her range of vocabulary, grasp of syntax and ability to choose standard forms correctly.

The fashionable emphasis on 'oracy' is in part a product of the tendency to regard English, not as a subject, but as an opportunity to acquire a haphazard collection of virtues (maturity, tolerance and so on); and in part an attempt to reduce the importance of standard English (which is the most usual form of the written language).

'Assessment should not concentrate on the pupil's errors'

No good teacher sets out to discourage and demoralise his or her pupils, concentrating on their mistakes to the exclusion of all else. But exponents of the new orthodoxy do not merely wish to insist on this sensible maxim. Their view, that it is 'more important to see what the child can do, rather than what he cannot', sounds tolerant and humane; but, in fact, it condemns those who speak and write badly to go on speaking and writing badly. The dire effects which it has are a simple consequence of other tenets of the new orthodoxy when they are applied to the question of assessment: the belief that English teaching should be child centred, and the belief that supposed mistakes in speech and writing are, at worst, examples of inappropriate use of language. If these tenets are rejected, then this view of assessment is left without support.

'Grammar is descriptive not prescriptive'

The error of this position is to assume that description must be an *alternative* to prescription. By describing how a certain language is spoken or written, the grammarian prescribes usage for those who wish to speak or write that language. The case is the same for varieties of any given language. A grammar which describes standard English prescribes English usage for those who wish to speak or write it.

Whether the grammarian should phrase his or her discussion in descriptive or prescriptive terms depends on the purpose of his or her work. If, for instance, the grammarian is writing a monograph for linguists, who know well how to speak and write standard English but who are interested in how its various usages are to be analysed and classified, he or she will rightly use a descriptive terminology. But if the grammarian is writing so as to teach schoolchildren how to write and speak standard English, it will be proper for him or her to prescribe. The prescriptive manner of old-fashioned school grammars, usually condemned by modern linguists, was entirely appropriate to their function.

Exponents of the new orthodoxy often use the statement that 'grammar is descriptive not prescriptive' as the slogan for their case against prescriptive teaching of standard English. In this way they manage to suggest that anyone who disagrees with them has simply misunderstood the nature of grammar. But the misunderstanding is theirs. Grammar prescribes by describing.

'No language or dialect is inherently superior to any other'

This principle of linguistic equality can be understood in three different ways. Exponents of the new orthodoxy believe that it is true according to all these three interpretations.

It might be taken merely as a recognition that there is no intrinsic link between communicative adequacy and the particular forms of any given language. By this interpretation, the principle of linguistic equality is almost certainly true.

By another interpretation the principle of linguistic equality means that all languages are equally regular and rule governed. This position is justified in one important way. Speech in, for instance, Cockney or West Indian Creole is sometimes described as 'ungrammatical'. The linguist is right to object to this description: although Cockney and West Indian Creole do not follow the grammar of standard English, they each have their own implicit rules, which modern grammarians have succeeded in describing. The linguist must, however, qualify this view. Whereas *all* the speech of someone who speaks standard English only will tend, by and large, to bear out the rules with which linguists describe standard English, *all* the speech of dialect or creole speakers is unlikely to bear out the rules which describe their dialect or creole. Parts of their speech will follow, not the rules of their own language, but those of the standard language; and, at moments, usage may reflect rules which belong to neither.

By a third interpretation, the principle of linguistic equality means that every language is wholly (and therefore equally) adequate to the needs of the speakers. There is a sense in which this statement is not just true, but truistic. The only measure of a man's linguistic need in a particular area of life is the language he actually uses in that area of life – a language which will therefore be by definition fully adequate, whatever it is. But exponents of the new orthodoxy do not usually take adequacy to need in so limited a way: rather, they assume that the needs of speakers of different languages and dialects are all roughly the same, and that every language and dialect is equally capable of fulfilling them. From these premises they draw the conclusion that no one language is intrinsically more subtle, logical or precise than another; no one language, except by accidental convenience, more apt than another for any particular type of use or activity. This is a remarkable position, and a mistaken one.

'Language use should be judged by its appropriateness'

One of the criteria for judging the use of language is certainly appropriateness: the man who speaks to his wife as if she were a public meeting, or addresses a scientific congress in the language of the nursery, cannot be said to use language well. But exponents of the new orthodoxy are not content with this commonsensical position. Since they advocate the principle of linguistic equality, not only in its first and second, but also in its third interpretations, they believe that appropriateness is the *only* criterion for judging one language or sort of language superior to another. They conclude that, whilst one language might, as a matter of fact, happen to be more convenient or appropriate for a particular sort of occasion, there is no way in which any one language is intrinsically better than another. They allow that standard English is a better language than Cockney or Scouse for writing a business letter, because most businessmen or women will receive a letter in standard English more favourably than one in dialect. But they deny that, in itself, any one language is more precise, logical, flexible or subtle than another. These conclusions cannot be upheld, once the third interpretation of the principle of linguistic equality is rejected.

The importance of standard English

At the centre of the new orthodoxy is its devaluation of standard English. From this derives its exponents' hostility to grammatical prescription: *because* they do not think that standard English is superior to dialect, they do not believe that its grammar should be prescribed to children (a position they try to support by mistakenly insisting that grammar cannot ever prescribe); *because* they cannot accept that standard English is superior to dialect, they insist that the language schoolchildren use can be judged only by its 'appropriateness'.

Why is standard English superior to dialect? One important reason has already been suggested. Standard English has been developed over centuries to fulfil a far wider range of functions than any dialect – from technical description to philosophical argument, from analysis of information to fiction and poetry. Only by using another language (such as French) which had been developed similarly, over centuries, by a similar culture, could the speaker enjoy a similar resource.

Standard English gains another advantage over dialect by the very fact of being standard. When a linguist formulates the grammar of a dialect, he or she is engaged in an exercise which is to a considerable degree artificial. Dialect is always changing: from decade to decade, from village to village, from street to street. Outside the textbooks of sociolinguists, it is never clear exactly which of the constructions that dialect speakers are using are grammatical and which are not, because it is never clear exactly which dialect they are speaking, or how consistently they are intending to speak it. Standard languages change too; but very, very slowly. The linguists may be quick to come forward with examples of constructions where usage within modern standard English is undecided. But, for the vast majority of constructions, all who know standard English will recognise instantly not only whether they are correct or incorrect, but whether they are usual or unusual in their context.

It is far easier to destroy a standard language than to create one. A standard language requires a body of speakers who have been trained to distinguish correct constructions from incorrect ones, usual forms from those which are unusual and carry with them special implications. Such training is neither short nor easy; and it is unrealistic to expect that English teachers can give it to their pupils if, along with teaching standard English (as one form of the language, appropriate for certain occasions), they are expected to encourage speech and writing in dialect and to attend to the multiplicity of other tasks with which modern educationalists have burdened them. By devaluing standard English, the new orthodoxy is destroying it.

HOW ENGLISH COULD BE BETTER TAUGHT IN SCHOOLS

The good English teacher's aims

A better approach to English teaching in schools would reject every tenet of the new orthodoxy. It would recognise English as a subject – no more and no less: the subject in which pupils learn to write standard English correctly and thereby to speak it well, and in which they become acquainted with some of the English literary heritage. As such it would contain a distinct body of material which teachers must teach and pupils must learn. English teaching would therefore be 'child centred' only in the very limited sense that all good teaching is child centred – that it engages the interest and efforts of the pupils. Improvement in pupils' powers of speaking and listening would be achieved by improving their literacy.

The teacher would not hesitate to prescribe to the children on matters of grammatical correctness. He or she would recognise the superiority of standard English and see it as his or her task to make pupils write it well and thereby gain the ability to speak it fluently. It does not follow from this that the teacher would scorn dialects or their speakers. On the contrary, the teacher would realise that many people use a dialect (or some dialect forms) in order to identify themselves as belonging to a particular social group. The teacher would not expect pupils to give up their dialect when talking to their friends or family, but would recognise that children come to English lessons at school in order to be taught standard English. The teacher would not, however, see it as an important part of his or her work to instruct the pupils in any specific sort of pronunciation of English (such as Received Pronunciation); but, just as he or she would try to avoid mistaking regional variations in pronunciation for errors in spoken language, so he or she would try not to overlook errors in spoken language by mistaking them for regional variations in pronunciation. And the teacher would recognise that some regional accents can make their speakers' English hard to follow, especially to those from outside Britain.

A teacher who followed these tenets would set tasks and exercises for the pupils, not as some inchoate attempt to induce self-criticism, tolerance, maturity or liveliness of imagination, but with the definite object of improving their use of language. The teacher would regard the tasks and exercises proposed both by older textbooks and by newer ones critically but with an open mind. If the old-fashioned textbooks and worksheets seemed dull, he or she would consider whether their dullness was merely an unnecessary obstacle to engaging pupils' interest or whether it was inevitable in what they sought to teach. The teacher would recognise that the process of learning is often laborious and makes considerable demands on children's self-discipline. If the task suggested by modern books on English teaching seemed strange to the teacher, he or she would nevertheless be willing to set them, so long as he or she was persuaded that they were the best way of making pupils learn an important aspect of correct speech or writing.

When such a teacher came to assess the pupils' work, he or she would be guided by the principle that, in English as surely as in mathematics or chemistry, there is right and wrong. Like any good teacher, he or she would mingle encouragement with correction, but would not let an exaggerated concern to dwell on the pupil's successes distract him or her from the duty to point out, clearly and firmly, the pupil's mistakes – the instances where writing is ungrammatical, words are misspelt or misused, sentences are mispunctuated. The teacher would know that the apparent kindness which spares children such admonishment is in fact a form of cruelty which denies them the opportunity to learn how to speak and write well.

NOTES

1 *A Language for Life. Report of the Committee of Inquiry appointed by the Secretary of State for Education and Science under the Chairmanship of Sir Alan Bullock F.B.A.*, HMSO, 1975, p. 50.
2 *Ibid.*, p. 143.
3 *Ibid.*, p. 166.
4 *English from 5 to 16*, HMSO, 1984, p. 3.
5 *Daily Express*, quoted in *English from 5 to 16. Second Edition (incorporating responses)*, HMSO, 1986, p. 27.
6 *Ibid.*, p. 17 (= unchanged text of first version).
7 *Ibid.*, pp. 16, 15 (= unchanged text of first version).
8 *Ibid.*, p. 36.
9 *Ibid.*, p. 43.
10 *Ibid.*, p. 44.

Chapter 3

The National Curriculum in English

Brian Cox

In July 1991, Kenneth Clarke, Secretary of State for Education, removed from their posts the two chairmen and chief executives previously in charge of the National Curriculum Council (NCC) and the Schools Examinations and Assessment Council (SEAC). Duncan Graham at NCC and Philip Halsey at SEAC were both men with considerable experience of educational administration. They were replaced by David Pascall, an oil executive who had once worked in Mrs Thatcher's policy unit at No. 10, and Lord Brian Griffiths, previously Mrs Thatcher's policy adviser on education. Both had strong links with the right-wing Centre for Policy Studies, a think tank supported by people with traditional views about English fashionable in the 1930s. From this time onwards, through 1992 when, after the General Election, John Patten became Secretary of State, the advice of professional teachers has been largely ignored by Ministers, and the number of right-wingers on NCC and SEAC has increased dramatically. Extreme right-wing educationalists describe teachers as the Enemy. The English group on SEAC was chaired by Dr John Marenbon, a Cambridge don who specialises in medieval philosophy, who, with his wife, Dr Sheila Lawlor, is a prominent member of the Centre for Policy Studies.

In 1992 this group of Conservatives proceeded to impose their ideas on both assessment and the curriculum. In September 1992, John Patten announced that the English curriculum would be revised by NCC, even though almost all teachers agreed it was working well. Soon afterwards Lord Griffiths announced assessment arrangements for Key Stage 3 which prescribed three Shakespeare plays and a short anthology of poems, stories and plays. The freedom of teachers to choose their own texts for their pupils to enjoy was taken away. Professional teachers pointed out that the best way to obtain high marks in these new arrangements for assessment would be by rote learning; in June 1993 teachers boycotted Key Stage 3 tests in English.

Why were these right-wing Conservatives allowed to take over the National Curriculum? Unfortunately the original arrangements for setting up a National Curriculum as laid down by Kenneth Baker in the 1988 Education Reform Act were deeply flawed. In his autobiography, *The View from No. 11* (1992), Nigel Lawson, previously Mrs Thatcher's Chancellor of the Exchequer, says of Kenneth Baker that

> not even his greatest friends would describe him as either a profound political thinker or a man with a mastery of detail. His instinctive answer to any problem is to throw glossy PR and large quantities of money at it, and his favoured brand of politics is the instant response to the cry of the moment (p. 606).

In his book on the intrigues and pressures which surrounded the foundation of the National Curriculum, *A Lesson for Us All* (1992), Duncan Graham describes how in 1988 he was called down to London by Kenneth Baker to be offered the job of chairman and chief executive of the NCC. The meeting, he says, was 'gloriously unspecific . . . he offered me a concept of what the job was even if the details were decidedly vague' (p. 9). Graham was an energetic administrator determined to make the curriculum work, and that meant careful attention to detail. As soon as he began to take action, he discovered that Baker's woolliness continually left him in an exposed position, unsure of his powers and responsibilities.

The main problem was that there were no clear guidelines about who should take final control over the curriculum. When I became chairman of the English Working Group, I assumed – perhaps naively – that my duty was to produce a curriculum which reflected the best of professional advice and classroom practice. Saunders Watson, who chaired the History Working Group, took a similar stance, and as a result Mrs Thatcher decided he had gone native, and let the country down. She was determined that the history curriculum should place great emphasis on the learning of historical facts; in contrast, the History Working Group rejected parrot learning, and said that names, dates and places provide only the starting points for understanding. The lack of firm rules about the power of the Working Groups and NCC created inevitable tensions.

Graham says that Baker told him shortly after his appointment that Ministers had insisted on a National Curriculum Council because they realised they would need totally independent professional advice over and beyond the kind they would get from civil servants. Teachers would also need a source of independent educational advice, and it would be better if schools were given that advice by people they saw as professionally credible. Perhaps the most important sentence in Graham's book deals with this issue. He writes: 'Both Baker and Rumbold (a junior minister) believed there were dangers in the national curriculum if it passed into the hands of an unscrupulous minister and that the existence of NCC with a strong professional view would be a bulwark' (p. 113).

Baker's failure to establish the independence of the NCC on a proper footing, to think hard about how a future unscrupulous Minister (Conservative or Labour) could be prevented from taking over the curriculum, caused me major problems when I chaired the English Working Group. When the Working Group's first report on the primary stages was submitted to Kenneth Baker in September 1988, he commented in his proposals, printed at the front of the report, that 'the programmes of study for writing should be strengthened to give greater emphasis to the place of grammatical structure and terminology'. He wrote this as a PR exercise in response to 'the cry of the moment' from right-wing Conservatives, not as a rational reply to our careful explanations that knowledge about language is best acquired in the process of writing and discussing real texts. Graham writes that my Working Group 'had simply failed to grasp that nothing else than a firm commitment to grammar, however it was described, would be acceptable to the government'. Instead, he says, we followed the Kingman Committee's recommendations, which, of course, reflected the views of professional teachers and linguists. Graham's account brings out the unresolved confusion about who should control the National Curriculum. Should I have adapted our report to satisfy the prejudices of politicians in opposition to professional advice about the real needs of children? For me and my Working Group such behaviour was out of the question.

While Graham was in charge of NCC, teachers welcomed the new frameworks for learning, and standards in English began to rise. Unfortunately, since Clarke placed right-wingers in charge of NCC and SEAC, these bodies have lost credibility. A crucial problem in the 1990s is for teachers and parents to devise strategies for keeping the curriculum free of political control.

Now the curriculum is in the hands of right-wing ideologues, does this not support the views of those opponents of the National Curriculum who argued that this experiment was doomed to failure? In the 1970s and 1980s many educationalists (including Duncan Graham) pointed out that schools from similar catchment areas often varied dramatically in their academic achievements. After the 11+ selection exams were abolished, schools were free to devise their own courses until pupils reached the age when the demands of GCSE imposed their prescriptions. Some excellent schools used the progressive ideas of the 1960s with imagination in carefully structured programmes of work. Others were of depressingly low quality, with children left to survive for themselves in badly organised classrooms where, for example, some teachers seemed to believe their pupils would somehow learn to read by osmosis. The aim of the National Curriculum was to raise the standards of these poor schools to those of the best.

I am still strongly in favour of a National Curriculum, but believe radical changes are necessary. As I have explained, the curriculum must not be dominated by one political party, and must reflect the views of the best professional teachers. I believe Key Stage 3 should be abolished; there is now too much bureaucracy and testing in the system, and teachers' time is being wasted. Key Stages 1 and 2 should be mainly assessed by the teachers themselves through coursework, and carefully structured observation over a period of time. There should be no published league table for Key Stages 1 and 2.

But even if these reforms are instituted, the curriculum will still create problems because the teaching of English language and literature raises crucial questions about our value systems and our concepts of national identity. This is particularly so in the teaching of grammar and in the choice of texts for study in the classroom.

In the 1930s and 1940s grammar was usually taught through mechanical exercises such as parsing and clause analysis. The clever children, of course, advanced quickly in their reading and writing skills, as they usually do whatever the quality of the teaching. They were selected at a very early age, and placed in an 'A' stream. Many of these children are now in their sixties and they look back with nostalgia to those golden far-off days. They forget that the less able children fared badly under this system, and received little individual attention. In those days the lower streams were usually allocated to the less experienced teachers. When I left the army in 1949 I spent four months as an untrained supply teacher in a secondary modern school at Immingham in South Humberside. Although I had no qualifications, I was asked to teach reading to a group of illiterate 13-year-olds. I was a complete failure, and did not know how to help them.

In the 1930s and 1940s children were taught rules about English grammar which are now recognised as false. Children were taught not to begin sentences with 'And' or 'But', and not to end a sentence with a preposition. They were told never to split an infinitive. The teachers of those days were applying Latin rules to the living English language, and all linguists today acknowledge that this is entirely inappropriate.

Great writers such as Byron and D.H. Lawrence split their infinitives. The excellent Reader's Digest *The Right Word at the Right Time* (1986) says that the rule that you must not split the infinitive is 'irrational'. Phrases such as 'to boldly go where no man has gone before' and 'begin to silently hope' are guaranteed to set the pedant's teeth on edge, despite the greater metrical regularity of 'to boldly go' and 'to silently hope'. In a witty entry in his *A Dictionary of Modern English Usage* (revised by Gowers, 1965), Fowler pokes fun at those pedants whose tortuous efforts to avoid split infinitives are deaf to the normal rhythms of English sentences.

Old people get very upset when they are told that the English rules they were taught at school are wrong. The way we write and speak is part of our identity, and it is destabilising to find that modern usage has left us behind. This is why many elderly Conservatives get so emotional about language. Some of these took over National Curriculum English in 1992. David Pascall himself, when asked what he meant by grammatically correct spoken standard English, replied that children should not split the infinitive. In my article 'English Studies and National Identity' (*Reassessing Language and*

Literacy, edited by Mike Hayhoe and Stephen Parker, Open University Press, 1992), I describe how this longing for traditional methods is common among Conservatives, how for them the connectives of grammar, rhyme and rhythm are seen as a form of resistance to the disorders and confusions of modern living. In an article in *The Independent* on 2 November 1990, Stephen Spender describes how before 1945 it was taken for granted that children of every social background (particularly from the working class) should ideally speak and write an English which conformed with the best speech and writing of the educated upper classes. This involved learning the rules of Latinate grammar, and an induction into the traditional classics of English literature. In those days there really were no other standards, but today we hear on the BBC new accents, new voices. Today our schools include thousands of children from various ethnic communities. The idea of 'correct' English as Latinate grammar plus Received Pronunciation is no longer valid. The great tradition of Milton, Keats or Jane Austen, Spender says, is growing even further away from the present very fluid, Anglo-American language. Like many of the older generation he finds this change unsettling. He writes: 'The idea of a future in which there is no single standard but a multiplicity of standards, each with its separate variety of correctness, is indeed terrifying.' He still believes, and my English Working Group followed him in this, that all children are entitled to be helped to use written and spoken standard English; this is the language of academic discourse, of national politics, of international usage.

Many research projects have shown that the old-fashioned teaching of mechanical grammar exercises does not raise standards (see, for example, Elley, W.G., Barham, I.H., Lamb, H. and Wyllie, M., 1975, 'The role of grammar in a secondary school English curriculum', *New Zealand Journal of Educational Studies*, 10, pp. 26–42; reprinted 1976 in *Research in the Teaching of English*, 10, pp. 5–21). Such research has persuaded many teachers to reject the old boring and inaccurate ways of teaching English. Unfortunately some of them went to the other extreme, and taught no grammar or knowledge about language. National Curriculum English gives due weight to spelling, grammar and handwriting, but instead of the old boring exercises, young children are encouraged to write their own stories, to discuss them with the teacher and their friends, and to improve them, perhaps for printing in a class or school magazine. Grammar and knowledge about language can be introduced in their discussions with the teacher to help children to improve their writing skills. Teachers are very excited about these new ways of teaching language. Instead of tedious exercises, children study language in use. English is treated as a living, not a dead, language. Unfortunately these stimulating new methods are opposed by the old-fashioned traditionalists who now control NCC and SEAC. This is another great battleground for the 1990s.

Conservatives who are nostalgic for the old disciplines and authority of

Latinate grammar are also usually in favour of a curriculum whose texts are taken entirely from the English classics. Dr Marenbon has pronounced that by the age of 16, children should have read Bacon, Dryden, Pope, Milton and Dr Johnson. When at the end of 1992 SEAC published its lists of texts for Key Stage 3 a passage from Johnson's *Rasselas* had been included. Few children under the age of 14 are likely to enjoy this work. Dr Marenbon and his wife, Dr Sheila Lawlor, believe texts for a National Curriculum should not include any written during the last thirty years; they say we need to wait until we are sure that these recent texts are going to achieve classic status. Teachers are made very angry by these pronouncements, because such policies will kill enjoyment of literature. The Cox Report insisted that all children should be introduced to a wide range of literature, that we should include texts in English from other cultures. In our multicultural society children should be introduced to the many successful writers in English from other countries (Chinua Achebe, Anita Desai, Toni Morrison, etc.). In an article in *The Times* on 1 January 1993, Sally Feldman, editor of Treasure Islands, the children's book series on Radio 4, said that the 1992 book lists drawn up by NCC were 'a betrayal of children, of their literature, and of the experience of reading'. She listed the many enchanting modern writings which can persuade children to enjoy reading, and pointed out that the NCC poets included no women and hardly any texts from a multicultural background. The list, she said, 'represents a swingeing denial of what is good and valuable in modern writing'. The canon of literature advocated by the Centre for Policy Studies would have suited the days of the British Empire. It treats English as a dead language, and ignores all those creative experiments which have changed our views of what is 'correct' English.

These conflicts will continue through the 1990s. I greatly admire the teachers of English I have met during the last five years, and I have seen some wonderful examples of classroom teaching. We need to encourage these teachers, to respect their expertise, and to ensure that decisions about the teaching of English are taken by these professionals, not by politicians.

Part II

Speaking and listening

The following three parts are concerned with speaking and listening, reading and writing. These well-known headings were used for two major reasons: first, because as Brian Cox in *Cox on Cox* says, 'This division of the English curriculum [is] familiar to English teachers and in accord with good practice' (p. 10); and second, as part of a PGCE course this reader needs to support student teachers in working with the National Curriculum, and these headings will facilitate an understanding of the structure of the National Curriculum for English. Importantly, however, these headings are grouped together under 'Issues' because:

> The profile components are inter-related. For example, group discussion may precede and follow individual writing; writing may be collaborative; and listening to stories is often a preparation for reading . . . . Because of the inter-relationship between the language modes, in good classroom practice the programmes of study will necessarily and rightly be integrated.
>
> (*English for Ages 5–16*: the National Curriculum Working Group Report. Quoted in the Non-Statutory Guidance: English)

Many of the chapters demonstrate this point by straddling at least two of the areas; for example, the newly commissioned chapter 'Standard English: the debate', by Professor Katharine Perera, while planned for the part on speaking and listening, inevitably refers to both reading and writing. The 'inter-relationship' is evident too in the chapters examining classroom practice, such as Jenny Des Fountain's 'Planning for learning through talk'.

In his paper on spoken English given in 1965 Andrew Wilkinson wrote: 'Oracy is not a "subject" – it is a condition of learning . . . it is not a "frill" but a state of being in which the whole school must operate' (*Educational Review*, Occasional Publication No. 2, University of Birmingham, 1965). Andrew Wilkinson's seminal work on oracy (a term he originated) was the foundation of much of the thinking in the National Oracy Project. The first chapter by the director of the project, John Johnson, records the development and some of the outcomes of the project. The two chapters following have both been written by members of the NOP: Alan Howe, Project Officer, and Jenny Des Fountain, NOP Co-ordinator. Alan Howe in 'Perspectives on oracy' looks at pupils' talk in the classroom and offers an 'oracy map' as an overview of classroom talk. Jenny Des Fountain's chapter outlines how planning for learning through talk is a way of achieving 'action knowledge'. The next chapter, on assessment, addresses strategies rather than issues for the reasons outlined earlier in this part. These strategies are the result of work undertaken by teachers as part of the project – chalkface advice! Diana Cinamon, writing on bilingualism and oracy, also discusses strategies in the context of the pupils' perspectives. The chapter was initially written in a primary school context; its inclusion demonstrates that good primary practice is also good secondary practice. The final chapter in this part, 'Standard English: the debate', by Katharine Perera, explores an area she describes as 'both complex and controversial' with clarity and coherence. Katharine Perera disentangles an issue which has become central to the English teaching debate.

Chapter 4

The National Oracy Project

John Johnson

INTRODUCTION

The National Oracy Project will complete its work during 1993, the year in which this volume will be published. I hope in this chapter to provide a summary of the work of the many teachers and others who participated in the project, focusing in part on the work of secondary English teachers but also acknowledging that the project was, in terms of age range and subject coverage, one of the biggest curriculum development projects seen in the English-speaking world.

SETTING UP THE PROJECT

The government had recognised that new demands were being made of schools in the area of spoken English, and in 1986 invited LEAs to apply for a modest number of education support grants for oracy. Over fifty-five LEAs applied for just five grants, and the government approved seven bids, after asking that some be reorganised (so that more money was not needed!). It was by then clear that the National Oracy Project, which was approved shortly afterwards, would need to help as many of the disappointed LEAs as possible.

The first thing that I did on appointment as Director of the project was to call a conference for LEAs to discuss a complete restructuring of the project. In brief, a number of LEAs made applications for individual membership and were selected and approved. Others formed consortia to work together, and all consortia were guaranteed membership. And a third group of LEAs became associate members, forging links with the project but not participating directly in the development work. With the additional inclusion of the LEAs directly funded by government, some forty-four LEAs were effective members of the development phase of the project which began in 1989.

Most LEAs appointed advisory teachers to act as their co-ordinators, and invited or selected schools to participate in the project. Centrally, a small professional and administrative team was appointed in the London headquarters of SCDC to co-ordinate the project. These were the aims and objectives which were set for the project:

- to enhance the role of speech in the learning process 5–16 by encouraging active learning;
- to develop the teaching of oral communication skills;
- to develop methods of assessment of and through speech, including assessment for public examinations at 16+;
- to improve pupils' performance across the curriculum;
- to enhance teachers' skills and practice;
- to promote recognition of the value of oral work in schools and increase its use as a means of improving learning.

We were given three years to undertake development work, and a further two years to disseminate that work as widely as possible.

A NETWORK OF PROJECTS

The National Oracy Project was really a network of LEA projects, which in their turn were also networks of school and classroom research and development projects. This approach was similar to some other SCDC projects, most notably the National Writing Project. There was enormous variety in the themes and areas which LEAs and schools chose to investigate and explore. Among the LEA themes were:

- talk in the early years;
- organising the classroom for talk and learning;
- developing the audience for talk;
- storytelling;
- small-group work approaches to secondary English;
- assessing talk;
- talk in the community.

Schools and teachers were also able to choose the particular areas they wanted to focus on. Assessment was a popular choice, partly because of GCSE and partly because by 1988 schools could see the imminence of National Curriculum Assessment, but the central team in many instances encouraged teachers not to start with assessment, but to get talk going purposefully in the classroom first, and take on assessment later. Many teachers simply wanted some time and support to concentrate on classroom language, often for the first time in their professional lives. And it was very exciting to mix mathematicians, scientists, historians, technologists and English teachers together in these investigations. Some of the initial questions teachers asked were:

- Who talks, where, what about? Is it related to work?
- Do some children use another language in school?

- Are there differences between boys and girls?
- Is that quiet child always so reticent?
- What sorts of talk happen in different activities?
- What about my own talk? Do I listen?
- What are my pupils' attitudes to talk?
- What is happening when groups are working together, without me present?

To find answers to their questions, the teachers gathered evidence in a variety of ways:

- they observed individual children at intervals during a day or week, jotting down details of where the child was, what was being said or done, and why;
- they tape-recorded groups of children working together;
- they recorded themselves working with a group, the whole class or individual children;
- they asked pupils about their perceptions of talk;
- they recorded or observed talk in particular curriculum areas or areas of the classroom;
- they 'followed' a pupil for a day, noting or recording the talk activities of a whole day.

With several hundred schools, and several thousand teachers, involved in these forms of small-scale investigation, it is possible only to generalise about their findings. Most teachers were surprised by the range and quality of the talk which children could produce, but disappointed by the limits and constraints which they as teachers often placed on pupils. They found that children did good, and important, work in small-group activities, particularly if they had or established fairly clear roles and purposes for their individual contributions and for the whole-group activities. Children astonishingly quickly picked up 'messages' about the value, or lack of value, of talk in the classroom, and often attributed less value to group activities than to individual work.

As a consequence, teachers looked for ways of 'getting talk going', so that children would have a variety of purposes and roles in their discussions. This is a summary of some of the approaches which proved popular with teachers.

Brainstorming

A large group, or even the whole class, will contribute ideas, or thoughts, or words, off the top of their heads, related to a particular subject or problem. All contributions are listed without comment, and then the children use their list to select tasks or topics for further work. Smaller groups, even pairs, can also gather thoughts in this way.

Jigsaw

This is an extremely effective form of co-operative learning. A topic is set and subdivided into areas. 'Home Groups' are formed, and each child in the Home Group is given one of the topic areas in which to become an 'expert'. The child then joins prospective 'experts' in the same area from the other Home Groups, to form an 'expert group'. Each expert group works on its chosen area, and then the members return to their Home Groups to make reports and to share in putting their whole set of discoveries together. Each 'Home Group' can then present its work to others. Jigsawing gives all children a key role to play in the work of a group.

Twos to fours

Children work together in pairs, perhaps upon a mathematical problem, or science experiment. They then join another pair to explain what they have achieved, and to compare this with the work of the other pair. This provides a valuable opportunity to express understanding, and to respond to the views of others in a supportive context.

Rainbow groups

A way of ensuring that children experience working alongside a range of others is to give each child in a group a number, or a colour. When the group has worked together, all the children of the same number or colour form new groups to compare what they have done.

Envoys

Often in group work, the teacher is concerned that he or she will be under pressure from many different directions. Envoying helps children to find help and support without necessarily having recourse to the teacher. If a group needs to check something, or to obtain information, one of the group can be sent as an 'envoy' to the library, or book corner, or another group, and will then report back. Another use is to ask groups to send an envoy to a different group to explain what they have done, obtain responses and suggestions, and bring them back to the group.

Listening triads

This strategy encourages children, in groups of three, to take on the roles of talker, questioner, or recorder. The talker explains or comments on an issue or activity. The questioner prompts and seeks clarification. The recorder makes notes, and at the end of the (brief) time gives a report of the conversation. Next time the roles are changed.

Critical friends

A group member is responsible for observing the ways in which the group works together. Using a simple guide list (which children can devise), the observer watches and listens as the children work. The information is then discussed by the group. This helps children to develop their own evaluative strategies.

DEVELOPING NEW ROLES

Teachers experimenting with these and other approaches to active learning, and finding them successful, often went through an uncertain phase. If their students were able to do so well without them, what exactly was their role? Were they no more than the initiator of activities, who set up a number of situations in which the students did all the hard work? Gradually, however, they realised that putting children and students into new roles also gave them the opportunity to take on new roles. This extract from a publication of the project describes this process:

> Active learning engages pupils in exploratory, investigative activities, using spoken language to discuss, question, clarify, describe, evaluate and justify ideas. All this places demands on the teacher's expertise and requires a diversified classroom role. Teachers exploring the implications of this in their work have found themselves acting as a potential:

ORGANISER:	*'Would you like to form six groups of four?'*
PROVIDER:	*'You might find what you need in the Library.'*
SUPPORTER:	*'Let me know if you want me to work with you.'*
ARBITER:	*'Try and make sure that you've heard from everyone before you reach a decision.'*
COLLABORATOR:	*'Perhaps we need to look at it another way.'*
WORKING GROUP MEMBER:	*'What would you like me to do?'*
DIRECTOR:	*'All groups will need to report back in half an hour.'*
EDITOR:	*'Where will this fit in?'*
FRIEND:	*'Are you feeling a bit better today?'*
ADVISER:	*'Have you considered any alternatives?'*

LEARNER:	*'I never knew that before.'*
EXPERT:	*'The map will show you where the river flows.'*
LISTENER:	*'Mmm . . . mmm . . . go on . . . this is very interesting.'*

Reflecting upon these roles, one teacher wrote: 'I am realising there is a time and a place for all manner of approaches and different audiences that I as a teacher can offer. I need now to view my skills beyond those of purely didactic pedagogy . . . . I felt therefore that I needed to look more closely at the implications this had upon my approach to teaching.'

This shift in teaching role had to be balanced by shifting expectations of the roles that children could fulfil. They could, and did, develop the confidence and self-esteem to take risks, to offer tentative thoughts, to make exploratory statements and offer hypothetical avenues for potential investigation and evaluation. They showed how well they could consider ideas and materials put before them, formulate questions for themselves, negotiate the ground rules and develop a sense of ownership over the whole learning process.

MEETING PUPILS' NEEDS

As their confidence in organising and managing more active learning situations grew, teachers had more opportunity to consider some of the more complex issues of oracy – gender and talk, linguistic diversity and variety, and children's special needs.

Amongst other things, they found that girls and boys often have different experiences of and attitudes to talk, hold different expectations of their role in talk, and therefore need the teacher on occasion to use different strategies in the classroom. In particular, boys may refuse to work with girls, may adopt the role of 'expert' or leader in group discussions, may be reluctant to talk sensitively or to express emotion, and may subject girls to verbal harassment. Girls may adopt non-speaking or subservient roles in group conversations, and may find it difficult to get equal shares of teachers' time and attention.

Teachers also found that their assessments of children's talk could be affected by subconscious bias or prejudice. There were dangers that teachers would give undue credit to boys for responsive listening, for good eye contact with other speakers, for supportive questioning or for building on others' contributions simply because these were unexpected features of boys' talk.

Although these are complex and difficult issues for teachers to address, many found it a valuable professional challenge to investigate. Identifying the hitherto unrevealed problems experienced by students helped them to enhance their professional understanding and practice in a way which benefited their students. The same was true for teachers of children with special needs, where extra care and attention was found necessary to enable children to participate fully in lessons. Among the strategies found to be successful were:

- pairing pupils with supportive partners;
- putting pupils into the role of questioner and interviewer;
- planning for well-structured small-group work, with clear time limits;
- asking for appropriate teacher interaction in small-group work;
- tape-recording individual pupils doing their tasks, using a microphone where necessary;
- providing pupils with a cassette player so that they can record their work orally rather than in writing;
- reducing extraneous noise and explaining tasks very fully and explicitly;
- using drama, role play, puppets and play to encourage participatory talk.

In general, teachers found it important to separate issues of special needs from issues concerned with linguistic diversity. There was too much danger that bilingual pupils, or children with strong regional dialects, would be described as having 'problems'. It was always better to consider such pupils as possessing linguistic strengths, which needed to be encouraged and nurtured. The following principles appeared to support this:

- pupils' home languages should be respected;
- displays and resources should reflect the cultures and contexts in which children's languages are used;
- all children's languages should be encouraged in presentations and public contexts such as school assemblies;
- all children's languages should as far as possible be reflected in the curriculum;
- assessment of pupils' work should not be affected adversely by any comparative weakness in English.

THE NATIONAL CURRICULUM

Like everything and everyone else in the education service, the National Oracy Project and its members and officers were from 1987 working through an unparalleled period of extensive change. The Education Reform Act shut down the SCDC, and replaced it with the York-based National Curriculum Council (NCC), which took over responsibility for administering the project. Statutory Orders for core and foundation subjects were prepared and published, making new demands on teachers and pupils to use and develop oral language in English and across the curriculum. And statutory assessment of pupils using both Teacher Assessment (TA) and Standard Assessment Task (SATs) was introduced for all pupils at the ages of 7, 11, 14 and 16. The first rounds of assessment occurred in 1991 for 7-year-olds, requiring teachers both to assess pupils' abilities in speaking and listening, the first attainment target in the new English curriculum, and to use spoken language as the medium for assessing much of the rest of the curriculum. At the time of writing the statutory assessments of 14-year-olds in English have become a matter of controversy, with many complaints that the timetable and demands are unrealistic and unfair.

These demands on teachers to use spoken language confidently and purposefully to develop learning, and to develop pupils' speaking, and listening, led them to look to the project for help and guidance. This chart, prepared by the project, shows some of the demands which the National Curriculum made of talk across the curriculum:

What? (Uses)	**How?** (Activities)	**Where?** (Contexts)
Expressing feelings and opinions about themselves, the subject or activity.	Preparing presentations to class/school/parents.	Across curriculum areas, e.g. the science laboratory, the technology room.
Taking part in group discussions.	Planning and designing tasks, and setting and solving problems within them.	In a variety of groupings (paired, single sex, small group, class, with/ without presence of teacher).
Presenting ideas, information, texts.	Identifying specific outcomes for their own work.	
Interpreting arguments and developing them.		
Discriminating between fact and opinion.	Making and testing hypotheses.	In contact with audiences beyond the classroom.
Summarising views to gain a consensus.	Reporting and discussing stories, poems, plays and other texts.	In representative roles, acting on behalf of others.
Instructing and responding to instructions.	Reasoning and arguing.	Using audio/video, radio, television, telephone, computer.
Conveying information.	Using talk in shared reading or writing activity.	
Role play.	Simulations and group drama.	In enquiry and survey work in the locality or on field visits/trips.
Reflecting upon their own talk and learning the talk of others.	Discussing and analysing language in use.	In mini-enterprise, work shadowing or industry liaison exercises.
Exploratory talk (predicting, speculating hypothesising).		
Demonstrating knowledge of language.		

The chart was published in a highly successful series of publications specifically designed to help teachers to implement the spoken language demands of the new Statutory Orders:

Teaching Talking and Learning in Key Stage One (published 1990).
Teaching Talking and Learning in Key Stage Two (1991) and
Teaching Talking and Learning in Key Stage Three (1991).
Teaching Talking and Learning in Key Stage Four (1993).

These and other publications also summarised the work of teachers in assessment. As I said earlier, this was an area which teachers found innovative, demanding and problematic.

For a start, talk is simply an unfamiliar medium for teachers to use in assessing children's achievements, their knowledge, understanding or particular skills. The methods used to conduct written assessment, and particularly the kinds of tasks set, are often wholly inappropriate for oral assessment. And there are additional problems in observing talk and in capturing talk so that it can be considered again later.

Yet teachers also noted from their own work that if assessment were not constrained by the demands of literacy, many pupils were better enabled to show what they 'know, understand and can do'. Through observing and listening to pupils at work, teachers obtained much fuller access to the processes of learning, not just the final outcomes. Assessment could be genuinely formative if teachers observed the first stages of a piece of work to check that the pupils both understood the task and had the required conceptual knowledge and information to undertake the task. And assessment became both more reliable and more valid in the areas of enquiry, communication and collaboration if talk was used as a principal medium of assessment.

One crucial distinction must be drawn, however, between two kinds of oral assessment:

Assessment of talk
Assessment of talk is an assessment of pupils' *use of spoken language*, especially their English. It looks particularly at such features of speaking and listening as appropriateness, diction, presentation, tone, register, responsiveness, interpersonal skills, and so on. In the National Curriculum it leads to assessment of the attainment target and profile component Speaking and Listening.

Assessment through talk
Assessment through talk is an assessment of *the knowledge and understanding of a subject*, displayed by pupils through their talk. It looks particularly at such features as accuracy, use of terminology, quantity and quality of knowledge and understanding, application of these to a new situation, and so on. In the National Curriculum it can lead to assessment in a subject area, including the attainment targets for Reading and Writing in English.

Teachers also found it important to remember that:

- When children and adults speak, they do not always make their knowledge explicit (like an iceberg, the greater proportion remains hidden).
- Pupils may find it hard to 'display' all their knowledge in conversation with teachers when they know that their teachers are more expert than they are.
- A misunderstanding of the task, or a difficult relationship between pupils, may prevent them showing all that they do through talk.

At times, therefore, teachers found that oral work would not produce valid evidence, and they needed simply to discount what they had observed, because it would not stand as valid evidence of pupils' achievements.

They also found that, for a variety of reasons, it was impossible to determine beforehand exactly how pupils would talk in any given situation. We may have general expectations of them, but their talk may follow totally different but still relevant paths and patterns. Teachers observing children, listening to or watching recordings of them, or analysing short transcripts, soon realised the limitations of any approach to oral assessment which only used predetermined criteria to evaluate pupils' work. Because of these problems, it was necessary to develop models of assessment which involved collecting information about children's oral work over a wide range of contexts and over a period of time, and which involved the pupils and teachers, and on occasion the parents, in discussing and reflecting on the information collected. The assessment process needed particularly to focus on the children's best, most interesting or most noteworthy oral work, often described as 'catching them peaking'.

CONCLUSION

This chapter, necessarily, is only a summary of the extensive and wide-ranging work of the National Oracy Project. If you would like to know more about this work, the following publications are available:

The 'Teaching Talking and Learning' series mentioned in the chapter is available from the National Association for the Teaching of English.
'Talk and Learning 5 to 16' is a major INSET pack on the project published by the Open University.
The project's journal *Talk* and a number of working papers on such matters as assessment are available from the National Curriculum Council.
The project's four final publications, autumn 1992 and 1993, are available from Hodder and Stoughton.

Chapter 5

Perspectives on oracy

Alan Howe

I have entitled this chapter 'Perspectives on oracy' because what I want to try and do is to look at children's talk in school from a number of different perspectives and to raise a number of issues connected with those perspectives.

I'd like to start by telling a story, a version of which I first heard told by Mike Newby. It's called *Raucous Little Sister*.

I'd like you to imagine a large Victorian house in the centre of Cheltenham: three storeys and a basement. There is a family living in this house; the father has married twice – two daughters by his first marriage and a younger daughter by his second marriage. Unfortunately the second wife died, the father's away on business a lot and the two elder sisters are the ones who rule the roost, forcing their younger sister to do all of the menial, dirty tasks around the house. It's the two elder sisters who go out into society and get invited to things and the younger sister who is always left at home. She's called 'raucous little sister' because she's always chattering, singing to herself little rhymes, little songs, talking to the neighbours over the fence and so on – but she never gets invited anywhere. Let's call her two elder sisters 'Ms Reading' and 'Ms Writing', and of course you know what happens: in 1985 all three of them get invited to the GCSE ball. The invites drop through the letter box and the little sister opens hers frantically and she says, 'I've been invited to the Ball; finally, finally I've been recognized!'

'Oh, it's ridiculous, it must be a computer error', say her two elder sisters.

She says, 'No, it's true, Sir Keith says come along to the GCSE ball.'

'Well anyway', they say, 'you can't come – you have nothing to wear', and you of course know what happens: they go off to the GCSE ball and the younger sister is left distraught.

But along comes a fairy godmother and suddenly she is transformed and has new clothes to wear.

She arrives at the GCSE ball late and it's in full swing. She enters through the double doors, walks across the hall and the prince (or shall we say Kingman?) sees her. He thinks, 'Who is she? I haven't seen her before, she's beautiful, I must get to know her.' He walks across to her and looks her in the eyes and says, 'I don't know who you are. You're beautiful, you must dance with me.'

She looks at him quizzically, then eventually answers, 'Yes, I will dance with you but don't forget you have got to assess me as well.'

'Fine, I'm prepared to assess you', the prince replies, 'but don't forget that you have got to satisfy my criteria.'

In a sense that is what has happened to talk. Talk has been the Cinderella of the language modes for years and years. It is commonplace in school, we have all recognised it, we have even recognised its usefulness, but when it comes to going out in society, when it comes to being invited to the ball, talk has been left behind. In the last four years or so, GCSE oral communication, the importance placed on active learning approaches through such initiatives as TVEI, and, more recently, the establishment of a National Oracy Project, with over thirty LEAs developing their own locally based initiatives, have all contributed to a situation in which the spoken word is being given much greater prominence in educational thinking and planning.

So where are we now? We are at a stage where spoken language in school has got some kind of official sanctioning – it's been officially legitimised. Cinderella has been invited to the ball. Why is that? Why suddenly would spoken language have this official recognition? I would like to think that it is because it is now generally recognised that children need to articulate their ideas, to make them their own; because it is recognised that children need to have their own vernacular language valued in the classroom; because it is generally recognised that children need to be given power over language, so that they can learn to discuss, to argue, to negotiate, to persuade, to respond in discussion, to resist and challenge spurious arguments, learn to ask questions, learn to engage critically with the world. I would like to think it is to do with all those things, but I somehow doubt it; and as well as this upsurge of activity and of initiatives and the very positive statements we get in official documents, we also get mixed messages, contradictory statements. For example, have a look at this extract from the Kingman Report:

36. In a class of 11-year-olds visited by the Committee, the pupils had been divided into groups of four to discuss whether the rights of individuals are threatened by establishing No Smoking areas in public places. One member of each group was elected to provide a summary of that group's discussion. The elected reporter gave a one-minute summary of his or her group's discussion, standing up in front of the class (with the lights at the front of the class being dipped 10 seconds before the minute

was up). Each summary was then commented on by a member of another group, in terms of, for example:

- how clear the summary was;
- whether the speaker kept repeating the same structure or vocabulary;
- whether the speaker made the discussion appear interesting;
- whether the speaker represented only one point of view or was able to represent several points of view;
- whether the speaker stood up straight and looked at all members of the audience or kept looking just to one side of the class;
- whether the speaker was fluent or paused too much;
- whether the speaker was adequately audible at the back;
- whether the speed of the speech was appropriate.

After each critique, other members of the class offered their observations, often including a critique of 'unjust' criticisms made by the previous speaker. This was clearly a familiar format and most pupils participated.[1]

It is as if children come to school with a language that is a bit like cholera. The job of teachers and schools is to engage in some kind of inoculation programme – to root out the debased forms. There is a view in this extract that suggests that there is a particular kind of spoken language that is better than another and the job of teachers is to replace the kind of language children come to school with, with this more acceptable form. There's also a focus on surface features and even some elements of an 'elocution model' of the spoken language. In a recent letter in the *Times Educational Supplement* the writer complained about the 'slovenliness of speech' exhibited by some school leavers heard on the radio, and offered the following solution:

Schools are their only hope. It would not take much time, though it would need persistence. A few speech exercises run through as a matter of course at the beginning of every English lesson, for instance, will soon train pupils in proper attention to consonants.

In a book entitled *Teaching Talk*, Gillian Brown *et al*. propose a hierarchical approach to the 'teaching' of the spoken language:

Since most pupils perform inadequately in transferring information in at least some types of information-related speech, we believe they should be explicitly taught to control the transfer of information in information-related speech.

If they are to be taught, then a syllabus must be devised. It is clear that the syllabus should be structured, so that pupils learn first to perform relatively simple acts of information transfer, and only gradually move towards the extremely demanding types of task . . . . The main aim of this book is to discuss how such a graded syllabus can be devised.[2]

I would like to contrast this perspective with a very different perspective offered by Douglas Barnes:

> It is when the pupil is required to use language to grapple with new experience or to order old experience in a new way that he is most likely to find it necessary to use language differently. And this will be very different from taking over someone else's language in external imitation of its forms: on the contrary, it is the first step towards new patterns of thinking and feeling, new ways of representing reality to himself.[3]

Here the emphasis is on using language for real purposes as part of the learning process, and the suggestion is that two things might happen: by using language in this way children are likely to learn more effectively and are also, simultaneously as it were, likely to develop as talkers and listeners – to develop their language use.

Now in a sense that has been the starting point of the work that we have been doing in the Wiltshire oracy project. We have tried to say to ourselves 'What does that mean in practice in the classroom, and how can we translate the implications of that into classroom practice?'

I want to take a slight sideways shift at this point, and just briefly say something about the word 'oracy' itself. In considering what we might mean by 'development' it might be useful to have some kind of map of the territory. The following is an attempt to devise some kind of 'oracy map' (Figure 5.1). Like all maps it is an oversimplified version of reality.

The four dimensions are actually interlocking. The first is what I have called 'learning' – this is the connection between the spoken language and understanding. Very often talking through something can help to clarify it – or even generate new ways of thinking about it. We can use talk to formulate ideas, to grasp at semiperceived thoughts and bring them into existence. One way of viewing talk in school is as a necessary bridge between the experiences and values that the pupil brings into the classroom and the experiences, concepts, understanding being met for the first time in school.

The second dimension is 'resources', 'the linguistic nuts and bolts' of oracy – the ability to use appropriate vocabulary; to use the spoken language for a variety of purposes; the ability to use non-verbal signs – gestures, eye contact and so on; the ability to 'organise' ideas in talk; the ability to switch register and code according to context.

'Reciprocity' is a clumsy word but the best that I have come across to describe this third dimension which is the 'interpersonal or social' side of oracy – working with others, getting on with other people, being a good listener as well as a good talker. You could say that oracy is as much about facilitating the word of others as it is about talking yourself. It is about helping other people say what they want to say in all sorts of ways.

The fourth dimension is 'reflexivity'. There are two sides to this. First, 'being reflective', using the spoken language to be reflective about your

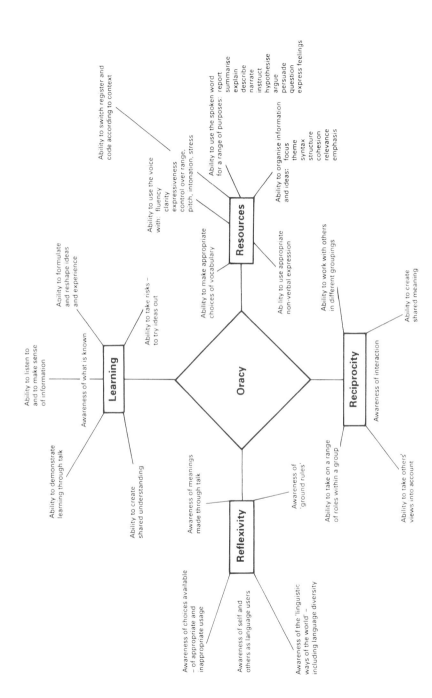

Figure 5.1 An oracy map

learning, doing what Jerome Bruner has described as 'looking back on your traces and telling yourselves what you know' through talk. This is an often neglected aspect of function of talk in the classroom, but one which has very powerful possibilities. So – being reflective *through* talk – but also linked with this is the ability to be reflective about yourself and others as talkers and listeners: to be *aware* of yourself and to be aware of *others* as talkers and listeners. It does seem to me that this is one of the key ingredients in developing children's oracy.

It may be that this map might be a useful starting point when we are beginning to think about where children's language might be developing, and how we as teachers might be able to assist in this process.

You can sum all of this up in one word – versatility. If you take this map of oracy and ask, 'what in the end might we be hoping to move children towards?', I would argue that we should be helping to move them towards being more versatile users of the spoken language, being able to make their language meet the demands of a wide variety of situations. So when I talk about versatility it is that sort of ability that I mean – the ability to make your language meet the demands of both the known and the unfamiliar.

WHAT CAN WE LEARN FROM EARLY LANGUAGE DEVELOPMENT?

Before we start devising grandiose plans for achieving that, before we start devising graded syllabuses and slotting in oracy as another bit of the curriculum jigsaw, I think it is useful to remind ourselves of what happens in the first four or five years of a child's life, before he or she actually arrives at school. Most children come to school already very effective talkers and listeners in the contexts in which they have grown up and the situations they have had to use talk for. If 5-year-olds coming into the school have managed to master most of the grammar of the language, have an active vocabulary of about 3,000 to 5,000 words, have understood many of the nuances and the subtleties of the language without any formal teaching, it might be useful to ask ourselves what has contributed to that and what we as teachers in schools can learn from it.

In a chapter of his book *Fair Dinkum Teaching and Learning*, entitled 'Oracy in Australian schools', Garth Boomer provides us with a list of 'The conditions most likely . . .' – features of the language climate in the early years which seem to be particularly conducive to language development.[4] The list includes the following:

1 'Tracking', where the adults try to work out what the child is seeking to say, or talk themselves as a commentary to accompany the child's activity.

2 'Caring and sharing' – which follows on from the previous condition, the adults engaging in activities along with the child.

3 'Talk serving needs' – obviously one of the reasons children learn to talk so effectively is that they very quickly realise that they can alter their world as a result of particular utterances. When my 2-year-old daughter says 'potty', it must seem to her as if she's uttered a magical phrase, so quickly do her parents start to attend to her!

4 'Adult time' – it seems to me that it is not so much the amount of time that is important as time spent with caring adults who are doing all of the above things as well as modifying their language, and their usual ways of responding to language, in order to give the language learner the opportunity to make meaning. Even parents of new-born babies start to behave with them as if the infant was an ideal conversational partner! Is it not strange that adult members of the species have long conversations with tiny members of the same species who do not speak the language? Of course, what we are doing is treating the child as an ideal conversational partner because we know intuitively that this is the best way of helping the child to learn all the complex skills involved in spoken interaction.

5 'Words to play with': children are quick to see language as a kind of Playdoh, a medium you can mess about with. This is partly because they get pleasure from rolling the sounds around, but I suspect it is more serious than that. In breaking the rules the child is learning them, and is attending to communication itself – it is a kind of code cracking.

6 'Challenge and involvement' – children need a stake in what they say, to be using the language for real purposes.

7 'A wide range of contexts' – to put it simply, language will grow in proportion to the breadth and depth of experiences the child is having, and the opportunity he or she is given to talk about a range of topics and to engage with others who are using talk for a variety of purposes.

8 'Exploratory talk' – asking questions and getting serious answers, using talk to hypothesise, to speculate about things, to take risks.

What seems to be emerging from this analysis, then, is the crucial importance, in early language learning, of mature speakers engaging seriously with the child and providing him or her with various kinds of verbal scaffolding within which the child can try the language out for size. The adult role is one of being 'reciprocal' – following the child as he or she talks and providing what Gordon Wells has called 'sustaining strategies' as a way of helping the speaker do his or her own extending.

In what ways might these insights inform our teaching?

AND SO TO SCHOOL

When we get to school, of course, we find that the picture is not quite as rosy as it might be.

HMI have this to say:

> The National Secondary Survey recorded curricula in many schools which, especially in years 4 and 5 [now referred to as 10 and 11], were heavily dominated by writing, largely of a kind requiring notes and summaries. In consequence, talk tended to be squeezed out, especially that type of talk which helps young people to handle new ideas, to develop a reasoned argument, to internalize their experiences and to find personal expression for them.[5]

Unfortunately, it does seem that when you look at the school system as children move up through it talk does get squeezed out of the classroom. There are, of course, lots of reasons why this happens.

Why is talk not encouraged? When I have asked this question of groups of teachers, these are the sorts of answers they give:

1 Concerns about noise, lack of control or handing over control, discipline problems and so on.
2 Syllabus constraints and lack of time, particularly in the secondary school.
3 The exam system: when it comes down to it in the secondary school particularly you show what you know you can do by picking up a pen and writing.
4 The difficulty of evaluating what is happening.
5 Organisational difficulties to do with space, layout of chairs and so on.
6 The fact that talk has got a life of its own; you cannot guarantee what pupils will do. This is a concern to do with control over knowledge and over what counts as being relevant in the classroom.
7 Finally, entrenched attitudes to methodology. In other words, teachers who operate with a model of learning which does not admit that talk is a vital part of the learning process. If you do not have that it seems to me that all of these other constraints are likely to get in the way. On the other hand, if you do have a view of the learning process which admits the importance of talk, that immediately enables you to start overcoming some of these other barriers – they are not insurmountable.

Some of these objections are obviously deeply rooted as part of the system we work in. Some of them are things you can overcome in your own classroom. More important than all of that is the need to recognise that all teachers everywhere suffer from these sorts of constraints and that there is no point in feeling guilty about it. Once you actually get over that business of feeling guilty then very often you can begin to find ways round some of the problems that are presented by talk.

GETTING THE CLIMATE RIGHT FOR TALK

Most of the research evidence points to the fact that pupils are rarely given opportunities to engage with a variety of spoken language contexts as part of their regular school experiences. What this reminds us of is the fact that the curriculum and the way it is taught are pretty impervious to change. To extend the metaphor a little, we can see the curriculum as a kind of solid bedrock covered by the soil of learning – rich and fertile in parts, but also with large areas of thin, poorly cultivated soil. Talk is one of the essential nutrients – without it there is little long-term growth and only the strongest plants manage to prosper. In such a situation, what is needed is not a bulk order for more watering cans, but a change in climate!

What is involved in achieving this – or at least in beginning to take the first steps? Having worked with a number of groups of teachers who have been tackling the challenge, I would like to offer a few tentative thoughts in response to this question myself.

1 Learning first, talk second – it is what talk can do for our pupils, as well as what they can do with talk, that is our main concern. Oracy is important, but not as important as understanding. The two kinds of development – learning through, and learning to use – are intertwined.

2 Excitement and development of talk first, assessment second – we need to ask 'What kinds of talk (and writing, reading, thinking) do I want to stimulate in my classroom?' and then 'How can I assess these?'

3 A repertoire of teaching approaches – we need to be on the alert for talking and listening opportunities as part of a wider repertoire of teaching and learning strategies. Oracy should be seen not as instead of other activities, but as one of a number of ways of helping pupils to make and communicate meaning. We also need to be aware of the particular value of talk as a way of exploring and sharing understanding – what we might call 'shared drafting' – and of reshaping and presenting understanding with others. There will be times when it is more appropriate for pupils to be silently reading, writing, listening to the teacher, and others when they will be busily talking, often within the same lesson or activity.

4 Flexible classrooms – in order to ensure that talk can be one of a number of currents of activity, classrooms will need to be flexible enough to allow for individual, pair, small-group and whole-class activities. Teachers will need to be flexible enough both to plan for such activities and to adapt what they are doing when the occasion arises. (One science colleague of mine said recently that the major shift of perspective he had undergone as a result of being involved in the Wiltshire oracy project was that 'now when I run out of things for the class to do I think of something they can talk about'.) In addition we need to build in flexible, open-ended

sequences of work which lend themselves both to classroom-based and out of school contexts for talk.

5 The task's the thing – we need to recognise the importance of context, and the way the spoken word is influenced by the nature of the task and the behaviour of the other participants (including ourselves). Because talk is usually interactive, we have far less control as speakers over what we say than we do in writing – we can be interrupted, sidetracked, steamrollered, ignored or we can receive offputting non-verbal signals which make us lose confidence, or lose our drift. It is consequently important that we try to set up conditions which are likely to work in favour of pupils' talk rather than against it. This certainly involves being able to seize the chance to build in some talk when the occasion arises, but it also means that we need to plan carefully for providing a range of opportunities. Oracy will not feature centrally if we leave it solely to chance or if we provide the pupils with vague, unfocused instructions, purposes and outcomes. If we want to encourage pupils to learn how to develop a reasoned argument, or to establish a hypothesis, then we need to think carefully about setting up tasks and contexts which are most likely to elicit this kind of talk.

6 Teacher intervention – we need to know when to intervene, when to keep out – and how. As a rough rule of thumb I tend to intervene less at the initial stages, reserving my interventions to the sorting out of groups which are having trouble getting started, and get more involved when pupils are ready to try their ideas out. The way in which we intervene can be crucial too. Individuals or groups of pupils will respond very differently to being asked 'How are you getting on? Any problems?' (teacher in stereotypical role as trouble shooter and assessor), compared to 'Tell me about what you've found out?' (teacher as listener – what I've called the 'attentive passenger'[6] role, in which the pupils are encouraged to take the driving seat, and the teacher adopts the stance of an intelligent, interested and at times knowledgeable listener). Pupils can so often feel powerless in interaction with an adult, particularly a teacher who 'knows it all already'. It can require a great effort on our part to counter the many ways in which schools make pupils feel that they don't have a legitimate voice in the learning process.

There are no hard and fast rules for this, of course – different teachers will develop their own styles for intervening and joining in as part of pupil talk. To illustrate this, here are some comments by a science teacher, reflecting on his role in promoting learning through talk in his lessons:

If you want discussion to fail in your classroom, keep a low profile, put vague or ambiguous questions to the whole group, and take responses only from the chosen few. The most successful sessions I have experienced have seen me maintaining a high profile, wandering through the groups, clearly 'listening in' and occasionally joining in, pushing where necessary, chiding where the occasion demands, encouraging. No one in the class dares to believe they are not observed and are likely to be called upon. This is not as threatening as it sounds. It is just that if I value the activity then I will be vigorous in encouraging involvement. It is, after all, part of my role as a teacher.[7]

What this all adds up to, then, is that if we want to encourage our pupils to talk, we have got to behave differently. Oracy will have more chance of flourishing in the classroom if we can succeed in providing a richer variety of roles for both sets of participants in the teaching and learning interaction.

Some suggestions for pupil roles:

1 Pupils working to their own agenda – having a personal stake in the activity, being provided with some degree of choice over what they are doing and how they are going to tackle it.
2 Pupils as experts – talking about what they know to someone who does not know. As well as the exploratory talk mentioned earlier, we need also to build in opportunities for more sustained talk, when there's a 'press' on the pupils' language, a demand, recognised by the pupils, that what is said needs to take into account the state of knowledge of the listeners and thus requires a degree of explicitness not necessary in collaborative talk.
3 Pupils 'in role' – through the use of drama approaches, simulations. This can have the effect of helping them to say things they would never otherwise have said, in fresh ways.

THE RADICAL SHIFT

Although a commitment to oracy *is* about techniques and strategies that we might try to build in, it is also much more than this. If we are serious about committing ourselves to children's spoken language, bringing it into the centre of education, allowing the child's voice to have more of a part to play, that entails a radical shift in our expectations of children, in the way we go about organising learning in our classrooms and the sorts of roles that are taken on by both teachers and pupils.

That is a major challenge. I think the important thing is for the teacher to begin to make the first steps and to recognise that there are ways of actually moving in that direction without feeling that it is too oppressive an idea.

We are at a most interesting time in the field of language and education, with the real possibility of the right sorts of developments being encouraged on the ground in schools which might begin to lead to 'the radical shift'. As will have become clear from what I have written so far, this is an issue that transcends the concerns of English departments in the secondary school, and is the rightful concern of all teachers. As another of the teachers who has been involved in the Wiltshire oracy project has written: 'We need to make oral approaches part of the stock in trade of all teachers, and in so doing help to make pupils more active in their learning.'[8]

I started this chapter by calling it 'Perspectives on oracy'. I have no doubt that the perspective that has developed gradually among those of us who have been working in Wiltshire has begun to seep through what I have been writing. In the end, of course, the story has only just begun. Maybe the tide is shifting for oracy in new and vigorous ways. There are, however, equally powerful voices which would pull us in a different direction. Cinderella has been invited to the ball – the question is, which tune is she going to be asked to dance to?

NOTES

1 DES (1988) *Report of the Committee of Inquiry into the Teaching of English* (The Kingman Report), London: HMSO.
2 G. Brown *et al.* (1984) *Teaching Talk – Strategies for Production and Assessment*, Cambridge: Cambridge University Press.
3 D. Barnes (1976) *From Communication to Curriculum*, London: Penguin.
4 G. Boomer (1985) *Fair Dinkum Teaching and Learning*, New Jersey: Boynton/Cook.
5 DES (1985) *The Curriculum from 5 to 16 (Curriculum Matters 2)*, London: HMSO.
6 A. Howe (1988) 'Releasing pupil talk', in *English Education*, Spring, NATE.
7 R. Essex (1987) *Oracy Matters*, Journal of the Wiltshire Oracy Project, Wiltshire LEA.
8 J. Smith (1984) *Oracy Matters*, Journal of the Wiltshire Oracy Project, Wiltshire LEA.

Chapter 6

Planning for learning through talk

Jenny Des Fountain

You learn a lot more if you can talk and communicate and discuss things with people rather than a teacher standing in front of you and drumming information into you: and I don't think that teachers realise that. But in practice, that does work better because we can all do better at a lesson if we're allowed to communicate and talk than if we're sitting behind a desk copying out a sheet about a Science experiment or something.

This was the way that a 15-year-old pupil in a Darlington school[1] summed up her perception of the centrality of the role of talk in learning. She is talking about the sort of learning which becomes part of our mental stock in trade. As she says at a later point, 'This way, you're not (just) learning it, but remembering it and understanding it as well.' Douglas Barnes[2] has defined this as 'action knowledge':

School knowledge is the knowledge which someone else presents to us. We partly grasp it, enough to answer the teacher's questions, to do exercises, or to answer examination questions, but it remains someone else's knowledge, not ours. If we never use this knowledge we probably forget it. In so far as we use knowledge for our own purposes however we begin to incorporate it into our view of the world, and to use parts of it to cope with the exigencies of living. Once the knowledge becomes incorporated into that view of the world on which our actions are based I would say that it has become 'action knowledge'.

In this chapter, I hope to show some of the ways that teachers have planned for learning which will result in 'action knowledge', using purposeful talk. As English teachers, we are aware of the inevitable interrelatedness of language and learning; we learn through talk, we reflect on our uses of talk, learning more about talk and about how we might wish to develop as good speakers and listeners, whatever that might mean to us at a particular time of our lives, or as members of a particular community. This chapter will focus on learning through talk but will, of course, also point to some of the ways that teachers can support young people's development as speakers and listeners. Its theoretical underpinning comes from the work of psychologists such as Vygotsky, Piaget and Bruner, whose work has indicated the ways that learners actively construct meaning, sharing experiences in words in order to make better sense of them.

WHAT ABOUT THE TEACHER?

Teachers will want to consider establishing the classroom conditions which are needed, in order to make learning through talk a reality in our classrooms. As teachers, we need to be aware of the importance of finding ways to listen carefully to what our pupils actually say, and to value their ideas. We need to plan for a range of tasks which highlight speaking and listening, and we need to find ways to make explicit to our pupils what we are asking them to do, and why. Most important of all, we need to have confidence in our pupils' learning, and in our own abilities to plan for it. As Douglas Barnes[3] has written: 'Whatever teaching methods a teacher chooses – question and answer, guided discovery, demonstration, or another – it will always be the pupil who has to do the learning.' Teaching is never simply a matter of transferring an idea from teacher or textbook or activity into a pupil's mind. It is about creating opportunities for pupils to work on their understandings, to engage with new information or interpretations in a way that supplements or challenges their existing concepts or frameworks. Talk, for most young people, is the most flexible and accessible tool for working on understanding.

The widely observed mismatch between the subtlety of observation, discussion and analysis when these are conducted orally rather than in writing can be redressed when oracy is truly valued in a classroom. Teachers and pupils can give credit for pupils' thinking in oral feedback and in written records and assessments. This works to highlight the learning achievements of all pupils, but especially, perhaps, those who are struggling with literacy in English. Discussing the difference between talk and writing as vehicles for reviewing their own work, an 11-year-old commented, 'Sometimes you can't describe as well on paper' and a classmate added, 'When you write it, you want to keep it short and brief because you don't like writing, but people like talking, so they give you more detail.'

At the early stages of a sequence of work, collaborative talk can help create a readiness to learn. It can help pupils to review their existing understandings about a topic, to begin to identify the areas where they themselves realise there is a gap, or simply to gather together the thoughts which the sequence of work will hopefully rework, challenge, and reshape, if learning has taken place. The ephemeral nature of talk is what works so well, at this stage, allowing pupils to make statements and quickly retract them as they recall a more 'accurate' version of their understandings, or develop ideas in response to others' contributions. It makes it possible to take risks, to try out ideas and hear how they sound. Pupils build themselves a stake in the next stage of the process, as they have already contributed their own ideas and know that the teacher has acknowledged the extent of their existing knowledge.

Teachers gain a valuable opportunity to listen and to learn about their pupils' starting points. This is essential, of course, when we find ourselves teaching a Year 7 class which has come from a large number of different primary schools or when we are planning for differentiated learning. Enabling pupils literally to gather their thoughts can also provide teachers with good opportunities to make cross-curricular links, too, as we hear pupils reminding each other, for example 'We did something like this in Drama, last year.'

CLASSROOM STRATEGIES

There are many ways to organise small-group work which will encourage pupils to review their current understandings. Three examples of classroom strategies:

1 Brainstorm, e.g. pairs quickly remember and write down three reasons why people write poetry, then share their ideas with another pair, rework them and appoint one person to feed back to a whole-class scribe.
2 Talk partners can be asked to interview each other to find out what their partner thinks or knows about x or y.
3 Talk partners can be given a minute to review what they did at the last session and what they hope to achieve in this one.

As pupils begin work on a topic, they will need opportunities to test out the strength of their existing understandings. As Douglas Barnes[3] has written: 'Most of our important learning, in school or out, is a matter of constructing models of the world, finding out how far they work by using them, and then reshaping them in the light of what happens.' Pair and small-group talk can provide a powerful arena for such learning. Talk's flexibility, the opportunities it presents to reformulate, to think aloud, to try out ideas and see how far they will work, allows pupils to decide how far their existing frameworks can assimilate the new knowledge, or must be changed to accommodate it, to use Piagetian terms. Well-planned tasks will provide opportunities for pupils to try ideas out for size, 'How do I know what I mean until I hear what I say?', and to do this in an atmosphere where tentativeness can be valued and supported, allowing connections to be made between the earlier framework and the new information or interpretation.

Year 11 pupils working on gender issues commented on a small-group discussion task, where they had been working to gather ideas: 'It makes you think of things you haven't thought of – and didn't bother to think about' and 'I think it makes you realise what you're actually thinking about, what you're saying before you say it.'

Two more examples of classroom strategies:

4   Statement games can provide a useful focus for a group's exploration, e.g. of ideas about the value of talk, where pupils were asked to discuss statements in order to come to an agreement about how they would sort them – into agree/disagree columns, or into rank order of importance.

5   Jigsawing, where a topic is set and subdivided into areas. 'Home Groups' are formed, and each child in the Home Group is given one of the topic areas in which to become an 'expert'. The child then joins prospective 'experts' in the same area from the other Home Groups, to form an 'expert group'. Each expert group works on its chosen area, and then the members return to their Home Groups to make a report and to share in putting their whole set of discoveries together. Each 'Home Group' can then present its work to others. In secondary schools this work might go on over several periods, or be done more quickly in one.[4] For example, 'expert' groups researching an aspect of Anglo-Saxon life, prior to reading *Dragon Slayer*, put together the questions from their 'Home Groups' and helped each other find answers from a range of information texts.

Pupils will find themselves able to renegotiate ways of handling the topic, and to make sense of new information, discussing it within their own set of cultural references and in the variety of English or in the community language which best suits their needs.

There will be space, too, to take risks, to 'play' with language and with ideas, to experiment with their own formulations of ideas, but also to try out other voices – the voice of the text, or of the teacher, for example. A teacher of Year 6 offered tapes and time to make tape diaries, on which pupils could record any item of particular interest to them. Some pupils used the tape diary to record their work – for example, the outcomes from their science experiments – whereas others chose to record more personal interests and concerns. Sometimes the tape diaries seemed to provide good opportunities for 'trying on' voices and ideas to see how far they suited their users. An 11-year-old boy, in his taped account of a football match he had seen, can be heard to try out a range of 'voices' as he chooses his words. We hear a TV sports commentator: 'He's gone past the goalkeeper, the two Derby County's players, he's done it, it's Kevin Keen!' We hear the voice of older spectators, perhaps the father who took him to the match, explaining the play to him: 'The big lanky bloke there got it away. Mark Patterson's got it away 'cause he's very tall.' We also hear him try out for size the rather aggressive swagger of the adolescent supporters: 'I'm going to Watford on Saturday with the junior members and we're going to beat them, no problem, so sit on that one.'

Teachers in the National Oracy Project found that some aspects of the 'teacherly' role of guiding and supporting pupils' learning could in fact be provided within well-planned and organised group work. Pupils working together can provide each other with an extremely productive social support system for their learning. There can be a sympathetic, but rarely sentimental, valuing and evaluation of each other's contributions. For example, here is a Year 8 pupil evaluating his own and his talk partner's work on a one-minute radio news item based on an incident in the class's reader:

> Me and Gary did a 'Crimestoppers' about the machine gun that had been stolen. We had an eye witness. I talked and listened quite good. Gary did very well considering what he would normally do but he thought he done badly.

In well-planned lessons, pupils can provide each other with authentic and immediate audiences – no need to wait to attract the attention of a teacher who has to hold the needs of twenty-nine other pupils in his or her head as he or she listens. Asking pupils to 'Find out what your partner thinks about x or knows about y' highlights listening skills and makes it much easier for quiet or shy pupils to speak and be listened to.

Working within well-defined ground rules for talk, pupil groups can provide support for the intellectual and linguistic risk taking which is an important part of working on understanding; learning through talk can make the learning audible, accessible, no longer hidden in the mysteries and silences of reading, thinking and writing – as they may appear to less confident pupils. Working in small groups can also be seen to be providing a kind of privacy, a safe place for trying out ideas before they need to be presented to a larger audience or to a teacher.

Whenever adults work together in small groups, they are aware of the need to take time out from the task, which may involve a sidetrack into social talk or into silence. Often this actually enhances our ability to return to the task after some time to think – or to find another way into thinking about the problem at hand. One teacher reflected on her experience of this, working in a group of adults at an oracy conference. She wrote:

> Intense silence followed either a decision being made or a 'dead end' being reached. These silences were broken by the group cracking jokes before returning to the task in hand.
>
> I didn't give any of this a second thought until I asked my Year 9 group to record themselves discussing a project they had been working on. Before the oracy weekend, I would have listened in on each group, nagged pupils sitting in silence and been suspicious of arguments and laughter. However, without realising it, I had learned the value of dis-agreement, witticisms and silences as ways of consolidating and freeing talk. For the first time I felt confident about leaving pupils alone while they were working.

Pupils working together in groups often operate to allow each other this sort
of space for thinking and learning and, given that the task is well designed
and that they feel they understand why they are working through talk, will
regulate themselves; 'Sometimes you go on to different things but you have
to be firm with yourself', as a Year 11 pupil commented.

Having provided time for reviewing what they already know about a
topic, and time to explore new materials or ideas, it is often helpful to build
into the sequence of work a time when pupils have an opportunity to share
where they have got to, to present to others what they have learned, or to
take up a position which they are now ready to argue and defend. At this
stage in the learning process, groups may decide to come back to ideas which
may have been put forward by one person but can now be interpreted and
expanded by others. It is a time of consolidation, of organisation of the
developed framework of ideas.

In a jigsaw structure, this is the time when pupils prepare to present their
ideas to their 'Home Group'. Of course, the presentation can be on tape, in
writing, on an overhead transparency, or in any appropriate form, but talk,
again, offers the flexibility which allows pupils to try out ideas but be
prepared to rethink and rework in response to the comments and feedback
they gain from the next round.

The pupils who return to their Home Groups now have an opportunity to
try out the 'expert' role, and to claim a 'long turn' (in Andrew Wilkinson's
terms[5]) to explain what they have found out or thought through. Long turns
allow pupils to clarify their own understandings, voicing them to an
audience which can be designed to be receptive – for example, if the group
knows that it needs this particular piece of information to complete its task –
or critical – for example, if each 'expert' is returning to the Home Group
with an argument which the others need to critique before deciding on their
group decision about the best place to site the new motorway in a simulation
exercise.

The 'presentation' talk, at this stage, is often a place where understandings
are once again tried out, to see how far they stretch, to test their strength. It
sometimes helps to find a new audience for the learning, at this time – for
example, another class in the year who are studying *Romeo and Juliet* could
be visited by the class who have already studied it and whose task has been
to devise an introduction for the second class. Many pupils respond well to
the challenge of planning ways of sharing their understandings with younger
pupils and blossom as 'experts' when they meet an audience of junior or
infant pupils – for example, when talking through with Year 6 pupils what
they might expect at the transition to secondary school.

Teachers in the National Oracy Project found that planning a reflection
time, when pupils could look back over what they had done and learned,
was to plan for yet another important stage in the learning process. In a
sense, reflection is built in at each stage, whenever pupils are asked to explain

how far they have got, or what they have noticed, or what their initial reactions have been. At the end of a lesson, or at the end of a sequence of work, even a minute or two to reflect on learning and to tell someone else – in speech or in writing – can help to consolidate work done and provide the first stage of identifying the way forward. It is a powerful way of establishing pupils' ownership of their learning, as they are defining it for themselves and for their teacher.

Planning time for reflection also allows the teacher time to listen to pupils, to learn about their learning, and, if necessary, to collect evidence of it for records of individuals' progress.

Other examples of classroom strategies:

6 *Talk diaries:* pupils can be asked to make very brief notes about what they have noticed or learned. Here are some Year 10 pupils' notes in response to the question 'What have I learned, so far?' scribbled in two minutes at the end of a three-lesson unit on poetry: 'Poems don't have to rhyme to be good.' 'If you don't understand a poem the first time you read it, don't put it down and give up. Persistence is really the most important thing I learned. The poem was better the second time round.'

A talk diary logs one Year 9 pupil's self-evaluation of his oral work on the class's reader. In this case, the teacher had begun some sessions with a brainstorm to establish the group's criteria for good speaking and listening, and her pupils were asked to bear these in mind when they wrote their talk diaries. For many students, this helps to clarify the aims for their oral work. In this pupil's case, it acted as a springboard for his sensitive analysis of both the task and his learning. For example:

> I find it easier to digest factual information in open discussion within a group because this does not only give you your own insight, but other people's. Although improvisation can help you understand people's feelings more deeply because you put yourself in their position.

7 *Discussion logs:* a pupil observer can be asked to make notes on the progress of a discussion, or can fill in a grid (again, preferably the items in the grid would be brainstormed with the class, e.g. identifying what makes a good storyteller for observation of a sequence of storytelling work). The pupil observer can then provide feedback for the members of the group.

8 *Pupil : pupil interviews:* talk partners can interview each other with the task of 'Find out what your partner learned about . . .' or, 'Find out what your partner enjoyed and what your partner found difficult, in today's work' instead of, or in preparation for, a written evaluation. This technique lead Samantha, a Year 8 pupil, to write this about her interview of her grandmother:

> I had a few problems on the interview because I had to do it on the phone, but I had gained a lot of evidence, and confidence from talking to my Nan. It was very good because I never talk to her all that much, and the discussion was done very well. I find it difficult talking to adults because they are older and it is hard. What I learnt from the interview is that you have to put questions in certain ways so that the person can understand. If I could do it again I would ask more specific questions and say what I mean. And I would try to be patient in waiting for an answer.

9 *Pupil group : teacher conference:* when the teacher has established the reflection stage of the learning process, he or she may draw up a rota of visits to groups in the class, finding out how the work has gone, where the group feel they were successful and where they feel they need help.

10 *Tape evaluation:* a teacher in a middle school in Dudley asked her Year 7 groups to review a section of tape where they had recorded their work on a statements game about foxhunting. They were asked to: 'Find an example of (a) you expressing an opinion, (b) you giving evidence to support your opinion, (c) you listening to the views of others' etc.

Dorothy Heathcote[6] has said:

> If you cannot increase reflective power in people, you might as well not teach, because reflection is the only thing in the long run that teaches anybody. Reflection is what makes the knowing something that can be touched on and assimilated for further use.

Teachers are able to create a strong and purposeful framework for learning through talk. We are able to monitor its effectiveness by learning to become skilful listeners at each stage of the process, but especially by considering the messages that we hear or read in pupils' own reflections on their learning.

Most importantly, we are building into our teaching repertoire sequences of work which enable pupils' new understandings to become part of the way that they interpret and analyse the world, when we plan for learning through talk.

ACKNOWLEDGEMENTS

I have drawn heavily on the work of the National Oracy Project in this chapter, and wish to make a special acknowledgement to Alan Howe, in discussion with whom many of these ideas were first formulated for a chapter in *Thinking Voices*. Douglas Barnes' analysis and descriptions of classroom practice have provided much inspiration. The work of Jo-Anne Reid, Peter Forrestal and Jonathan Cook, in *Small Group Learning in the Classroom*, English and Media Centre/NATE, 1991, has also been influential.

My thanks to the following teachers, whose classrooms provided many of my examples: Margaret Beck, Deborah Berrill, Angela Dale, Lynne Johnson and Janet Shaw in the London Borough of Havering; Marina Cash in the London Borough of Enfield; and Brenda Madeley in Dudley.

NOTES

1 On the videotape which accompanies *Learning Together Through Talk; Key Stages 3 and 4*, ed. Hilary Kemeny, Hodder and Stoughton, 1993.
2 Barnes, Douglas in *From Communication to Curriculum*, Penguin, 1976.
3 Barnes, Douglas in *Thinking Voices*, ed. Kate Norman, Hodder and Stoughton, 1992.
4 NCC/NOP, *Teaching Talking and Learning in Key Stage Three*, NCC, 1991.
5 Wilkinson, Andrew in *Spoken English Illuminated*, ed. Andrew Wilkinson, Alan Davies and Deborah Berrill, Open University Press, 1990.
6 Heathcote, Dorothy quoted in *Drama as a Learning Medium*, ed. Betty Jane Wagner, Washington, DC, National Educational Association, 1976.

Chapter 7

Talking and assessment in secondary English

National Oracy Project

SEAC says in its leaflet, 'Teacher Assessment at Key Stage 3' (1991):

> Teacher assessment is an integral part of teaching and learning in the classroom. Teachers discuss with pupils, guide their work, ask and answer questions, observe, encourage, challenge, help and focus. In addition they mark and review written work and other outcomes. Through these activities they are continually finding out about their pupils' capabilities and achievements. This knowledge then informs plans for future work. It is this continuous process that comprises teacher assessment. It should not be seen as a separate activity necessarily requiring the use of extra tasks or tests.

THE PROCESS OF ASSESSMENT

How well pupils talk about any subject, or in any situation, depends on a number of factors. Among them are:

- their understanding of what the task in hand is, and how they should respond;
- the nature of their audience, or those responding to what they say;
- their interest in and commitment to the task;
- their knowledge and understanding of the subject;
- their fluency in English or other languages;
- their gender;
- their personality;
- the grouping in which they are working;
- their previous experience of similar situations;
- the general atmosphere of the classroom.

As a result, it is impossible to determine beforehand exactly how pupils will talk in any given situation. We may have general expectations of them, but their talk may follow totally different but still relevant paths and patterns. Teachers observing children, listening to or watching recordings of them, or analysing short transcripts, soon realise the limitations of any approach to oral assessment which only uses predetermined criteria to evaluate pupils' work.

For these reasons, teachers in a variety of oracy projects have developed models of assessment which involve collecting information about children's oral work over a wide range of contexts and over a period of time, and which involve the pupils and teachers, and on occasion the parents, in discussing and reflecting on the information collected. The information particularly concentrates on the children's best, most interesting or most noteworthy oral work, often described as 'catching them peaking'.

In such models the central and crucial activity is not evaluation but planning: planning for purposeful talk to occur in the classroom; planning for pupils to work more autonomously; planning for observation and record keeping of pupils' oral work; planning the accumulation of evidence on which summative judgements can be made.

Teachers in different situations will use different vocabulary to describe these models. For the sake of simplicity, this chapter identifies a single cyclical process of oral assessment which embraces these models. It involves planning; managing the learning environment; observation; recording; summarising; evaluating; making judgements; and reporting.

PUTTING THE PROCESS INTO ACTION

> Assessment should be a continuous process which reinforces teaching and learning.
>
> *(English for Ages 5 to 16*, HMSO, 1990)

Surveys of secondary schools often refer to the professional isolation of teachers within their different disciplines and the way in which they find it hard to recognise the wholeness of the experience offered by the curriculum. In schools in a wide range of oracy projects, talk is increasingly being seen as a focal and unifying area for curriculum development. Ways of developing talk, awareness of its importance in shaping learning, as well as its assessment, are becoming priority areas for INSET. Establishing such whole-school approaches to curriculum, language and assessment was recognised by HMI in the 'Secondary Schools' report as characterising best practice: 'In the majority of schools which had overall assessment policies, these not only contained guidance to teachers about the importance of assessment in relation to their other commitments but also provided advice on approaches to assessment.'

This suggests, too, that the clearer the links between the different stages and forms of assessment and the learning across the curriculum, the less time consuming and more effective it will be. Where better to start than with talk?

One Secondary school has set up an 'Oracy Working Party', aiming to develop a school 'oracy policy'. One member from each faculty in the school acts as a representative and feeds back to the faculty, setting 'talk' as a major curriculum development area for the whole school. Teachers have been encouraged (and freed!) to work in pairs for four half-days, spread over the school year, looking carefully at work in their respective subject areas, in different age groups (e.g. Year 7 and Year 11). They will try to chart the characteristics of talk at different developmental stages, to check out their observations together, and to begin to recognise the broader elements of progression, using samples they have collected.

It is important, then, that whole staffs develop the assessment policies that will best fit, both with existing practice in their schools, and with the requirements of the National Curriculum. Coming to broad agreements about the place of talk within learning will help to develop whole-staff awareness and confidence, and will generate important discussion about the nature of language and learning.

Planning

Above all, it is important to check first that learning is being managed in a way that allows the teacher sufficient opportunity to observe pupils' talk. The following short 'checklist' may serve as a reminder when drawing up schemes of work:

1 Will there be different kinds of talk, and will the pupils experience different roles and purposes for talk?
2 Is there a variety of groupings?
3 Is the classroom resourced and organised for talk?
4 Is there the right amount of time for talk?
5 Are there mechanisms for recording talk?
6 Are the pupils to be involved in the overall process?

Managing the learning environment

Teachers who have looked closely at their own and colleagues' work and roles in the classroom have been struck by how complex and varied teaching is. A teacher's day is characterised by many conversations with pupils on many different topics, in each of which there are specific demands on the teacher to come to terms with their pupils and to help their learning. It does not seem helpful to try to find additional time and space for conducting assessment. Rather, teachers who have developed oral assessment success-fully have done so by first reducing the other demands placed on them in the classroom. This often means managing the learning environment in a new way, reorganising furniture, resources, the way classroom tasks are set up and negotiated, the ways in which groupings operate, and so on, with the objective of increasing the autonomy and self-motivation of the pupils, and allowing the teacher more time to observe pupils at work.

Observation

Observation should be considered in its broadest terms, including using audio and video recorders, pupils' own observations and journals, and teacher observation which can be done both from a distance and when working with pupils, or listening to their conversations. The aim is that information both of immediate value (for formative assessment) and for later use (in summative assessment) should be gathered through this observation, and recorded in suitable form so that it can be understood both by you and by others.

Allowing time for reviews with pupils, wherever possible, makes assessment through talk less of a 'snap' judgement and more of a discussion of ways forward. The formative element in assessment should clearly indicate to pupils what steps they can take in order to extend learning or achievement, but this should be done in as supportive a way as possible. Such dialogues can help pupils to discover their own resources, to take responsibility for their own learning, to improve, to feel more confident. In turn, 'dialogues' can help teachers identify how pupils made sense of the challenge, how they felt during the work, what strategies might help them to develop and how the curriculum might be influenced or changed as a result. It is probable then that, through talk, it will be the pupils' perceptions of the task that will be uncovered and the next step negotiated in such a way that they feel confident and challenged to be successful. In a review session such as this, the assessment of talk will be given a proper context. It will not seem false, and it will give proper attention to the role of talk in developing learning and understanding.

You may also consider adopting other approaches to gathering evidence:

- Note one group's work only, for a period of five minutes or more, and review later what each pupil was doing.
- Focus on one particular pupil, perhaps because of some direct concern about her or his work or progress.
- Encourage pupils to tape-record and to evaluate their own discussions.
- Ask pupils to keep a 'talk diary' in which they comment on how their own task has helped their learning and that of others.
- Keep a journal, or a set of file cards or monitoring sheets, in which your observations can be written instantly.
- Use a hand-held tape recorder (dictating kind) to record short extracts of talk and your comments about it.

Recording

In the last decade schools have revolutionised their record-keeping procedures, so that much more information is now available about pupils' achievements across the curriculum. Yet surprisingly little of this evidence is in a form appropriate to oral assessment.

> Teachers in one school compared notes on the record-keeping of various departments. They found that much of the information being gathered was duplicated in several subjects, but that it was mostly limited to descriptions of completed written work. They reviewed the procedures to try to get more knowledge about learning as it occurred.

By following the principles suggested in earlier sections of this chapter, it is possible to keep a record which gathers your own observations, pupils' and others' comments, and perhaps some tape-recorded examples of pupils at work. These may be kept in a record book, a file-card index, a loose-leaf file, a box file, or any similarly accessible place.

> In one middle school, teachers encouraged pupils to keep an audio-cassette of their own oral work in different subject areas. On occasions the teachers would ask to listen to children's recordings, and would talk with them about the work.

Periodic quick reviews of the records will show if there are any pupils whose work has not been recorded adequately, or where there are gaps in the records which suggest that you should look for some particular evidence.

Records will also build on those previously maintained by teachers. These should be used in the whole planning and management of learning, and will be especiallly useful in ensuring a progression and continuity of learning experience and achievement.

Summarising

At various points in pupils' progress teachers may wish to make a summary of their achievements. If sufficient evidence has been collected, even if it is in a variety of media, it should be possible to summarise what pupils' oral work has revealed. Teachers have devised a number of frameworks for doing this. For the assessment of speaking and listening, this framework might consist of the following:

- using language effectively;
- taking part in discussions and group work;
- telling stories and giving accounts;
- preparing presentations and performances;
- language awareness;
- other.

The following strategies may be helpful:

- Focus particularly on what developments are indicated since the previous summary or review.
- Use language which other readers will be able to understand.
- Check that the summary covers all necessary aspects of the pupils' work and the subjects/attainments targets required for your assessment.
- Halt the summarising process if you find you are lacking important evidence, and make some further observations.

Consider particularly such aspects of work as:

- the use of evidence, supporting material, etc.;
- evidence of reasoning;
- ability to develop a personal viewpoint;
- ability to respond to alternative viewpoints;
- ability to engage in fresh thinking;
- understanding of concepts;
- ability to use knowledge, to sustain an argument, to organise ideas or explanations for a listener;
- the quality of the research, planning and preparation;
- the quality of listening and response.

Evaluating

As was said earlier, the process of assessing pupils orally requires teachers at some point to differentiate between the *talk itself* and what is *shown through the talk*.

An example of the first came when a teacher working with two partially hearing pupils who spend part of their week in a mainstream middle school came to evaluate their progress. She wrote:

> I have been very aware this year of an improvement in their group discussion skills. In the Unit, they tend to dominate their group in a way which does not readily accommodate others. Obviously they are not in a position to do this in the middle school and they usually try very hard to concentrate on the others' contributions, as well as being ready to join in themselves . . . . I hope to analyse more closely their ability to be a part of the group in the various tasks they undertake and to see if there are ways in which this can be facilitated. I am keen for them to be in charge of the use of sign interpretation, rather than for everything to be directed through me. It also offers an opportunity for me to assess their skills in comparison with their hearing peers.

Here the emphasis is clearly on the developing social and communicative abilities of the two pupils, and less on the cognitive development arising from the group discussions.

An example of the latter occurred when three Year 9 pupils were working together. One was asking another about what she had observed when a fabric was heated. The teacher noted that although in the whole conversation the children sometimes strained for the right language, they nevertheless used non-technical language to good effect in gradually building a picture of what had been observed. Here it is the scientific technique of observation which is being assessed, although the pupils' use of questioning and responsiveness plays a major part in revealing what they know.

These teachers are starting to evaluate the evidence which they have gathered and recorded. Both have shown that evaluating talk is not alien to teachers; rather, it helps them to make explicit understandings and insights which had often hitherto been internalised and remained hidden. Of course, the process of evaluation also involves being open and honest about the criteria for evaluation, and there is a need to be wary of the inner prejudices and false assumptions that everyone holds concerning talk. There is also a risk of bias in the way talk is perceived. It is very hard to avoid valuing one accent more highly than another, or to apply the same positive criteria to evaluating all children's oral work.

Making judgements

Teachers will be required to make judgements about the overall levels of attainment achieved by pupils. Teachers have been encouraged to keep records of the kind described in this chapter, and schools are required to issue reports on pupils' work and progress which will no doubt draw on such records.

Certain preparatory actions can nevertheless be taken which may assist you with the eventual task of making these judgements. In particular, it is helpful if your department or school records some children working, in such a way that groups of teachers can talk about the work and try to reach provisional agreement about what judgements should be made. Talking about a number of children from different years may also give you some feel for pupils' progression and development.

Reporting

Reports on children's oral work are needed by several groups – most importantly, children themselves; their parents; and other teachers and relevant educational staff. The establishment of reporting as part of a statutory process – of offering written reports to parents summarising performance by profile component and subject, combining the results of Teacher Assessment and SATs – may blind us to the broader task of providing information and feedback to children, parents and others about success in oral work. In many instances, schools have had to find new ways of doing this, since so many of our reporting conventions are based on work in literacy. For example, at parents' evenings and on open days, schools have found ways of demonstrating children's oral achievements – *'listen to your child's audio-tape'* or *'please allow these two children to show you around the school'*.

Reporting, if we think of it in broad terms, may occur at any stage in the assessment process, from the first observation onwards. It involves responding to pupils in ways which show that we have understood and appreciated their achievements, and it involves teachers making direct reference at particular points in any learning process to the success or failure of work which has been going on around them. Many oracy project teachers have discovered the value of this kind of 'interim' or 'progress' report, whether to individuals or to whole groups.

Chapter 8

Bilingualism and oracy

Diana Cinamon

What are the implications for the bilingual children in our schools of a heightened interest in oracy? For all children there will be greater awareness of the role of talk in learning, more thought given to planning for talk, and more emphasis on *oracy* as a skill to be developed. For bilingual children this should have positive advantages. Talk has long been recognised as essential for supporting the acquisition of a second language. If talk is accompanied by practical activities and concrete experiences it helps children to understand concepts, develop skills and learn English while doing so. But what if the talk that is valued and encouraged is English only? What about the crucial relationship between language and learning?

Clearly all children need to be able to use the English language for a variety of purposes if they are to have equal opportunity within our schools and society. A monolingual English classroom which provides practical activities and encourages talk between children creates a learning environment which makes it possible for children who are new to English to understand something of what is going on around them and what is expected of them. But this experience of school is inevitably different from one where the teachers understand the child's language, and where this language can be shared with peers.

I became interested in bilingualism when children with home languages other than English first joined my class. At the time I did not think of the children as bilingual, but as children learning English as a second language. Referring to the children as bilingual came at a later stage when I realised that the ESL concept had negative connotations. The children were operating in two (or more) languages in their daily lives and therefore were bilingual, or even multilingual.

My concern was to help the children gain in understanding and take part in class activities alongside their peers. Having experience of group work in a withdrawal situation I knew this was not a solution. Despite the seductive cosiness of the small group, children do not get access to the same curriculum as the rest of the class, so even in that pre-Calderdale era I was committed to mainstream support. (In 1986 the separate ESL provision of this Local Education Authority was found to contravene the Race Relations Act 1976.) Withdrawal also cuts children off from their peers who provide models of English and the inevitable message for all is that bilingual children are not fit to participate fully in the ordinary class.

I began to reconsider the content of the curriculum I was offering to all the children. I knew that the bilingual children's motivation would be affected by what was offered, and that this would also influence the attitudes of the other children. How were our activities chosen? Whose views were represented? What about the language policy? How should we approach reading and writing? What about resources? Were the books and materials offensive? Did they portray stereotyped images of people of different racial backgrounds? What were my attitudes, and what would be the effect of these on the achievement of the children? I also needed to monitor the children's learning in order to help them progress, so I began to find ways of responding to the needs of the children without relying on what they could tell me as the main indicator of their understanding. This involved closer observation of the strategies the children used when approaching tasks.

To develop their learning and their English I planned more collaborative work to increase the opportunities for all children to work and talk together. Being part of an interactive group provides opportunities for bilingual children to:

- be involved at an appropriate conceptual level, learning, contributing, listening, gaining in understanding without having to speak until ready to do so (children's receptive language is always in advance of their productive speech and trying to get them to speak before they are ready may hinder progress);
- take part (a silent part perhaps) in conversations about events and things in which the children are engaged, which is the natural way to acquire language, whether first or second;
- hear models of the English language. The language the children will learn the most readily will be the language of their peers. Even when most of the children are bilingual there will still be those who are more proficient than others in English to provide models;
- make language their own by using it in a variety of situations, which includes the opportunity to return to some learning via different routes. This gives essential rehearsal and practice, more effective for language learning than sterile drills or exercises;
- experiment as they learn with the language structures they have acquired to express meaning. The first language will not *interfere* with learning a second and such errors as do occur are likely to be evidence of learning in the same way that young children acquiring their first language make errors as they sort out the structure of the language.

Despite the advantages of the above approach for all the children in the class it was not long before I realised that there was a contradiction between what I understood as *good* practice, which values and builds on the knowledge and understanding children bring to school, and an educational system which disregards one of the most fundamental attributes anyone has – their language. Although I had, or thought I had, positive attitudes to the children, some children I knew lived in bilingual communities claimed not to speak languages other than English and certainly these were rarely used in school. They had clearly imbibed an ethos which devalued their linguistic background. Considering the emphasis given to the role of language and its influence on learning and achievement this ethos was discriminatory in effect.

I needed to use a major resource I had in my classroom, namely the languages of the children. The community was linguistically diverse, so that at one time in the classroom there were speakers of Gujerati, Spanish, Urdu, Sylheti, Cantonese, Farsi, Arabic (Moroccan), Singhalese, Portuguese, although often only one speaker of each language.

As it was never going to be possible to have teachers who spoke each of their languages the children needed a learning environment which actively valued, encouraged and used these in the classroom.

Where home languages have not been used in the classroom, strategies encouraging these require careful planning and preferably a whole-school commitment. Bilingual children will not be able to use their language to further their learning in an atmosphere which is hostile, or where such attitudes are subtly expressed. Where a school is sure of the advantages of using home languages in the classroom for all the children and can present this positively, it will be better able to prevent some of the insecurity which often accompanies change. Valuing the talk of bilingual pupils, and finding ways to use this positively, encourages teachers to take more account of the role of language in learning, and to plan more effectively to ensure talking and listening are an integral part of the curriculum with consequent benefits for all children.

SOME STRATEGIES TO ENCOURAGE THE USE OF HOME LANGUAGES

School level

Valuing and supporting bilingual staff:

- The role of the mother tongue teacher in relation to the class teacher. Who plans the curriculum, takes the register, writes reports, sees parents, goes on courses . . .?
- The bilingual class teacher. How to use this teacher's skills without *steering* him or her into bilingual issues. The school may benefit more if a bilingual teacher has responsibility for maths, for instance.
- What about attitudes to other bilingual staff?

Display notices, signs and children's written work in home languages.

Translation of letters home

- Difficult here not to overburden bilingual staff. A way of involving members of the community perhaps, or older children in either junior or secondary schools who would have a real purpose and audience for their writing. Links could also be made with community schools.

Language policy

- Include the role of talk in learning, the relationship of talk to literacy in home language and English, resources and assessment procedures. Ensure that home language teaching has a considered place in the curriculum (separate mother tongue teaching when others are doing maths will not lead to equal opportunity for bilingual children).
- Share with parents.

Class level

Plan collaborative work with clear purposes for talk. The benefits of collaboration outlined earlier are equally applicable to situations where the children are encouraged to use their home languages as well as English. In addition bilingual pupils can:

- Continue to learn: there does not have to be a learning freeze while they wait for their English to catch up.
- Use their home languages to sort out concepts when working with others who share these languages, either peers or bilingual adults.
- Use both languages (code-switch) as the need arises – bilingual children have no problems with this, and can move in and out of the languages even in mid-sentence with amazing facility. Both languages will develop without confusion.
- Bring in their own experiences naturally if their language is valued in the classroom.

Sensitive groupings of children

- Groups can be engineered to allow those who speak the same language to be together sometimes. The learning context will influence the children's willingness to use their home language. If bilingual children are in the minority they may need support to help them to do so. Groups can be together for different purposes. A pair makes an excellent group.

Tapes of stories in community languages

- We need strategies for their use which do not isolate bilingual children. Story props accompanying tapes could be used in mixed-language groups. Books with tapes can be shared. Children can talk about them in either language.

Parents/aunts/uncles etc. coming in to tell or read stories in the class languages to all the children

- Include the English-speaking parents. This will enhance the status of all parents in the eyes of the children who will also love the sounds and the experience. Once you get one parent in, the children will do the rest of the persuading for you.

Members of the bilingual community to come and work in a group

- Could be involved in an activity, working with the children and perhaps using their home language.

Books in home languages

- Fiction, preferably not dual texts but books in their own right. The message with the former is that a language has no value unless accompanied by English. There are also problems with translation, the direction of the book (e.g. is it read from left to right?), which language comes first, etc.
- Information books, increasingly available in Indian subcontinent languages. Perhaps parents visiting their home countries might be able to help? Children literate in their own language could find these invaluable, and all children will see that knowledge is not confined to English.

Opportunities for talk which consider bilingual audiences and purpose

- Could include using home languages to report back from a group discussion, presentation of science experiments, storytelling, plays, interviews, etc., involving children in the school, bilingual staff, and the community.

Classroom topics on language

- Useful as a way of getting home languages on the agenda. Starting with languages other than those spoken by the children in the class may be a way of breaking the ice, enabling bilingual children to bring in their own experiences without being singled out as different. The children's ideas about what constitutes a language may differ. Everybody needs to be able to contribute. The ultimate aim would be to get the home languages used in the classroom.

As can be seen from the above, the distinction between using home languages for learning and being positive about them in school can become blurred. What is important is for teachers to appreciate the difference. Language awareness activities are intended to increase knowledge about language, but if English is the only language spoken in the classroom such activities are tokenistic. At the same time, encouraging home language use without considering how this will help bilingual children gain access to the curriculum will disadvantage them. At least as much care and attention should be given to materials and the organisation of this work by the teacher, as to all other aspects of the curriculum. To set up home language groups without clear learning objectives is another way of marginalising bilingual pupils.

When the school or class encourages the use of home language, teachers find ways of assessing and responding to learning in a language they do not speak. This requires a big leap in thinking, but it is an exciting process because it challenges notions of how we find out what children know. Do we rely on questioning? How much can we gauge of children's understanding by what they say in response to our questions?

There are also issues of trust. If children are talking together in groups we have to trust them to get on with the task, and also to trust them as they express opinions, argue points, disagree with what we think. It's not such a big step to encourage some of this to take place in a language we do not understand. We need to think about the control we exercise and how to hand over some of this within a clear structure, with objectives the children understand. Bilingual children will not exclude teachers who do not share their language and will usually switch in groups according to the needs of the task as well as the composition of the group.

Using the languages in the class will change the ethos of the school. When community languages are valued and actively encouraged this opens the way for incorporating and making good use of dialects in addition to the standard English dialect, which encourages more positive attitudes to the language all children bring from home.

Many children have succeeded in school without the benefit of home language support, although at some cost to themselves, to maintaining family relationships and cultural links. Others have been less successful. Often it is the attitude towards the social or racial group which is the key factor. A *civilised respect* for languages other than English is endorsed in the draft proposals for the National Curriculum ('English for ages 5 to 11', November 1988). How this is to be achieved, and how this will affect learning, should be clear from the school's policy and practice. A school which genuinely values linguistic variety and has re-examined the curriculum to ensure access for bilingual pupils will have higher expectations of the children with consequent effect on their achievement.

An interest in and commitment to the role of oracy in learning will benefit bilingual children if their bilingualism is used positively. The term *oracy* was coined within the context of English, but as a concept it has been around for a long time, and concepts cross over language barriers.

BIBLIOGRAPHY

Dulay, H., Burt, M. and Krashen, S. (1982) *Language Two*, Oxford University Press.
English for ages 5–11, November 1988 (DES).
Issues in Race and Education No. 54 Shelving Books Part 1 1988.
Saunders, G. (1982) *Bilingual Children: Guidance for the Family*, Multilingual Matters 3.
Teaching English as a Second Language. Report of a Formal Investigation by the Commission for Racial Equality into the Teaching of English as a Second Language in Calderdale Local Education Authority. Commission For Racial Equality (1986).
Wells, G. (1981) *Learning Through Interaction*, Cambridge University Press.
Wiles, S.(Spring 1985) *Learning a Second Language*. English Magazine No. 14.

Chapter 9

Standard English
The Debate

Katharine Perera

The notion 'standard English' seems at first sight so obvious and straight-forward that it is hardly necessary to write about it. In fact, though, it is both complex and controversial, with different scholars holding widely divergent views on the topic. This short chapter necessarily provides a simplified account, generally following the position established in the Kingman and Cox Reports (DES 1988, 1989, more easily available in Cox 1991). There is a useful overview of the broader picture in McArthur (1992), while the processes of standardisation are described in Milroy and Milroy (1985) and Joseph (1987).

Here, I shall work with just a two-way distinction between standard and non-standard, whereas Wells (1982) and Trudgill and Chambers (1991), for example, refer to 'general English' and 'mainstream English' respectively, both of which encompass standard and non-standard varieties and are contrasted with 'traditional dialect'.

A BRIEF HISTORY OF STANDARD ENGLISH

From the eleventh to the fourteenth centuries the languages of Church and State in England were Latin and Norman French; it was not until 1362 that English was officially used in Parliament, and Chancery documents were written in Latin or French until the 1430s. During this period English was rather rarely written and its spoken forms differed substantially from one dialect region of the country to another. At the close of the fourteenth century, Chaucer chose to write his literary works in English, using his own East Midlands dialect. These works were among the first books to be printed in English, after Caxton had set up his printing press at Westminster in 1476. The advent of printing both made it necessary to have a form of English that was widely understood throughout England and, in its turn, contributed powerfully to the establishment of one nationwide written variety. As most of the scholars who wrote studied at the universities of Oxford and Cambridge, and as official documents of administration were produced in London, it is not surprising that it was from the dialects of this midland and eastern region that modern standard English grew. The publication in the seventeenth century of the King James Version of the Bible (1611), Shakespeare's plays (1623) and the Book of Common Prayer (1662) had a profound influence on the development of a standard written form. As this form, closely associated with the educated and the powerful, gained currency, other coexisting varieties came increasingly to be downgraded in status.

The next stages were the codification and prescription of the standard, which began in the eighteenth century with Samuel Johnson's *Dictionary of the English Language* (1755) and grammar books such as Lindley Murray's *English Grammar* (1794), and continue to the present day, e.g. Henry Fowler's *Dictionary of Modern English Usage* (1926), and *The Oxford English Dictionary* (1928,1989), although modern grammars have a more descriptive than prescriptive emphasis, e.g. *A Comprehensive Grammar of the English Language* by Quirk *et al*. (1985).

Four points can be made on the basis of this thumbnail sketch. First, it was an accident of geography that selected the East Midlands dialect as the forerunner of standard English, not any inherent superiority over other fifteenth-century dialects. Second, a number of non-standard forms of modern English are direct descendants of early English dialects, rather than (as is sometimes suggested) careless corruptions of the standard. Third, there is a very close relationship between the written language and the development of standard English. Finally, the standard language has come to serve a wide variety of public, formal functions. Other dialects of English have been much less used for these purposes, because the introduction of English as the language of administration roughly coincided with the invention of printing, which was the first major step in the process of standardisation. For this reason, standard English is a much more fully elaborated variety of English than any non-standard variety.

STANDARD ENGLISH AND PRONUNCIATION

In the approach that I am taking here, standard English refers to the structure of the language, i.e. its grammar and vocabulary, not to its pronunciation. Standard English may be spoken in an accent that does not reveal the speaker's geographical origins – in England such an accent is called Received Pronunciation (RP). Much more frequently it is spoken in a regional accent. The following sentence would sound different in the local accents of Liverpool, London and Newcastle:

1 They go by bus, train or boat every week.

Whatever its pronunciation, though, it is still a standard English sentence. In contrast, the next sentence is non-standard, because, in standard English, the verb form *goes* occurs only after third person *singular* subjects:

2 They goes by bus, train or boat every week.

Such a sentence is never pronounced in RP but always in a regional accent, in this case probably one from Oxfordshire, Hampshire or Dorset. These examples make the point that non-standard English is always evident in writing, whereas a regional accent is not, unless the writer uses unconventional spelling to try to convey the sound of speech.

When the National Curriculum stipulates that pupils should be using standard English to fulfil statements of attainment in Speaking and Listening, this does *not* mean that they are required to change their accents. The Cox Report was emphatic on that point: 'We do not see it as the school's place to enforce the accent known as Received Pronunciation' (Cox 1991: 26).

WHAT IS STANDARD ENGLISH?

The first point to make is that standard English does not necessarily mean good English. The label is a technical term used to identify a particular variety of English that has characteristic forms and functions. Like any other variety, it can be used well or badly. For example, the following sentence, produced by an MP in the House of Commons, has the vocabulary and grammar of standard English but is ridiculous none the less because of the conflict between metaphorical ups and downs:

3 The rise in unemployment has become an avalanche.

The common identification of standard English with good English derives from the different meanings of *standard*. There are twenty different definitions listed in the 1991 *Collins Dictionary*. Some of these cluster into two distinct groups:

(a) 'an authorized model of a unit of measure or weight'
    'an accepted example of something against which others are measured'
    'of the usual, regularized, medium or accepted kind'
(b) 'a level of excellence or quality'
    'a principle of propriety, honesty and integrity'
    'of recognized authority, competence or excellence'

The definitions in the first group relate to ideas of uniformity, those in the second to notions of excellence. It is easy to see how the second set came to affect the interpretation of the term standard English.

After that negative point, a positive characterisation of standard English can begin with three statements which relate to its forms, speakers and functions respectively. Standard English is:

(i) *relatively* uniform throughout the English-speaking world;
(ii) used by educated native speakers;

(iii) used in public, formal contexts, e.g. Parliament, law courts, churches, radio, television, and particularly in education and published writing.

Unfortunately, each of these three characteristics presents some problems, which we can consider in turn.

(i) 'Standard English is relatively uniform'

In comparison with non-standard varieties, standard English *is* relatively uniform but even so it varies along at least three dimensions – spatial, temporal and stylistic. As far as the spatial dimension is concerned, there is well-known variation in vocabulary and, to a lesser extent, grammar between different national varieties, most notably British and American English. So where an American might say,

   4 I've gotten a new vest and pants

an Englishman would say,

   5 I've got a new waistcoat and trousers.

In fact, it is more accurate (though fairly unusual) to speak of standard Englishes, rather than standard English. Even if we confine our attention to Britain, there are still differences between the standard English used in Scotland and in England. Where an English person would say either,

   6a These essays need marking

or,

   6b These essays need to be marked

a Scot is likely to say,

   7 These essays need marked.

Then there is also variation across time, since all living languages inevitably change. For example, George Eliot wrote this in *Silas Marner*, which was published in 1861:

   8 to him this would have been an effort of independent thought such as he had never known; and he must have made the effort at a moment when all his energies were turned into the anguish of disappointed faith.

In today's English the clause following the semi-colon would read,

   9 and he would have had to make the effort . . . .

It is easy to accept a change that occurred over a hundred years ago. The difficulty comes with changes that are currently in progress. For example, older speakers of standard English can say,

  10 You ought to leave soon, oughtn't you?

Younger speakers, though, find *oughtn't* awkward or odd and tend to say either,

  11a You ought to leave soon, shouldn't you?

or,

  11b You ought to leave soon, didn't you?

This use of *didn't* strikes older speakers as non-standard, although after lexical verbs it is perfectly normal, e.g.

  12 You wanted to leave soon, didn't you?

What is happening, in fact, is that *ought* is changing from an auxiliary into a lexical verb. One reason why it is difficult to define standard English precisely is because what is standard for the younger generation may be non-standard for older speakers. The fact that language changes over time means that codification in grammars and usage manuals *follows* the practice of speakers, so such books are inherently conservative. This leads us to the second characterisation of standard English and to the difficulties that arise with that. (The third, stylistic, dimension of variation within standard English is touched on in (iii) below.)

(ii) 'Standard English is used by educated native speakers'

Most obviously this statement raises the question of what is meant by an 'educated' speaker. It is often taken to mean a person who has had a university education (though such a formulation does not mean, of course, that standard English is not spoken by those without such an education). In practice, it often turns out that there is some circularity in this criterion, since people are frequently judged to be more or less educated by the way they speak. The further problem, though, is that educated native speakers do not always agree about what is acceptable. In a study of attitudes to a number of possibly disputed constructions, e.g.

  13 He is in London but his family *are* in Bournemouth

Mittins *et al.* (1970) found a great variety of response, even from people with similar educational backgrounds.

(iii) 'Standard English is used in public, formal contexts'

The problem with this statement is that it seems to restrict standard English too narrowly. Although it undoubtedly *is* used in formal contexts, many people would accept that there are also notably informal expressions which nevertheless form part of standard English. If this is not the case then it leads to the curious conclusion that when educated speakers of standard English are chatting casually with their friends they are no longer using standard language. Andersson and Trudgill (1990) give the following example, which they describe as informal standard English:

    14 He's *bust* his collar-bone.

And Mittins *et al.* (1970), who questioned their educated informants about the acceptability – in informal speech – of various colloquial expressions, recorded a positive rating of 84 per cent for

    15 The instruments were *pretty* reliable.

While these two examples are unlikely to be used in writing (except in personal letters, diaries, etc., and written dialogue), there are informal lexical expressions and grammatical constructions which can be used both in speech and in all but the most formal writing, e.g.

    16a They got angry and said they wouldn't put up with his behaviour.
cf.
    16b They became angry and said they would not tolerate his behaviour.

    17a The reporter photographed the children Chelsea had been speaking to.
cf.
    17b The reporter photographed the children to whom Chelsea had been speaking.

A person who habitually used the more formal expressions even in familiar, informal contexts would run the risk of being regarded as pompous.

SPOKEN STANDARD ENGLISH

Despite the problems I have outlined with the three characterisations of standard English, they still work reasonably well when applied to printed written language, where uniformity is so great that it is possible to read scores or even hundreds of pages without being able to detect any linguistic clues to the writer's background. It is much harder to arrive at a workable description which will include *spoken* standard English. Yet the National Curriculum requires that pupils are assessed on their ability to speak it, so it is essential to have some agreement about what it is. First, it is necessary to itemise five ways in which speech differs from writing, since spoken standard English has all these characteristics.

(i) Speech contains false starts, hesitations, mazes and incomplete sentences. These features are quite unlike writing. Even written representations of speech, in plays or dialogue in a novel, rarely convey them fully because they are difficult to read; authors tend merely to insert the occasional *er* and to allow some sentences to trail off in a series of dots. In addition much of the 'speech' we listen to as hearers (as distinct from our role as participants in a conversation) is actually written or prepared text read aloud or performed. This is true of lectures, sermons and a great deal of the spoken language on television and radio; the reporter who is apparently speaking to us fluently in complex and complete sentences is, in all probability, reading from an autocue. Therefore, we tend to have an unrealistic view of what the naturally occurring speech of educated speakers sounds like. It is worth being aware that completely fluent speech in a conversational setting sounds rehearsed and may give the impression of glibness, or even insincerity.

(ii) Speech contains items known as 'discourse markers', e.g. *well, you know, sort of, I mean*, which serve to help speakers relate to each other within a 'participation framework' (Schiffrin 1987: 316). It is true that they can be irritatingly overused and some are socially stigmatised, e.g. *like* in

18 I tripped over like

(which would not, I think, be regarded as standard English). But if informal speech is stripped of these features it sounds like a lecture or an address to a public meeting rather than a shared conversation among equals.

(iii) Speech depends heavily on the context in which it occurs. Meaning is derived from the situation, which includes any previous speech, as well as from the language itself. This means that face-to-face spoken language does not need to be as full or as explicit as written language. The utterance at (19a) might be said by a person speaking to a delivery man, whereas something like (19b) would be needed for a written note left on the front door:

19a Leave it there please.
19b Please leave the ironing board in the porch, in the corner behind the umbrella stand.

It is socially abnormal to use spoken language that is fuller than the situation requires and can actually sound rude. For example, if a visitor is asked, 'Would you like a cup of coffee?', it is normal to decline by saying, 'No thank you'. To reply in the complete sentence, 'No I would not like a cup of coffee thank you', sounds sarcastic or aggressive.

(iv) Speech contains characteristic constructions which do not normally occur in writing and which, indeed, look strange written down. These increase redundancy and make processing easier for both speaker and listener. The following utterance by Prince Charles recapitulates the subject noun phrase *all the people in my office* with the pronoun *they*:

20 All the people in my office they can't speak English properly, they can't write English properly.

In most of the newspaper reports of this speech, the redundant *they* was omitted. A rather similar construction starts with a pronoun and tags a co-referential noun phrase on at the end, e.g.

21 It was good, that book.

(v) Speech is, on the whole, less formal than writing. There are good reasons for this. Once written, a piece of writing can end up anywhere and be read by anyone. When we write we seem to have, probably unconsciously, a feeling that what we are writing may be read by strangers. When we speak we know who we are speaking to and, most often, we speak to people we know well, with whom it is appropriate to be informal. Good use of language entails being able to select the right style for the occasion, not always trying to use a formal style in the mistaken belief that it is the best English. So the assessment of spoken language always needs to take proper account of the context.

The crucial point about these five characteristics of spoken language is that they all have an interpersonal function. If we do not allow these into a description of spoken standard English but require what is, in effect, an oral version of written English, then we are failing to understand the nature of spontaneous speech.

It will be clear, though, that once we admit into standard English forms that are not used in writing and that are mentioned only rarely in grammar books it becomes very difficult to draw any boundaries around the variety. One way to proceed is to use the following two statements. Spoken standard English:

(a) is spoken by educated native speakers;
(b) does not contain features that are widely stigmatised by educated native speakers.

The first statement raises the problems that were outlined above in relation to a characterisation of standard English in general, with the additional difficulty that we do not currently have a full description of the structures of spontaneous speech (educated or uneducated). The second statement has to include the qualifier '*widely* stigmatised', since many individuals express strong and sometimes idiosyncratic hostility to particular uses of language and if all these were included the list would be both unhelpful and punitively long. In fact, there is a rather small set of frequently occurring features which are recognisably non-standard and serve as social shibboleths. These include negative forms, e.g.

22 He ain't here
23 I didn't want no-one to hurt nobody

verb forms, e.g.

24 She seen him yesterday
25 They was laughing

and pronouns and determiners, e.g.

26 He liked the play what I had wrote
27 I want them books.

(For more details, see Hughes and Trudgill 1979.) Although this focus on stigmatised features probably captures a truth about spoken standard English, it is unappealing to have to define it in this negative way.

ACQUIRING STANDARD ENGLISH

Some children grow up amongst people who speak standard English and so that is the form of the language that they learn. When they are 3 or 4 they may well say things like *I digged a hole* but that is simply a transient form which will in time be replaced by the irregular past tense form *dug*. An important characteristic of standard English is that its functions and forms have been elaborated over time. This is especially true of its vocabulary. When children go to school, and particularly when they learn to read, they become increasingly exposed to those words and grammatical structures of standard English that are characteristic of its more formal, public and written uses. For these children, learning standard English means extending the language that they have already begun to acquire.

Other children grow up in families where a non-standard variety of English is spoken. Naturally enough, they learn that variety. For them, the mismatch between the language of home and school is greater than for children who have standard English as their mother tongue. During the primary school years, as they are increasingly exposed to the forms of both spoken and written standard English, they begin to replace their non-standard features with standard features in writing (where there is time for planning and reflection). This replacement happens more slowly and errati-cally in speech. By about the age of 11, some pupils from non-standard language communities are likely to speak differently in the classroom with their teacher and in the playground with their peers. There is some evidence (e.g. Cheshire 1982) that girls take on these different speech forms more readily than boys. Certainly issues of attitude will be involved, since adopt-ing a different language variety entails aligning oneself with the social group that speaks in that way; for some the loss of identity will be too big a price to pay for the not always apparent benefits of speaking a more prestigious variety. The Cox Report recognised some of the social and emotional problems involved in adding the forms of standard English to pupils' linguistic repertoires:

> Teachers should never treat non-standard dialect as sub-standard language but should recognize the intimate links between dialect and identity and the damage to self-esteem and motivation which can be caused by indiscriminate 'correction' of dialect forms. All children should be supported in valuing their own dialects . . . but they should also be able to use standard English when it is necessary and helpful to do so in speaking as well as in writing.
>
> (Cox 1991: 128)

REFERENCES

Andersson, L.-G. and Trudgill, P. (1990). *Bad language*. London: Penguin.

Cheshire, J. (1982). Dialect features and linguistic conflict in schools. *Educational Review* **34**, 53–67.

Cox, B. (1991). *Cox on Cox*. London: Hodder & Stoughton.

DES (1988). *Report of the Committee of Inquiry into the teaching of English language* (The Kingman Report). London: HMSO.

DES (1989). *English for ages 5 to 16* (The Cox Report). London: HMSO.

Hughes, A. and Trudgill, P. (1979). *English accents and dialects*. London: Edward Arnold.

Joseph, J.E. (1987). *Eloquence and power. The rise of language standards and standard languages*. London: Frances Pinter.

McArthur, T. (ed.) (1992). *The Oxford companion to the English language*. Oxford: Oxford University Press.

Milroy, J. and Milroy, L. (1985). *Authority in language: investigating language prescription and standardisation*. London: Routledge & Kegan Paul.

Mittins, W.H., Salu, M., Edminson, M. and Coyne, S. (1970). *Attitudes to English usage*. Oxford: Oxford University Press.

Quirk, R., Greenbaum, S., Leech, G. and Svartvik, J. (1985). *A comprehensive grammar of the English language*. London: Longman.

Schiffrin, D. (1987). *Discourse markers*. Cambridge: Cambridge University Press.

Trudgill, P. and Chambers, J.K. (1991). *Dialects of English. Studies in grammatical variation*. London: Longman.

Wells, J.C. (1982). *Accents of English* Vol. 1. Cambridge: Cambridge University Press.

Part III

Reading

Reading is much more than the decoding of black marks upon a page: it is a quest for meaning and one which requires the reader to be an active participant. It is a prerequisite of successful teaching of reading . . . that whenever techniques are taught, or books chosen for children's use, meaning should always be in the foreground.

(English in the National Curriculum 16.2)

Reading is a complex area. We can use the term to mean the process itself, or a response to literary text. It can mean the retrieval of information in a non-literary text, or take on wider meanings like 'reading the situation'. Reading is not confined to print in a book. It is central to the debate about meaning and the construction of the reader. It is linked to issues of standards in education, and to one of the functions of education itself – the production of a literate society. Peter Traves in the first chapter begins with the observation that 'Few things in education excite the public imagination more than reading.' He looks at each of these interrelated areas and, in exploring reading, offers a 'charter . . . a basic minimum' of entitlement for readers in schools, concluding: 'The overarching aim of school ought to be the production of confident, ambitious and critical readers.'

David Buckingham and Julian Sefton-Green's chapter looks at reading media texts. They examine the idea of reading as 'an inherently social process' and the ways in which the reconstruction and renegotiation of meaning transforms 'readings' into 'culture'. Using examples from media texts they explore the 'cultural experiences and competencies' evident in the classroom and reflect on the implications for our future society of neglecting these reading experiences. The demands of this future society are evident too in the way that the concept of reading is now understood to include information skills – a need for information literacy. Colin Harrison approaches this area by analysing the requirements in the (1989) National

Curriculum, using DARTs (Directed Activities Related to Texts) activities as a mechanism for accessing information in non-literary texts.

The role of the computer in the classroom has developed considerably from the time when its sole use was that of word processing. The chapter by Sally Tweddle and Phil Moore contends that effective use of information technology equips pupils to work 'within a new literacy' described in the quotation they give from Margaret Meek: 'literacy itself . . . has to be redescribed, at least as *literacies*, to match the new, emergent contexts and kinds of literate behaviours that are prevalent in modern societies' (*On Being Literate*, 1991).

Integral to the reading curriculum is the study of literature. Alastair West challenges the current approaches to teaching literature through his development of the notion of 'critical literacy . . . modes of relating to texts . . . look[ing] to the range of possible meanings . . . [and] what was at stake in their differences'. Suzanne Scafe, in her chapter, takes up a similar theme in questioning the current practices in teaching black literature, discussing both the choices and approaches evident, and looking at possibilities for change.

Another challenge to established ways of teaching came from the project Shakespeare and Schools, directed by Rex Gibson. In his chapter 'Teaching Shakespeare in schools', Rex Gibson addresses two major questions: why teach Shakespeare; and how should Shakespeare be taught? He looks beyond the compulsory element to the integral values of teaching Shakespeare, and suggests strategies to teach Shakespeare not as a text, but 'as a SCRIPT to be brought to imaginative life through action'.

As Chief Examiners, Stella Canwell and Jane Ogborn are well placed to comment on the demands of A level examinations. In their chapter, 'Balancing the books', they look at the AEB 660 examination, and the ways in which planning at A level needs to forge coherent connections between course and examination work.

The final chapter in this part is by Margaret Meek, 'How do they know it's worth it? The untaught reading lessons' and looks at three of the themes of this part. How do we teach reading? What are the messages we give in that activity? How do we access texts? By using three learning situations, Margaret Meek demonstrates how readers develop, how they deal with literary texts and how inexperienced readers can be helped to discover that reading is indeed 'worth it'.

Chapter 10

Reading

Peter Traves

Few things in education excite the public imagination more than reading. Periodically we are informed by the press that there is a crisis: reading standards have reached a new low; our children do not read as well as those in our competitor nations; they do not read as well as they did in the past; they do not read as well as we all know they should at 6 or 7 or 11 or 16. It's a scandal. Behind this is the assumption of a golden age of reading just disappearing over the horizon.

The nature of the concern and controversy reflects a more complex and deeply rooted dilemma about reading, its nature and its function. On the one hand we see reading depicted as a 'basic skill', a functional activity to be mastered at an early age. This skill is demanded in our education system and in our society at large. On the other hand we see reading in terms of books or literature. It is linked then to a literary heritage, to a canon of texts. This leads on to a consideration of what and how children should be reading.

The National Curriculum places a premium on reading in both the senses outlined in popular debate. It is unambiguous in its requirement that all children should be equipped for the demands of a literate society and equipped as effectively and early as possible. It is equally emphatic that children should be offered access to a wide literary experience and should be helped in the development of critical reading.

It seems to me that there is a series of key questions that need to be addressed before we can get to grips with the teaching and learning of reading:

- What impact do we want reading to have on the lives of the children we teach?
- What does it mean to be a reader?
- What is involved in the process of reading?
- What implications do these questions have for schools in general and for English teachers in particular?

When we speak about reading we usually have in mind the reading of a particular kind of text – one that is in the form of printed language.

Sometimes the assumption is even more specific, referring only to books or even to particular kinds of books termed literature. In general parlance we use the verb 'to read' much more widely. We talk, for example, of reading faces, tea leaves, the weather, people. There is a common expression, 'I can read you like a book'. This broader definition is highly significant. It is indicative of the fact that the reading of print is only one instance of a much more widely applied human faculty. Paulo Freire and Donaldo Macedo subtitled their book on literacy *Reading the Word and the World*.[1] That is what we all do; we read the world around us. We give meaning to the patterns we see in it. We are active makers of meaning: we read meaning out of or into the world. Each of us reads our own unique version of that meaning but we do so within the constraints and conventions of the cultural networks in which we live our lives.

This chapter concentrates mainly on the reading of print. However, it is important to bear in mind the wider meaning of the word. We read the world in order to make coherent sense of it; in order to exercise greater control over it. We are not passive receivers of meaning from our world; we are active constructors of shape and sense. This applies to the reading of print as much as to anything else.

In defining the nature of reading and readers we must also consider the role reading plays in our society. We live in a society that assumes print literacy (it also increasingly assumes other forms of media literacy such as computer and television literacy). Every day demands are placed on us as readers of print. We read at work, as we drive, as we shop. There are few aspects of our lives that are not linked in one way or another to the reading of print. The institutions of our economy, our government and our culture rest upon written language and depend upon the capacity to read. Reading is a major source of pleasure in our society. Millions of books, magazines and papers are read every day. Reading allows access to generations of thought, to vast numbers of facts, to images of the world remote from our daily experience.

Reading plays a particularly important role in education. Not only does our education system demand a lot of reading in the process of learning, it also tends to use the capacity to read fluently as an indicator of more general intellectual ability. This tendency to assess intellect through reading is misplaced but prevalent and therefore cannot be ignored. It is part of the function ascribed to literacy, albeit one we need to resist and reform.

What does reading involve? What do readers have to do to make meaning from the page? The answer to this depends in part on the purpose behind the reading activity; whether the reader wishes to extract a single fact, like a name from a directory; come to terms with new and difficult concepts; or follow a narrative over hundreds of pages or even several volumes. If we look at what is involved in the reading of narrative there will be aspects peculiar to that form but there will be many others that are common to other texts and purposes.

Readers first have to make a correlation between the shapes on the page and the language in their heads. The recognition that shapes on a page relate to the meanings ascribed to spoken words represents an enormous leap of conceptual development for the small child. It is a gigantic step on the road to being a reader. To be effective readers it is necessary to be able to relate particular shapes to particular sounds and meanings. This is the process often referred to as decoding. In mainstream schools children do not normally arrive at secondary level without a general recognition that written language correlates to spoken language. However, there is a significant number of pupils who need a great deal of help in developing the skills to recognise the specific correlation between the shape on the page and particular sounds and words. They are unable to identify the sounds made by particular groupings of letters; they are unable to recognise a sufficient number of printed words to cope with the demands placed upon them in and out of school. The help that is provided has to be part of a broad approach to reading but it also has to address the specific needs of these pupils and it has to address them in a systematic and coherent manner.

In the reading of narrative readers need to be able to relate to a large number of conventions. They need to be able to read within or against the rules of particular genres. These rules help the reader to decide what is acceptable, plausible rather than possible, within the world of that story. Writers also often deliberately break the conventions in order to achieve effects. Children need to be given access to the widest range of genres. They also need opportunities to explore the conventions of genres and to explore the ways in which texts are structured if they are to internalise these conventions and thus become powerful readers, and writers, of narrative.

Texts are not entirely self-contained; they refer to the world. Texts assume knowledge on the part of the reader. Sometimes the knowledge is factually based and refers to objects, events and people. Even at this level the facts may carry values and connotations that can become more elusive as time passes. When James Thurber refers to Calvin Coolidge in his tale of Red Riding Hood it may require no great act of research to find out that Coolidge was President of the United States. However, part of the wit of the passage depends upon a shared image of the man as a taciturn and dim-witted politician that is more difficult to grasp today.

There are many references in texts which depend not on a grasp of facts but on an understanding of cultural institutions and practices. This can be made more difficult by the fact that while the word may be common to writer and reader the assumptions behind it may not. Texts may be written in a world that took for granted one set of values and read in a world which calls them into question. Readers are required to divide themselves into two parts: one which reads within the world of the text and one which calls it into question.

The teaching of reading involves movement beyond the confines of the text out into the world to which it refers and the world inhabited by its readers. The relationship between the perceptions, understandings and values of these two world views must be explored. At times teachers will be referees in a debate between the two, at others they will be interpreters adding facts and ideas that may be helpful to less experienced readers.

Like any other form of language activity, reading always takes place in particular historical circumstances; in real times and places. The meaning made by the reader depends in part on the situation in which the reading takes place. Reading *Jane Eyre* on the beach as part of holiday relaxation is quite different to reading it for a GCSE examination or as part of a PhD on the construction of women in nineteenth-century literature. In all three cases the words on the page remain the same but the experience and meaning of the reading varies significantly. Even more dramatic would be the difference in meaning made by a reader of the text at the time of its production, in mid-Victorian Britain, and one made by another reader over a hundred years later. This must be acknowledged in teaching. Readers must be given opportunities to see how the meanings they make are related to the circumstances within which they read. They must be offered opportunities to compare the possible meanings the text might have had for its intended audience and the meanings it has for them. They must also be allowed the chance to note how their own readings of a text change with time and experience.

Reading in school must take account of the role of reading in our society and the nature of reading as a process. Schools need to give clear signals that reading is a valued activity. In order to do this resources must be put into reading right across the curriculum. HMI annual reports consistently make the case that the money spent on books in schools is inadequate and yet for many children school remains the main source of reading material. Many children, particularly adolescent boys, need positive encouragement to read and a time set aside on a regular basis specifically for reading.

The encouragement and teaching of reading is a whole-school responsibility and each department should be clear about its own role in this process. Schools must teach children a wide range of reading skills to meet the varied requirements of education and the outside world. This means that opportunities must be created for a variety of kinds of reading activities to fulfil a variety of purposes. It also means the explicit teaching of some skills. Reading for information, for example, involves skills that can and should be taught. All too often important aspects of reading development, most of which are now requirements of the National Curriculum, are left to chance.

English teachers ought not to have the sole responsibility for the development of reading. Nevertheless, English teachers do have a very important and particular role to play. They are responsible above all for the development of active and critical readers. But what does that mean?

First of all, it means encouraging an enthusiasm for reading, or at least creating the conditions in which such an enthusiasm can flourish. It means ensuring access to a wide range of books. In this way there is more chance of engaging the interest of most pupils. One implication of this is that the teacher cannot rely too heavily on whole-class readers. There must be time set aside that allows pupils to read in groups or on their own. It also requires the communication of interest and enthusiasm from teachers to pupils. Teachers provide a model of more experienced readers. It is also vital to make space for the activity that dominates much discussion between avid adult readers – the sharing of reading experience which is relatively unstructured but which is so rich as a source of pleasure and as a stimulus to wider and more ambitious reading.

Second, it involves drawing attention to the ways in which the text itself offers particular meanings: how it is explicit about some of the values it offers and how it 'naturalises' others so that they appear no more than common sense or part of the onward drive of the plot. There are times when authors make it clear that they are offering a point of view. It is then possible for the reader to respond to those ideas and values. There are other times when what happens in the story and the tone in which this is conveyed appear so natural a part of the fabric of the text that we are unaware of the values implied. The happy ending that depends on the marriage of the hero and heroine may embody values about romantic love and the institution of marriage that may or may not be shared by the reader. Pupils need to be engaged in activities that return them to the detail of the text. They need to be able to explore the choices that have been made in the ordering of plot, in the construction of character and in the detail of the setting. This inevitably involves the posing of alternatives – how would it have been different if . . . and what does this tell us about the text? Powerful readers are in a position to see how effects are being achieved. They can then make more informed judgements about not just the craft of the author but the nature of their own pleasure or displeasure. They then cease to be consumers of texts and become participators in the making of meaning.

Finally, critical readers are able to place their own values and experiences in relation to those of the text. They are able to read from a position. They may read sometimes as a boy or girl, man or woman, young person or old person, black or white, insider or outsider and so on. We all occupy many roles at different times in our lives and our position as a reader will vary accordingly. Texts may challenge or affirm our view of the world; they may diminish or ennoble us. Schools should encourage the view that reading ought to be a dialogue between the reader and the text. Readers should be confident that their experiences are valued as a starting point for exploration and challenge.

To conclude, we are in an era of charters. Here is one for readers in schools.

Readers should be entitled to the following as a basic minimum:

1 Being literate must involve the capacity to deal with the day-to-day demands of print in our society. This is not the ultimate goal of literacy but it has to be one of its staging posts, part of the process at least. We cannot accept a situation in which even a small minority of pupils leave school functionally illiterate.

2 Pupils must be able to cope with the reading demands placed on them by the education process. Children are entitled to receive the level of support necessary to sustain them as readers right across the curriculum.

3 Readers employ different reading strategies according to the nature of the text and the purpose of the reading activity. Children need to be equipped to deal with the range of texts and purposes they will meet. This should be organised in a coherent and systematic fashion across the school.

4 Readers should learn how texts and readers make meaning. Books like *Making Stories, Changing Stories* and *Reading Stories*[2] show how enjoyable and accessible activities can be which explore the making of meaning in texts.

5 Texts work to achieve effects on their readers. Pupils should be helped to understand how this operates. They should be students of rhetoric.

6 Pupils should be made aware that print carries values. These values always have a relationship with the wider world. Active and critical reading involves the capacity and confidence to explore that relationship.

7 Every reader has a history of experience as a reader. This experience is important and plays a key role in further development. Time should be set aside for exploration and consideration of that history and of its impact upon the individual.

8 Reading can be a great source of pleasure. The nature of that pleasure is varied. Schools need to set aside time and resources in order to ensure that reading for pleasure is nurtured.

9 Pupils should be encouraged to be adventurous in their reading, both in terms of what they read and how they read it. This is a challenge to well-intentioned conceptions of relevance. We should make fewer assumptions about what will interest children at a particular age or from particular backgrounds. Pupils should be encouraged to develop a more extensive sense of cultural ownership through their reading. Schools ought to develop in children a defiance of cultural boundaries that will allow them to gain real powers of choice. Choosing not to read Milton or N'gugi Wa Thiongo because you don't like their work is real choice; choosing not to because you think they lie beyond the limits of your cultural horizons is not.

10 Readers ought to be able to value what they bring to the process of

reading in terms of their language, culture and values. They need to be able to test their own resources against the resources of the text. Reading ought not to be a process of being set in awe of the greatness of the text.

11   The experience of reading in schools should help pupils to be aware of what is peculiar to the reading of print. It should also help them to see that it has much in common with the reading of other media. Our definition of reading needs to keep pace with the kinds of reading available to our pupils.

12   Reading is a language activity and ought not to be divorced from other language activities in school. Reading, writing, talking and listening ought to work in harmony.

The overarching aim of schools ought to be the production of confident, ambitious and critical readers who see reading, like other aspects of their language facility, as a key part of their engagement in and understanding of the world.

NOTES

1 *Literacy: Reading the Word and the World* (Routledge and Kegan Paul; 1987).
2 *Making Stories*, B. Mellor (The English Centre; 1984); *Changing Stories*, B. Mellor (The English Centre; 1984); *Reading Stories*, B. Mellor (Chalk Face Press; 1987). All three books available through NATE publications.

Chapter 11

Making sense of the media
From reading to culture

David Buckingham and Julian Sefton-Green

The view of young people as the 'dupes' of popular media has a long history, and is regularly espoused by critics of all political persuasions. For many on the Right, the media are often seen as a major cause of moral depravity and violence, while they are routinely condemned by many on the Left for their reinforcement of racism, sexism, consumerism and many other objectionable ideologies. Yet what unites these otherwise very different views is a notion of young people as helpless victims of manipulation, and as extremely vulnerable and impressionable. In this account, the text is seen to be all powerful, while the reader is powerless to step back or resist: 'reading' or making sense of media texts is regarded as an automatic process, in which meanings are simply imprinted on passive minds.

In this chapter, we are seeking to challenge the familiar notion of reading as an isolated encounter between reader and text. Broadly speaking, we are attempting to move away from a notion of reading merely as a matter of individual 'response', and to redefine it as part of a broader process of social circulation and use, which we might term 'culture'.[1]

The material we are drawing upon is part of a much more extensive study,[2] which arises from a collaboration between a schoolteacher (J.S.-G.) and an academic working in teacher education (D.B.). The research was carried out over a four-year period in an almost exclusively working-class North London comprehensive school, and involved a combination of 'ethnographic' audience research and classroom-based 'action research'. The study as a whole builds upon the theoretical issues raised in the book *Watching Media Learning*,[3] in particular the connections between academic knowledge and common-sense knowledge, and the relationship between language, identity and learning in media education.

Our aim in this research is to develop an account of reading as an inherently social process. This has two main dimensions. First, it involves a recognition that the 'meaning' of a text is not established by the reader in isolation. On the contrary, meanings are defined in and through social interaction, and particularly through talk. As John Fiske has argued, talk about popular media can be seen as part of a broader 'oral culture'.[4] The meanings which circulate within everyday discussion of texts are 'read back' into individual responses, thereby generating a dynamic interplay between 'social' and 'individual' readings – and perhaps ultimately rendering the distinction itself irrelevant. What we 'think' about texts and how we use them in our daily lives depend to a great extent on how we talk about them with others, and the contexts in which we do so. Reading is thus inevitably a process of *dialogue*.[5]

Second, looking as it were in the opposite direction, talk about popular media also serves functions in constructing and negotiating social relationships. In considering how individuals use and talk about what they read, therefore, we are effectively examining the ways in which they socialise themselves into group membership, and thereby construct their own cultural identities. In defining their own tastes, individual readers also develop hypotheses about how *other* people read, for example by distinguishing between 'fans' and less committed readers, or in terms of gender or ethnicity: they define themselves as readers in terms of what they are not, as well as what they are. This process is likely to be complex and tentative, particularly when it comes to 'buying into' membership of other social groups. Yet it is also, crucially, an active process. Tastes and preferences are socially distributed, and they serve as markers of social distinctions and positions – and thus of power relationships: yet the *meanings* of those distinctions and positions – what it means to be black or white, male or female – are not simply given, but actively reconstructed and renegotiated through social interaction. It is through such processes that 'readings' become 'culture'.

RETHINKING READING: PROFILES, HISTORIES AND POSITIONS

One of the difficulties of the approach we have outlined is that it can easily lead to the assumption that social groups are much more homogeneous, and the boundaries between them much more rigid, than they actually are. Such an approach leads to a determinist account of reading, in which readers are seen to read in a particular way *because* of their gender or ethnic background, or some other given 'fact' about their social position.[6] We need to develop a theory of reading that does not collapse the individual into the social, or merely efface the social within the individual.

As we have suggested, different readers may make sense of the same text in quite different ways – and to a greater or lesser extent, this diversity of readings is something texts may well invite, or at least allow. Furthermore, individual readers will inevitably read a range of different texts, and any given text they read will be perceived in this broader context. Perhaps particularly for young people, the kinds of texts they read and prefer will change quite dramatically as they mature. By comparing what they read with their other experiences of reading, both contemporaneously and historically, readers will come to recognise what *kind* of thing it is they are reading, and what it can and cannot do.

These points may all appear quite obvious, but they do begin to identify some of the parameters of the *social process* of reading. There appear to be three related dimensions here, which we will term reading *positions*, reading *profiles* and reading *histories*. To restate: each text (for example, by virtue of its specific textual properties, its address to its readers, and its relationship with other texts) makes available a broader or narrower range of *reading positions*, and also closes off others; that is, it invites the reader to read it in some ways and not others, and demands and thereby develops particular kinds of competencies. Readers also have *reading profiles* – that is, they read a range of texts at any given time, not just one, and they situate a given text by comparison with other texts, in terms of what it is and is not. This process also changes over time: readers have *reading histories*, and as their tastes change and develop, so the way they define and judge the text also changes. It is through these processes that young people develop their cultural competencies as readers, while simultaneously constructing identities for themselves, as particular *kinds* of readers. We would like to illustrate these points by considering three brief examples.

The first is drawn from a series of interviews relating to Britain's most popular daily newspaper, the *Sun*.[7] What was particularly striking about these interviews was the remarkable degree of ambivalence students expressed. On the one hand, they were all regular readers of the *Sun*, and actively chose it in preference to other newspapers. While there were clear gender differences here – with the boys reading it primarily for the sports coverage, and the girls preferring the 'gossip' about stars and royalty – there was also a way in which the paper seemed to speak to their shared sense of class and generational membership. Unlike the so-called 'quality' newspapers, which were seen to be directed at middle-class readers, the *Sun* was defined as being for 'working people' like their parents, and by extension themselves; and it was also described as 'easy to read' and therefore more appropriate for young people. The political news featured so heavily in other newspapers was often condemned as 'boring', and as the domain of adults. For the few students who expressed any interest in politics, this seemed to be catered for by their other reading: Anthony, for example, also read black newspapers such as the *Voice* and the *Gleaner*, which he described as 'more realistic, more true'.

On the other hand, though, the *Sun* was also condemned by many of the students for its hypocrisy and dishonesty and its tendency to 'exaggerate'. While these complaints related primarily to false predictions about the soap operas and scurrilous gossip about the stars' private lives, they occasionally extended to 'straight' news stories.

Ultimately 'reading the *Sun*' was not seen as an exercise in responsible citizenship, but simply as a means of relaxation, and as something it would be wrong to take too seriously. To imply that the paper is a kind of biblical text which is studied and obeyed, or that it is responsible for merely imposing reactionary views on its passive readers – as many critics appear to suppose[8] – is thus to miss the point.

These students' reading of the *Sun* was thus part of a broader 'reading profile'. Their sense of its limitations and of its positive functions for them derived partly from a comparison with other texts. Yet, as we have noted, this process may also have a historical dimension. An explicit instance of this notion of 'reading history' comes from an interview with two comic readers, Darren and Mark. Darren was increasingly becoming involved in the specialist networks of comic readers, going to comics shops and marts, trading back issues and buying a readers' newsletter. In the process, he had developed clear preferences for particular writers and artists. Both boys had been comics fans for many years, having begun by collecting *Dandy* and *Beano*, and subsequently moving on to *D.C.* and *Marvel*. Within this, Darren also saw himself as having made the transition from simpler comics, such as *Punisher*, aimed at children – which he described as being simply concerned with 'action and fighting' – to more complex 'Mutant comics' aimed at older teenagers and adults.

The long history of some comic heroes was also significant here: having a collection of comics, which one could 'flick through for reference', made it possible to recall characters' past lives and thereby fill out the background to current storylines. It was almost as though Darren had 'grown up' with characters such as Batman, Spiderman and the Incredible Hulk, as they themselves had become more complex and mature, and had developed 'realistic' and 'normal' private lives in addition to their less realistic public personae. For example, he noted the changes that had occurred in the character of Batman: 'he's changed, 'cause he never used to come out at night and be a dark man, like a vigilante, he's bad as well as good . . . I think it's a bit more for adult readers now'. In the case of the Batman films, he argued that a different kind of reading was available to a specialist reader such as himself, when compared with the general audience:

DARREN: I think it helps if you read the comic, if you read a few Batman comics, before you see the new film, so you get an understanding of the character, what he's really like. 'Cause some people thought it was rubbish, but they didn't really know what he's really like, didn't understand it.

What Darren defined as more 'adult' comics were also distinguished by their engagement with 'realistic' social issues:

DARREN: *X-Man*, that's a good comic, it may talk about racism or something like that, and things like that . . . . It slips into the plot as well. And it changes with the times. Like before they may

> talk about, 'cause it's an American comic, like the Cold War and stuff like that, to do with Russian spies and stuff like that . . . [they tell you about] like people on the streets, like poverty and stuff like that.

Darren was thus actively constructing a sense of his own 'history' as a comic reader, with a past and a potential future – and in the process, coming to define himself as a particular type of reader. His knowledge of the wider comics culture enabled him to recognise that this was not simply a 'childish' preoccupation. While he had not attended comics conventions himself, largely because this was beyond his means, he knew that there were adults who did so; and while he felt he had now 'moved on' from his earlier preferences, he acknowledged that there were other comics and graphic novels aimed at what he called 'mature readers' that he might come to enjoy in the future. Typically, however, neither boy claimed to read books outside school – although the emphasis on long-term engagement with more 'realistic' characters, and on the seriousness and complexity of the themes, might suggest that in many ways reading comics served similar functions to those which reading books might serve for some adult readers.

Finally, these processes can also be traced more closely, in the ways in which individuals interpret specific texts or genres. Studies of television soap opera, for example, have provided very clear illustrations of the ways in which the genre enables readers to move between different 'reading positions'.[9] Talk about TV soaps often fluctuates between a position of close engagement with the text, in which it is described as, to all intents and purposes, 'real', to one of considerable distance, in which the artificiality and implausibility of the characters and storylines are criticised and mocked.

This was certainly the case with the students we interviewed here. Elizabeth and Manivone, for example, were both regular viewers of at least four soap operas. In our interview, and in some cases in lessons, they would engage in extended debates about the moral rights and wrongs of the characters' behaviour. Yet their discussion of the programmes was also characterised by a constant barrage of satire and condemnation. They complained about implausible and predictable storylines, poor acting and wobbly sets, and professed great amusement at the prospect of characters being 'killed off'. This distanced perspective also appeared to derive from the 'secondary texts' that surround the programmes, for example the plot predictions and the information about the actors' private lives that regularly appear in the popular press.

Here too, there was a sense of the girls having a reading history – although their move towards more 'adult' viewing led them to be more critical, both of the realism of the programmes and of their ideology. Thus, the girls discussed the marriage of Scott and Charlene in *Neighbours* (which had taken place roughly four years previously) as follows:

ELIZABETH: Because I was younger, I thought that was really good . . .

MANIVONE: Yeah, but you know, they give people what they wanna see, isn't it? They think it's aaahh, it's sweet. That's what people wanna see.

ELIZABETH: When I think back to it, I think, like little girls, they're sort of expected to get married at, how old was she? She was really young. Get married and start going all lovey-dovey, and get a family and go and move to Brisbane . . . . Is that what they expect us to do?

Yet the fact remains that both girls were regular viewers of these programmes – as indeed were most of their peers. The enduring popularity of soaps might thus be seen to derive from the diversity of 'reading positions' they make available – not merely in terms of distance and engagement, but also in terms of the range of characters (and thus possibilities for 'identification') they seem to provide. In effect, they offer diversity within commonality: they represent a form of 'common culture' that permits difference, even if it does not directly encourage it, and that enables viewers to exert a degree of deliberate control over the reading process that may be less possible with other genres. There is a sense in which the critical distance these programmes permit enables the reader to experience a kind of personal 'empowerment', a sense of superiority to the text and to the characters. Yet while it would be tempting to see this as broadly positive – and even as 'educational'[10] – we need to be wary of reaching easy conclusions about its political consequences.[11]

The implications of this view of reading in terms of media education remain to be explored. Clearly, we would reject the dominant notion of media teaching as a means of 'inoculating' young people against the influence of the media. This approach is, in our view, largely ineffective in terms of classroom practice, not least because it seriously misunderstands the nature of young people's relationship with the media. Yet in so far as they neglect the cultural experiences and competencies of the vast majority of young people, current changes in English teaching will merely result in irrelevance and incoherence. The social, cultural and technological changes that await us in the next decade will *inevitably* require a much more progressive rethinking of our conception of literacy, and of education itself.

NOTES AND REFERENCES

1 See Charles Sarland, *Young People Reading: Culture and Response* (Milton Keynes, Open University Press, 1991).
2 David Buckingham and Julian Sefton-Green, *Cultural Studies Goes to School: Reading and Teaching Popular Culture* (Falmer Press, forthcoming).
3 David Buckingham (ed.), *Watching Media Learning: Making Sense of Media Education* (Falmer Press, 1990).

4 John Fiske, *Television Culture* (Methuen, 1987).

5 Our approach here derives from the work of Bakhtin and Volosinov: see Buckingham, *Children Talking on Television: The Making of Television Literacy* (Falmer Press, 1993).

6 See David Buckingham, 'What are words worth? Interpreting children's talk about television', *Cultural Studies* vol. 5, no. 2, 1991, pp. 228–44.

7 For a fuller account of this research, see David Buckingham, 'Sex, lies and newsprint: young people reading the *Sun*', *English and Media Magazine* no. 26, 1992, pp. 38–42.

8 For example, Chris Searle, *Your Daily Dose: Racism in the Sun* (Campaign for Press and Broadcasting Freedom, 1989).

9 See, for example, Ien Ang, *Watching 'Dallas': Soap Opera and the Melodramatic Imagination* (Methuen, 1985); David Buckingham, *Public Secrets: 'EastEnders' and its Audience* (British Film Institute, 1987); Christine Geraghty, *Women and Soap Opera* (Cambridge, Polity, 1991).

10 An argument made, for example, by R. Hodge and D. Tripp in *Children and Television: A Semiotic Approach* (Cambridge, Polity, 1986) and by Tamar Liebes and Elihu Katz in *The Export of Meaning: Cross-Cultural Readings of 'Dallas'* (Oxford University Press, 1990).

11 See the Conclusion to Buckingham, *Reading Audiences: Young People and the Media* (Manchester University Press, 1993).

Chapter 12

Information skills

Colin Harrison

INTRODUCTION: WHAT ARE INFORMATION SKILLS?

In the 'Main Findings' section of its report *The Teaching and Learning of Reading in Primary Schools* (DES 1990a), Her Majesty's Inspectorate make the claim that in their survey of 3,000 schools, by Year 6 (age 10–11) 'three-quarters of the children assessed were reading widely on their own, but the majority were not being challenged to develop advanced reading skills'. This is a somewhat tantalising assertion, since the report goes on to give little indication of precisely what these 'advanced reading skills' are. Paragraph 52 of the report gives some clues, and refers negatively to the Inspectors' finding an overemphasis on reading as an individual task in Year 6, with little time given to developing 'more discriminating choices' of books, or to specific additional instruction on how 'to use reference books effectively'. There are also references to textbooks and non-fiction in the section, which make it clear that 'advanced reading skills' are particularly important in relation to information texts.

The meaning of the term *advanced reading skills* is, in some respects, even more difficult to pin down than that of the topic of this chapter, *information skills*. Advanced skills are presumably those which beginners do not possess, but in this sense the use of the term *advanced* may be misleading. To take two examples, skimming (looking swiftly through a text to identify main points or gist) and scanning (looking swiftly through a text to find a specific item of information, such as a name or a date) are thought by many teachers as 'advanced' skills, but in fact they are used by many readers from the earliest stages. The key aspect of these 'skills' (if they are technically skills at all – *strategies* may be a better word) is not whether a reader has them available, but whether a reader is able to use them appropriately in a study situation; it is therefore perhaps confusing to think of these as 'advanced' skills if even beginning readers are at least potentially able to use them. The term *information skills*, by contrast, while being capable of many definitions, perhaps presents fewer real difficulties. In this chapter I propose the following simple definition: *information skills are those which enable one to select,*

comprehend and integrate information, usually from a number of sources.
On this definition, information skills are clearly part at least of what HMI
felt needed further attention from teachers.

HOW IMPORTANT ARE INFORMATION SKILLS?

In the United States, as in England, there has recently been an increased
interest in information skills, and before looking at the demands of the
National Curriculum in England and Wales, it is worth considering why this
should be, since the answers will lead to some worthwhile comparisons. In
the United States, the 1986 National Assessment of Educational Progress
(NAEP) study found that, although the processing of written documents
was becoming increasingly crucial in the workplace, 95 per cent of high
school graduates made errors in simple tasks which required skills such as
searching a bus schedule for information. Furthermore, 79 per cent of
fourth-grade students failed to answer simple questions based on searching
tables or bar charts (Applebee *et al.* 1988, Kirsch and Jungeblut 1986, cited
in Guthrie *et al.* 1991). The US interest in the development of information
skills is underpinned by detailed research evidence which is published and
made widely available to the academic community, and this contrasts with
the situation in England, where the evidence upon which the DES report
was based is not accessible to teachers or other researchers. Nevertheless, as
we shall see, if the National Curriculum is followed, teachers and pupils in
England and Wales will be required to give a considerable degree of attention to this part of the reading curriculum.

What are the information skills required by the National Curriculum?
The specification for *Attainment target 2: reading* is prefaced by the following statement: *The development of the ability to read, understand and
respond to all types of writing, as well as the development of information-
retrieval strategies for the purposes of study.* The statement might lead us to
expect a heavy emphasis on handling information, and this is indeed the case.
Table 12.1 gives a summary of the topics listed in the National Curriculum
programmes of study for Reading (DES 1990b), and since the Speaking and
Listening attainment targets also mention information a good deal, a summary of these is also included. Clearly this selection from the skills and
activities listed in more than forty-two pages of the National Curriculum
document on English is a personal one, but even if it omits some areas (such
as writing) it still represents a fairly challenging and extensive range of topics
for teachers to cover.

The statements in Table 12.1 indicate an emphasis on information skills
from the earliest stages of school language development, including attainment Levels 1 and 2. Throughout the National Curriculum, information
skills are related not only to handling information from a wide variety of
printed texts, but also to working with other media. Listening to a radio

Table 12.1 Summary of the information skills in the Programmes of Study of the National Curriculum (HMSO, 1989)

Speaking and Listening

Key Stage 1: 'Development of listening skills' (e.g. to radio programmes).
All activities should 'draw on examples of speaking and listening across the curriculum', including 'explaining and presenting ideas, and giving and understanding instructions'.
Activities should include 'securing responses to visual and aural stimuli' (e.g. pictures, TV, radio, computer, telephone), and also 'giving and receiving simple explanations, information and instructions'.

Key Stages 2–4: Pupils should learn how to:
'present factual information in a clear and logically structured manner' and 'discriminate between fact and opinion and between relevance and irrelevance, and recognise bias' and 'report and summarise in a range of contexts'.

Reading

Key Stage 1: Reading material should include 'labels, captions, notices, children's newspapers, books of instructions, plans and maps, diagrams, computer printout and visual display'.
Activities should ensure that pupils:
'refer to information books, dictionaries, word books or simple data on computers as a matter of course. Pupils should be encouraged to formulate first the questions they need to answer by using such sources, so that they use them effectively and do not simply copy verbatim.'

Key Stage 2: Pupils should:
'be shown how to read different kinds of materials in different ways, e.g. "search" reading to find a scientific or geographical fact'.
'learn how to find information in books and databases, sometimes drawing on more than one source, and how to pursue an independent line of enquiry'.
'be taught how to use lists of contents, indexes, databases, a library classification system and catalogues to select information'.
'be taught how to interpret and use organisational devices such as chapter titles and headings, subheadings, changes in print or typeface, and keys to symbols and abbreviations'.

Key Stages 3 and 4: The programmes of study give a list of twenty-one types of text in a variety of media which pupils should be taught to handle, for a range of purposes, such as finding a fact, getting the gist of a passage or making a summary or synthesising information from different sources.
The detailed provisions emphasise the need for pupils to be able to respond to the way information is structured so that they are able to identify key points.
Pupils should be able to deduce authorial points of view in non-fiction as well as fiction.

programme, for example, requires a good deal of selection, comprehension and integration of information, and this is included as part of the Key Stage 1 curriculum. Indeed, the very nature of information skills implies transformation of knowledge from one form to another for some purpose, and it is therefore very difficult to see how information skills could relate solely to one curricular area or attainment target. Within the National Curriculum there is a good deal of evidence that despite the separation of topics into the attainment target areas of Speaking and Listening, Reading and Writing, the language modes interrelate and overlap. For example, all the statements of attainment for Reading require the pupil to respond through talk, and all of the statements of attainment for Reading above Level 4, and for Speaking and Listening above Level 7, require the pupil to make some response in writing. What all this means is that information skills are not in any sense purely reading skills.

The activities summarised in Table 12.1 do, however, cover many of the areas traditionally associated with the reading development literature, namely the reading of a wide range of texts, the use of a variety of reading strategies to interrogate these, and skills of selecting and then transforming and representing the information which has been selected.

For the teacher, then, a number of priorities are clear. From Key Stage 1 onwards, the concept of a *text* must be widened to include not only newspapers, labels and maps, but also visual and audio texts from TV and radio, the computer and telephone. Computer databases are specifically mentioned from Key Stage 2 onwards, as are information retrieval systems within libraries and signposting devices within books. From Key Stage 3 onwards (i.e. from age 11), as well as being introduced to a variety of literary genres, pupils are to be taught to deal with texts as challenging as consumer reports and contracts, and study aids as complex as thesauruses.

The problem for the teacher is twofold: even if he or she is able to help the pupil to gain access to this great variety of texts, there are likely to be difficulties in assisting pupils to come to terms with their content. The ability of a reader to select and summarise key points from a text is not simply a matter of practice, nor is it aided greatly by semi-mechanical formulae, such as 'Identify the topic sentence; if you can't find one, make one up', although such formulations can help some readers sometimes. The biggest problem is with overall text difficulty, and this is often increased in the case of what have been called 'inconsiderate' texts, which have an information structure that is not clearly signposted. Lunzer and Gardner (1979) found in their study of readability that the most difficult texts school students were likely to encounter tended to be those which they were required to read on their own, and it is when children are reading on their own that they perhaps feel least confident in making judgements about the meaning and information structure of a text.

WHY IS IT SO DIFFICULT TO STUDY INFORMATIVE TEXTS?

The National Curriculum has laid down that as part of Key Stage 1 children are to be taught not to copy verbatim from information books, but this is not something which can be achieved simply by legislation. Copying verbatim is fairly common at Key Stage 4 (GCSE level) in project work, and is not uncommon at college entrance level or even in higher education. Readers copy verbatim when they do not have confidence that any selection, summary or transformation of what they are reading would be an adequate representation of the original. In general, such readers are not simply being lazy, nor are they unaware that it is unsatisfactory and unethical to plagiarise. The point is that in order to write a synopsis or summary, a reader needs to be able to do two things: to identify the deep structure of a text, and to find superordinate terms in order to transform the sections that are most important in that deep structure into one's own words. The ability to do this is not a 'skill' which one does or does not possess; it is a function of the reader's vocabulary knowledge and his or her ability to identify the information structure of that particular text, ideally in a hierarchical form. This is why 'considerate' texts are much easier to summarise than 'inconsiderate' texts: if the information structure is clearly signalled, half the job is done for you; the only problem remaining is that of vocabulary. In this sense, therefore, the National Curriculum programmes of study are overoptimistic in suggesting that 'pupils should be taught to skim-read so that they are able to discover the structure and gist of a text quickly' (Programmes of Study for Reading, paragraph 23). Such a prescription could only be successful if all texts were 'considerate'. For 'inconsiderate' texts, they need another, much more complex ability, namely that of being able to probe confidently and effectively beneath the surface, and to construct for themselves a representation of a text's deep structure.

It is by no means the purpose of this chapter to suggest that the National Curriculum for English is generally naive or wrong headed in its treatment of information skills. There is much to praise, and if the information skills curriculum demands are extensive and daunting, they are also exciting and potentially empowering for children, since they should encourage and prepare readers to be able to engage in the independent study of adult material, and to be alert to the bias, rhetorical techniques and unacknowledged or implied subtexts which such material might contain. Nevertheless, there remains the question of how teachers can best support readers in approaching difficult and possibly 'inconsiderate' texts effectively, independently, with confidence.

THE STRUCTURE OF INFORMATIVE TEXTS

To answer this question, it is necessary to consider not just reading 'skills', but the much wider issue of reading comprehension. What is it that enables a reader to identify the main points of a difficult text, of a passage that is poorly written or badly signposted, to penetrate beyond the surface text, and identify the deep structure underpinning it? In the helpful phrase of the Bullock Report (DES 1975), a reader needs to be able to 'actively interrogate the text'. When the reader does this, and asks questions of the text which go beneath the surface, another important issue must be confronted, which is the nature of that text's structure. It is commonly acknowledged that, to a greater or lesser extent, most fiction texts make use of elements of what is, in effect, a standard narrative structure, one which is in many respects universal across cultures. In general, folk tales, legends, fairy tales and other stories from oral traditions tend to follow the paradigmatic or canonical structures reported in the literature on 'story grammars' (see, for example, Mandler and Johnson (1975) for one of the best-known papers on the subject from a cognitive psychology perspective and Arthur Applebee (1978) for a thorough treatment of children's awareness of story structure), but all stories and novels make some use of certain commonly accepted structural elements. Canonical stories tend to have a setting, with a location, characters and time mentioned; there is a theme, usually related to a problem to be overcome, and a series of episodes lead to an eventual resolution of the problem, often followed by a coda in the form of a moral. But what of non-narrative texts? Do these have one type of deep structure, or many, and if the answer is that they have many, what are the pedagogical implications of this?

This was one of the questions which the Schools Council project *Reading for Learning in the Secondary School* set out to answer, and their conclusion was that there were at least ten major text types encountered in the work-sheet, textbooks and reference books which children encountered in schools (Lunzer *et al.* 1984). Lunzer and his co-workers drew upon the seminal work of Meyer (1975), who had provided an analogue to story grammars, but based upon relationships within the content of non-fiction passages. Meyer's initial premise was that if narrative structure was not the glue which held ideas together in expository text, this coherence had to be accomplished through two other types of linkage, which she called *lexical* and *rhetorical predicates*. The lexical links were mostly to do with how semantic relationships were established, while the rhetorical links related to the way the argument was developed. For example, *problem–solution* and *cause and effect* are relationships which are shown through rhetorical predicates. Using Meyer's approach as their starting point, Lunzer's group worked with teachers in a variety of subjects across the curriculum to identify generic text types. Their classification system for texts was broader, and not as complex as that of Meyer, and neither was it in some respects so rigorous, but it had two great merits: teachers could use it fairly reliably, and the classification system was systematically related to a range of reading development activities. The ten text types were as follows: *Narrative, Structure or mechanism, Process, Principle, Theory, Problem–solution, Historical situation, Classification, Instructions,* and *Theme.* Lunzer *et al.* give details of how to identify each text type, but equally importantly, they suggest activities for encouraging close reading and interrogation of each text type.

HOW CAN DARTs DEVELOP A READER'S ABILITY TO COMPREHEND INFORMATIVE TEXTS?

Can we teach reading comprehension? To this Lunzer's group would emphatically answer 'yes', but they would add that traditional comprehension exercises are no way to proceed in order to develop comprehension. Their preference was for directed reading activities, which they called DARTs (Directed Activities Related to Texts), but this was not all. They insisted that reading should be part of learning, and that a text-based lesson should arise naturally out of the teacher's curricular objectives. They added one bonus of DARTs, however, which was that the techniques permitted the teacher to offer pupils more difficult texts than might usually be chosen. One further tenet of DARTs must be emphasised, and this is the central value placed on exchanges by pupils in small groups. This small-group work around the text is absolutely fundamental to DARTs, and the reasons for it are important ones. Lunzer *et al.* stress the value of every pupil participating in interrogating the text, which does not necessarily happen in a whole-class lesson, and they also emphasise the unthreatening atmosphere within a small group, where hypotheses and hunches can be offered, exchanged and reconsidered in confidence.

A further point which is relevant here is the fact that comprehension exercises (including cloze exercises) which are tackled independently, and without immediate feedback, are, in terms of their structure, no more than tests, and tend to confirm the level of a child's reading, without raising that level. It is only in the context of group discussion that researchers have found that activities such as cloze or sequencing contribute to reading development. The reason for this is simple: it is through being offered a model of what it is to read more closely and attentively that a reader can develop. From the earliest stages in literacy development, adults provide models of how to behave like a reader, how to read and how to respond to what one reads. In tackling difficult information texts, children still need that modelling, and DARTs provide a framework for it to be offered. What happens when children undertake DARTs activities is that they lay bare a model of fluent reading, and just as all teachers learn from teaching, so readers learn from themselves and from each other what it is to read attentively, to spot the signals which identify certain types of text and certain types of information structure.

DARTs include all the well-known favourites of reading development, going back to the 1970s, as the full list of DARTs activities in Table 12.2 shows. Cloze procedure is expanded to a variety of text completion activities, within the category of Reconstruction of text. Sequencing and prediction are also in the Reconstruction category since they involve pre-editing of the text in some way. The same applies to table and diagram completion, which are important Reconstruction DARTs, devised initially in collaboration with teachers who were frustrated at the problems their students had with tables and diagrams in textbooks which were inadequate and difficult to interpret. Analysis DARTs do not involve pre-editing of text to any great extent, although it is axiomatic that a passage used for a DART should have been read and analysed in detail by the teacher in preparing the lesson. Analysis DARTs which use underlining, segmenting and labelling are crucial in offering pupils opportunities to identify gradually elements in the structure of a passage, which is the first stage in being able to do some more demanding things such as identifying main points, irrelevancies, fact versus opinion, and so on. Underlining and segmenting (i.e. saying where the breaks come in a passage), for example, can be done before a reader feels that he or she has anything like full comprehension of the text, but this externalisation of the reader's tentative notions which these DARTs encourage enables others to learn, test and examine their own ideas against those of others, and to acquire procedures and models for eventually doing the same things as independent readers. Some Analysis DARTs require a fairly high level of confidence in handling the text; networks or Venn diagrams can only be written for some passages when a reader has already developed a reasonably complete idea of the information structure of the text. If confidence is low, however, working together can be extremely valuable, and devising a network diagram in pairs can encourage a very deep level of text analysis. By contrast, diagrams can also be very individual and personal representations of knowledge, and those devised in relation to a poem, for example, could be personal and idiosyncratic and still prove valuable in offering a basis for discussion and exploration. DARTs can thus fill a role in providing reading activities which are on a long continuum of open to closed, in terms of the teacher's intended task.

In concluding this description of DARTs as tools for exploring texts, with particular emphasis on reading to support information skills in the National Curriculum, it is appropriate to link Lunzer et al.'s text types to the DARTs activities, in order to provide teachers with an indication of how one can begin to make principled choices of reading activity according to the type of lesson and type of text. Table 12.3 gives a matching of text types to DARTs activities, to enable us to make at least a start on this. Clearly the list is

Table 12.2 Directed Activities Related to Texts (Lunzer *et al.* 1984)

Reconstruction of text	Analysis of text

1 Text completion
  – word completion
  – phrase completion
  – sentence completion
	1 Text marking
	  – underlining certain parts

2 Sequencing
  – time base
  – other base
	2 Labelling
	  – text
	  – diagrams

3 Prediction
  – pupils predict next part
  – pupils write next part
	3 Segmenting

4 Table completion
  – pupils fill in cells
  – pupils devise headings
	4 Table construction
	  – pupils construct headings (and fill in cells)

5 Diagram completion
  – label completion
  – diagram completion
	5 Diagram construction
	  – e.g. flowchart, network, Venn diagram

	6 Question generation

Table 12.3 The ten major text types identified by Lunzer *et al.* (1984), and the DARTs activities recommended as most effective for each

	Text type	Suggested DARTs activities
1	Narrative	Underlining, labelling, diagram completion, prediction, sequencing, question generation.
2	Structure or mechanism	Underlining, completion, diagram completion, flowchart, sequencing.
3	Process	Segmenting, tabulation, flow diagram, sequencing, prediction, diagram, question generation.
4	Principle	Tabulation, hierarchical diagrams, completion.
5	Theory	Tabulation, underlining.
6	Problem–solution	Segmenting, labelling, completion, prediction, diagram construction.
7	Historical situation	Underlining, listing, flow diagram, diagram completion, prediction.
8	Classification	Labelling, tree diagrams, segmenting, ordering, tabulation.
9	Instructions	Flow diagram, tabulation, sequencing.
10	Theme	Listing, diagrams.

tentative, but it is related to what the classroom teachers working with the project team found effective and workable, so every pairing of text type and DART is based upon classroom experience and extensive trials.

CONCLUSION: FOCUSING ON THE 'INFORMATION' RATHER THAN THE 'SKILLS'

There is not space in this brief review to give examples of all these DARTs in action; Lunzer's group devoted a whole book to this, and it is to that book that we should turn for detailed guidance. In this chapter the intention is more modest: it is to argue for an approach to teaching what we call *information skills* in a way that emphasises a DARTs approach rather than what one might call a 'study skills' approach. The ability to handle information from a wide variety of sources is essential, not only for the minority who go on from school to college, but for all readers, since everyone in our society benefits from the empowerment which access to information brings. Some study skills approaches are valid and useful, but what we need to recognise is that an ability to which we can give a name is not necessarily one which must be taught as if it is underpinned by a discrete skill. In other words, just because it is important to be able to 'discriminate between fact and opinion' and to 'report and summarise in a range of contexts', we should not imagine that there are entirely separate sets of 'fact discrimination skills', 'opinion discrimination skills', 'reporting skills' and 'summarising skills' each of which needs to be taught separately. What determines whether a reader can do the task in a specific instance is his or her ability to understand the text or texts upon which the task is based. To put the point even more bluntly, the reading 'skills' or 'strategies' needed for a person to be able to summarise a Shakespeare play are not different from those needed for a person to be able to read a biology textbook and to be able to draw a flow diagram illustrating the action of kidneys. What is very different in the two cases is the content and structure of the text, and it is this aspect of the reading task that we have tended to neglect. On a surface level, these tasks seem very different, and so, understandably, we might assume that they imply different types of processing during reading, and therefore use different reading 'skills'. What this chapter is arguing is that it might be more helpful to concentrate not on skills but on increasing the familiarity of readers with a wider range of information structures within expository prose. Giving children précis and summary practice may be entirely useless – unless it is done in such a way as to increase a reader's awareness of how different types of information text are structured.

Information skills are an important part of the National Curriculum, and deserve serious attention from teachers and pupils, but the best way to develop them will be to reduce the emphasis on 'skills' as such, and to pay more attention to developing readers' understanding of the way in which information texts work, and this will be accomplished most effectively through an approach which incorporates the DARTs philosophy.

BIBLIOGRAPHY

Applebee, A.N. (1978) *The Child's Concept of Story*. Chicago: University of Chicago Press.

Applebee, A.N., Langer, J.A. and Mullis, I.V.S. (1988) *Who Reads Best? Factors related to reading achievement in Grades 3, 7 and 11*. Princeton, NJ: Educational Testing Service.

Department of Education and Science (1975) *A Language for Life* (The Bullock Report). London: HMSO.

Department of Education and Science (1990a) *The Teaching and Learning of Reading in Primary Schools*. London: HMSO.

Department of Education and Science (1990b) *English in the National Curriculum (No.2)*. London: HMSO.

Eden, J.E. (1991) Helping pupils to read for information. *Reading* **25**/2, July, 8–12.

Guthrie, J.T., Britten, T. and Barker, K.G. (1991) Roles of document structure, cognitive strategy, and awareness in searching for information. *Reading Research Quarterly* **21**/3, 300–24.

Kirsch, I.S. and Jungeblut, A. (1986) *Literacy: Profile of America's Young Adults*. Princeton, NJ: Educational Testing Service.

Lunzer, E.A. and Gardner, W.K. (1979) *The Effective Use of Reading*. London: Heinemann, for the Schools Council.

Lunzer, E.A., Gardner, W.K., Davies, F. and Greene, T. (1984) *Learning From the Written Word*. Edinburgh: Oliver and Boyd, for the Schools Council.

Mandler, J.M. and Johnson, N.S. (1975) Remembrance of things parsed: story structure and recall. *Cognitive Psychology* **9**, 111–51.

Meyer, B.J.F. (1975) *The Organisation of Prose and its Effects on Memory*. Amsterdam: North-Holland.

Reutzel, D. and Hollingsworth, P.M. (1988) Highlighting key vocabulary: a generative-reciprocal procedure for teaching selected inference types. *Reading Research Quarterly* **23**/3, 358–78.

Chapter 13

Working within a new literacy

Sally Tweddle and Phil Moore

> but if he is not taught good English he will be perfecting himself in bad
> English . . . . Even while the schools may be teaching good English, the
> surroundings of street and home will be teaching bad English.
>
> (George Sampson, *English for the English*, 1921)

> The print that offers beginning readers the most insights into the mean-
> ingfulness of written language tends to lie outside books in the far more
> personal and pervasive world of their own lives.
>
> (Frank Smith, *Reading*, 1978)

> I wish [children] to understand the multiplicity of media through which
> their society attempts to inform and to form them, to have an understand-
> ing which is detailed enough for them to become productive users of
> some of these modes of communication.
>
> (Gunther Kresse, *TES*, November 1992)

Increasingly, definitions of literacy have moved outwards from the classroom context to embrace the context of students themselves. It is now many
people's belief that, in Margaret Meek's words:

> literacy itself . . . has to be redescribed, at least as *literacies*, to match the
> new, emergent contexts and kinds of literate behaviours that are prevalent
> in modern societies.
>
> (*On Being Literate*, 1991: 203)

One of these emergent contexts, that produced by information technology,
demands new kinds of literate behaviours and it is this context and these
behaviours which will be explored in this chapter.

Computers are an integral feature of twentieth-century living. Computer-
related texts surround youngsters – whether displayed on computer screens
or produced by means of a computer – and computers are slowly but
steadily being made available in schools for the purposes of students'
learning. Yet it is still not sufficiently the case that computers are used in
schools to support and enhance students' developing literacy.

There are two areas of computer-related literacy which need examination. One relates to what may reasonably be called 'computer texts' – those which are read on a computer screen. The second relates to the texts which have been produced using a computer, which can include books but which also includes database printouts, bank statements and 'junk' mail.

COMPUTER TEXTS

The concept of computer texts is relatively new to English teachers. Traditionally, text has been taken to mean printed words; more recently, however, the Language in the National Curriculum Project has led to a redefinition of the term. For example, Nick Jones suggests:

> In its origin [text] means *something woven*, which implies a purposeful working upon the available resources of meaning. The *realisation* of this meaning, and the completion of the work, is nonetheless dependent upon the reader.
>
> *(Reader, Writer, Text in Knowledge about Language*, Hodder and Stoughton, 1990)

Within such a definition it would seem reasonable to accept the principle that what is displayed on a computer screen is text and that the capacity to read that text is part of the literacy with which English teachers must be concerned. Therefore, just as the bus timetable is a text, so too is the information screen at the railway station giving departure and arrival times. So too, amongst the texts used by young people, are the teletext database, which provides information in the home by way of a television screen, and the cashpoint dispenser screen, which many a youngster will have used on a parent's behalf.

One of the key differences between printed and computer texts is that the former remain the same each time you look at them: the reader cannot change the words and images, though each time he or she reads them, he or she may produce a different meaning of them. Any one of the computer-related texts mentioned above, however, will present different displays at different times. And learning to know that, and to read accordingly, is one of the key factors in a student's developing competence with such texts. Indeed in *Language for Learning*, the APU reported that children's performance was affected by the medium in which they were reading and recommended that students 'should be given experience of reading and manipulating material in different forms on screen' (*Language for Learning: Assessment Matters No. 4*, APU, SEAC, 1991).

There is a multiplicity of ways in which electronically displayed texts differ from those that are printed: Tweddle provides a starting point for considering these differences in 'Towards Understanding a New Literacy' (*English in Education*, vol. 26, no. 2, summer 1992, NATE). She suggests that texts as displayed on a computer screen – whether encountered within school or in the wider environment – can differ from printed texts in the following ways:

- *in structure* – they are not necessarily linear unless the computer is being used as a tool to prepare text for printing;
- *in organisational conventions* – images, icons, screen messages are amongst the conventions used for helping the reader around a text;
- *in style* – the conciseness of expression and the use of a specialist vocabulary result in what may amount to a dialect;
- *in presentation* – the size of the screen, the facility to represent words, images and sound dynamically and in different combinations are characteristic qualities of the medium;
- *in content* – different types of information may be differently represented on every occasion.

In combination, these features offer possibilities which mean that computer texts can fulfil a range of functions which printed texts cannot.

TEXTS PRODUCED USING A COMPUTER

Of the texts whose features are considered above many will be designed to be read only on screen: they will never be printed. Other computer-related texts are intended only to be printed, in which case the computer is a tool for writing and the screen only a temporary medium for display. A letter to a bank manager or an annual update sent out with Christmas cards would fall into this category, as do novels, pieces of journalism and research. The literacy to which such texts best belong is the traditional print-based literacy with which teachers are familiar. However, the technology now offers possibilities which require an adjustment in thinking about the nature of such printed texts. It is increasingly possible for a number of people to be involved in the composition of any text and it is possible for that involvement to be unwitting and unacknowledged, for the technology now enables information and ideas from different sources to be accessed, manipulated and transformed so that their origin is untraceable.

In a different category are texts which will be read on screen and subsequently printed, such as database searches. The cashpoint dispenser with the proffered receipt is an everyday example of this kind of text. Some such texts do not fit neatly within traditional representations of text because the conventional relationship between the writing, the writer and the reader is altered: the writer is invisible and apparently non-existent and there is a temptation to assume that the computer itself has generated the text. However, computer-related texts are generated with the technology and not by the technology: in all cases there has been a process of composition in which an individual or individuals have been involved.

The question of authorship is a key one and it pertains to all computer-related texts, whether the text is a computer game, the result of a database search, or a letter from a friend. In the case of computer games, it is difficult to identify the voice of an author; likewise the database search. But the business of becoming critical centres upon the ability to recognise where authorial choices have been made and how they could have been different. It is important, therefore, that students are enabled to understand the authorial decisions that may have been made in the process of producing computer-related texts.

COMPUTER-RELATED LITERACY

Pupils will be encountering computer-related texts outside and within the school environment. They will develop attitudes to and expectations of those texts which will evolve in response to the particular characteristics of the texts and as a result of the pupils' experiences of reading those texts. Elizabeth Freund, in her analysis of developments in reader-response criticism, represents the process of reading as private and silent (*The Return of the Reader*, Methuen, 1987). This view of reading comes from a cultural context within which many serving teachers were educated. As has been suggested, that culture is changing and with it the way that the act of reading is perceived – no longer simply an interaction between writer, text, context and reader but an activity in which a number of readers may collaborate. Indeed, with a computer text, the reading process is rarely silent or private: not only can computer texts include sound but also the screen is a public medium. In the classroom where groups of students are working together around a screen many feel compelled to read the text aloud and are drawn into talking about what they are reading.

Whilst many students are confident with computer texts, it is important to acknowledge that the experience of reading them may alienate or disenfranchise some groups. It is widely recognised that boys tend to feel more at ease with computers than girls and that most computer games are male oriented. Many teachers have acknowledged this and have accordingly evolved approaches to the use of the computer which are designed to ensure equality of access. However, less apparent as an issue is the fact that the language which is used on screen, both for words embedded as part of the program and for the words which can be entered by the user, is almost invariably English, precluding the possibility of work being represented in any language other than English. Further, while youngsters with special needs may use computers to gain access to the curriculum, many of the texts which their peers will use outside school require a dexterity and accomplishment with keyboard or joystick which some may not have.

Through this exploration of computer-related and print-based texts, and the experience of reading them, it is important not to lose sight of the commonalities between the two. Reading is a complex process which involves skills, processes and understandings, many of which will be the same, whatever the type of text being read. Additionally, it is wise not to differentiate too widely between the reading that takes place with a computer and that with a book, because it is important that teachers value all their pupils' reading experiences. Indeed, one of the main purposes in urging a reconsideration by teachers of their definition of literacy is in order to encourage them to build upon the experiences youngsters have had with a whole range of texts. The key is to validate all successful reading experiences and to enable students to build upon the commonalities across those experiences and to recognise and understand the differences. Once that process is under way it is possible for teachers to focus on helping their pupils to develop critical approaches to the texts they will be encountering. And in the case of computer texts in particular, there would be some consensus about the need for developing critical responses.

There is one other aspect of computer-related literacy that should be raised before considering what these issues mean for classroom practice. In a world in which printed text is increasingly generated on computers, youngsters need to know for themselves how the technology can be used. Shortage of resources, however, means that many are still limited, for the purposes of their own writing, to the pen, a tool which prevents them from doing easily what a computer enables: making small changes, adapting one piece of writing for the needs of different audiences, revising the same piece of writing again and again, combining and moving words and images, producing professional printed copies.

As readers, when they receive a mass-mailed 'personalised' letter, or they react to somebody's choice of picture as an illustration of words, or they reflect upon the amount of space afforded to a headline in a popular newspaper, they need to know how these effects have been achieved. And they can only really understand this by having themselves used the technology which enables such effects. Only through creating their own texts do students have a chance of fully appreciating the decisions that have been made by the authors of the texts they read.

IMPLICATIONS FOR PRACTICE

So what are the implications for the classroom? One of the main consequences of developing understanding about the new literacies of the twentieth century is that teachers have re-examined their assumptions about the place of the computer in English teaching. In 1983 A. Adams and E. Jones concluded:

All this brings us to what is, necessarily for the Language Arts teacher, the primary application of the micro computer to the classroom – that is its use as a wordprocessor.

(*Teaching Humanities in the Microelectronic Age*, Open University Press, 1983)

Nine years later, Peter Nightingale wrote about the process of using *Developing Tray*, a 'reading' program:

The year 8 students had got to know the poem by working on it 'from the inside' as a cloze procedure. They were writing about the poem's effectiveness, not offering judgements about its literary merit.

('Karen's poems: collaboration in the writing process', Peter Nightingale in *Looking into Language*, ed. R. Bain *et al.*, Hodder and Stoughton, 1992)

Teachers have been exploring the role of the computer in the teaching of literacy and there have been some interesting and important outcomes. While acknowledging that the computer is a valuable publishing tool enabling the production of well-presented text, they have discovered that the technology can, in addition, support processes of learning and the development of understandings about language that are much wider than those involved in publishing.

The use of the program *Developing Tray*, for instance, as demonstrated by Peter Nightingale's account, has experienced a revival under the influence of the LINC Project. The program's capacity to provoke students into making explicit their implicit knowledge about language has been recognised for some time and it has largely been used to enable students to develop critical responses to literature, particularly poetry. Thus, students would be presented with a partially revealed text and encouraged to explore the possibilities of that text during a process of prediction which leads to the completion of the original text. Recently, however, new possibilities have been suggested. So, Nightingale describes a situation where students used the program in the writing of their own poetry, the computer supporting the critical reading and analysis of what they had written by their peers.

Other students have been involved in work which involves an exploration of a number of genres of IT texts, including teletext news services, on-line databases and computer games. Their questions about these texts were the same as they would ask of a print-based text: who wrote them, why did they write them and for whom and how were the texts produced? And as part of their exploration of those questions they were making IT texts themselves, in order that they could understand the processes more fully (The Trojan Horse, NATE, 1993).

An important issue for users of IT is the status of the information that is mediated by technology. While this may not be an explicit focus for all teachers, some have contributed to their students' understanding of some of the relevant issues through imaginative uses of databases. In *Sylvania* (Wendy Lynch, *Planning for Language*, NCET, 1991) students contributed information to a database which held details of settlements within an imaginary country. They had invented the information, but when they went to the database as a source of information for their reports as journalists, the information they had entered was indistinguishable from that which their teacher had previously produced, or from that which they would have seen in a 'real' database. Likewise, students involved in drama work which explored the influence of criminal records on people's lives were able to go through, and come to understand, the process of producing the kind of computer texts – database records – which are used by the police (Jonothan Neelands, *Drama and IT: Exploring the Human Dimension*, NATE/NCET, 1993).

A relatively new area of work for teachers of English is mixed media. The technologies that are now becoming available in schools make it possible to take photographs – with an ion camera, for instance – or to scan pictures and 'import' them into text produced on the computer. Sound can also be recorded. Students can therefore produce their own mixed, or integrated, media texts as well as reading those produced by others.

In *Authoring – an Educational Perspective* (unpublished paper), Phil Moore contrasts books where pictures may provide a different narrative from the words, as in John Burningham's *Time to Get out of the Bath, Shirley*, with animated stories on CD-ROM where each picture is animated to echo the words of the narrative but where additional narratives can be uncovered by the reader through selecting certain parts of the picture. He argues that the writer of integrated media texts explores the tension between various aspects of the text in different ways from the writer of books. But he suggests that it is possible that the narratives which students create for themselves when reading books may be replaced in integrated media texts with actions predetermined by the writers and which are the same with each reading.

Students in the classroom have explored the characteristics of integrated texts through creating their own animated stories, as described in *Planning for Language* and *Developing English* (NATE, 1993). In particular, work on branching stories has demonstrated the potential of the technology to support exploration of notions of authorial choice and narrative structure.

CONCLUSION

It is important to recognise that the approaches to literacy with computer texts which are characterised here rely heavily upon the use of the technology for those things which a computer can do well: supporting the processes of collaborative exploration, experimentation and investigation. Through such approaches, youngsters can begin to acquire the tools which will enable them to become truly literate: developing the understanding and experience which produce critical readers. If such outcomes are not acknowledged as amongst the most important when identifying how and why computers should be used in the classroom, we need to consider quite carefully what our motives are in using the new technologies with the students of today.

Chapter 14

The centrality of literature

Alastair West

Let me make clear at the outset that I fully endorse the proposition that literature is, and should remain, central to the teaching and learning of English in the secondary curriculum. So too, however, does almost everybody else who has expressed a view in recent years on secondary English teaching, not least 'those who have put themselves in charge of the nation's destiny' (Bolton 1992) and introduced the National Curriculum legislation. And therein, of course, lies the rub, for the seemingly widespread agreement as to the centrality of literature in schooling is deceptively reassuring and disguises substantial ideological differences. Since the inception of the National Curriculum, for example, there have been heated debates over the definition and assessment of the secondary English curriculum, with literature being a particular sticking point. There must be many within, let alone beyond, the world of education who are baffled at how all the parties in a dispute of this kind can subscribe to the same notion of the centrality of literature. But this is neither new nor unusual.

The centrality of literature has always been a powerful rallying cry in education to which many have responded, and a substantial chapter of the history of state education could be taken up by the arguments as to what precisely has been rallied to. Indeed, the proposition is the source of such deep confusion that I think it likely to be more helpful if we unpick the rhetoric of what is often no more than a slogan and try to say what we mean in some other kind of way. We could make a start perhaps by looking at three questions:

- what counts as literature?
- what are the educational benefits claimed for literature?
- and what is literature central to?

Some clarification on these points could help in two ways. In the first place it would help to resolve the muddle that exists in the English Working Group Report (DES 1989) about how English as a subject is to be construed for our times. The report describes five versions of English – skills, adult needs, cultural heritage, personal growth and cultural analysis – all of which ascribe a very different role and function to literature. These versions are not new, the main lines of disagreement being traceable back to debates at the time of the introduction of mass public education in the mid-nineteenth century (Williams 1965). Despite the report's claims that these versions of English are by no means *mutually exclusive*, each version leads to quite different classroom practices, expectations and notions of what counts as success and failure. They all make different assumptions as to what is possible and desirable in the classroom and have led to very different educational practices and outcomes, some of them extremely undesirable.

Some views on English need not detain us long, for example the skills version, because they see no role for literature at all. Ever since the mid-nineteenth century, there have been those who would restrict mass educational provision to a basic or functional literacy and subordinate full individual development to the narrow requirements of the workplace. Such a view has little to commend it in terms of either children's language development or economic efficiency, let alone social justice. It is the cultural heritage, personal growth and cultural analysis versions of the subject with which we are concerned here, all of which reject the instrumentalism of the skills approach. But whilst they all agree on that point, they are by no means easily reconciled and so there are choices to be made if we are to be clear about our own professional intentions, clear both to ourselves and to those to whom we are formally accountable.

There is a further, more urgent and practical reason for addressing these questions. In various formulations, and with varying degrees of intensity, these questions will come at us insistently in the classroom from our students: *why do we have to read this book? what is this supposed to do for me?* There can be no guarantee that the centrality of literature will be a self-evident truth to our students who will press us for answers that are persuasive at the time and who deserve ones that are durable enough to carry conviction when they later reflect upon their own, or perhaps their children's, education. And in those same classrooms many situations will arise that will lead us to ask very similar questions of ourselves: *why do I have to teach this book? what have these students learned from this literature?* The questions will not go away, nor can they ever be answered fully by legislation.

What is offered here is one set of answers within a framework which assumes that if, in the broadest terms, our business involves 'learning to be literate in a democratic society' (NATE 1989), then we have a good deal more thinking to do than present legislation has allowed for. I want to argue for a view of the subject which differs from those on offer in the English Working Group Report. I refer to this as *critical literacy*, a term associated with the work of Freire (Freire and Macedo 1987).

WHAT COUNTS AS LITERATURE?

Barthes' blunt comment that *literature is what gets taught* is particularly helpful in the present context. It gets to the nub of the difficulty that continues to confuse so much discussion about English teaching, which is that what distinguishes a piece of work as literature is not its formal or aesthetic properties, nor its subject matter, nor its popularity or effects upon audiences, but the particular uses to which it is put. A text becomes literature when it is incorporated into a quite specific set of institutional practices which confer authority, distinction and a hallmark of quality. As a category, literature is not given, but socially constructed. It acts as a device for the exclusion and separation of some texts from others. Beyond the circle of literature lie those texts which are merely read. This boundary between literature and non-literature is used to mark difference, not just of usage, but also of quality.

Nor is it simply a question of the distinction between the social valuations accorded to texts and the uses to which they are put: the distinction is subtly extended to include their readers. For a text that is taught as literature tends to be read in very particular ways and in quite specific institutional contexts as part of a highly complex process of cultural induction, social stratification and occupational qualification. This process whereby social distinctions are validated through the education system is, of course, by no means the only function of literature, nor has it ever been the one which most draws people into teaching. But it is there, is important and has to be acknowledged because the judgements that are made in relation to it make material differences to people's lives. Much contemporary discussion of literature in education is taken up, quite properly, with questions of access and entitlement. This is fine so long as we remember that, in the current disputes over the curriculum, more than the simple right of entry is at stake, for entry is to be obligatory and the entrants to be subject to judgement as they leave. Entitlement and access for all to Shakespeare is one thing; the assessment of all on the nature of their engagement with those texts is something else. Which is why what counts as literature is so important.

The curriculum is, as Williams (1965) pointed out, *a selection from culture*. But who gets to make the selection, and by what criteria and on whose behalf? Can there be just one culture in a multiethnic, multilingual society? Do all social classes share the same culture? The cultural heritage view of English is confident in the face of such questions: 'it emphasises the responsibility of schools to lead children into an appreciation of those works of literature that have been widely regarded as amongst the finest in the language' (DES 1989). Historically, this was a straightforwardly hegemonic approach in which the interests, language and literary tastes of the dominant social group subordinated those of other groups in society. The debates around the Newbolt Report (1922) indicate how closely this view was allied to sociopolitical concerns of empire abroad and social unrest at home. Comparable developments may be seen in education services in other countries, particularly at moments of instability and major social change. In essence, it is a process of appropriation both of voice and speaking position, of being defined by somebody else's terms. Ahmad describes the process well in his comments on how the category of Third World literature is currently constructed:

> 'literature' from other zones of the Third World – African, say, or Arab, or Caribbean – comes to us not directly or autonomously but through grids of accumulation, interpretation and relocation which are governed from the metropolitan countries. By the time a Latin American novel arrives in Delhi, it has been selected, translated, published, reviewed, explicated and allotted a place in the burgeoning archive of 'Third World Literature' through a complex set of metropolitan mediations . . . it arrives here with those processes of circulation and classification already inscribed in its very texture.
>
> (Ahmad 1993)

The heritage version of English is primarily concerned with the task of nation building, the literary heritage being the vehicle whereby the standard form of the language is established in its dominant role. Whilst it is important to clarify administrative ambitions in this way, it is equally important to record that the actualities of such intentions as they were lived out in classrooms and elsewhere were never quite so neat. After all, it is a very special kind of ignorance that seeks to prescribe the details of the nation's linguistic usage and coerce its literary tastes. Generations of teachers and their students can testify to the complexity of that particular kind of dialogue between the rulers and the ruled: enthusiastic acceptance, temporising compliance, outright rejection, mockery, the assertion of alternatives.

What counts as literature, then, in this version becomes highly particularised, a canonical selection of texts chosen from a loosely defined range of imaginative writing in a variety of genres. This view was challenged in the 1960s by what became known as the personal growth model of English, on the grounds that it was not appropriate and relevant to children's language development, their interests, creativity and culture. Teachers sought out and argued, often in the teeth of opposition, for the inclusion of texts that spoke to and of the experience of contemporary adolescents. The gains have been very substantial, but the literary heritage – whose it was, how it was constituted, how it had changed – was not so much challenged as side-stepped. Indeed, in many ways what occurred was the creation of a subsidiary canon of texts deemed to be appropriate and relevant to children's interests (*Of Mice and Men, Lord of the Flies, Cider with Rosie*, and so on) and which had many common features in terms of subject matter, generic features and ideology.

In the personal growth model of English teaching, therefore, literature –
albeit a different selection of texts – was accorded an equally important place
in the curriculum as in the heritage version, and equally important – but
different – claims were made for it. Substantial and worthwhile changes in
classrooms ensued, but there were also continuities. These continuities
became important in the 1980s when Conservative pressure groups began to
urge the restoration of the heritage model because 'they correctly identify
changes in English teaching with a radical change in English national identity
alien to their own interests' (Cox 1992). These pressures derive from the
transformation of the country 'from a racially and linguistically homogeneous society into a miscegenated and polyglot one, and the desire to reim-
pose an English identity on the country' (McCabe cited in Cox). The result
is that 'right wing conservatives wish to impose a Christian culture on all
children, together with national pride heavily dependent on a thorough
knowledge of English history and English literature' (Cox 1992).

Throughout the 1980s and 1990s, the English curriculum was one of the
key areas in which the ideological conflict to (re)define national identity was
waged. The contest has been made all the more slippery by the comparatively late realisation by English teachers that the terms of their discourse,
with its emphasis upon individualism, literature, entitlement, have all been
very effectively appropriated by the educational right for very different
purposes. The broadly liberal terms employed by many mainstream English
teachers seeking to acknowledge the complexity of their students' linguistic
and cultural experience and, through their work with literature, to promote
students' personal development, proved capable of a very much more auth-
oritarian inflection. The view of English teaching characterised by Barnes *et
al.* (1984) as *cherishing private souls* had few defences against the aggressive
culture of privatisation developed in the 1980s.

The controversy over the extent to which the National Curriculum should
prescribe what is read by children has opened up very explicitly the question
as to whether or not there is a shared culture, or even the memory of one.
Moreover, the illusion that this matter is simply to do with classrooms is
dispelled by the regularity with which official rhetoric in recent years has
linked issues of language in education very explicitly to wider social and
economic concerns. If, as has been argued, the main task facing our contemporary politicians is *the management of decline*, then literature has a very
specific ideological function in that process of social reassurance.

What counts as literature, then, remains a highly contentious matter in the
politics of education. It remains an even more important pedagogic problem.
Whatever shape the English Order finally takes, teachers will require classroom approaches which help them to acknowledge the ideological status of
English. None of the versions of English mentioned in the Working Group
Report enable this, primarily because the highly particularised sense of the
word *literature* gets in the way. We desperately need to recover something

of its eighteenth-century usage, in which the connections with literacy and letters were more evident and what was referred to was the whole body of books and writing rather than the highly particularised range of work now denoted. We need in fact to start with texts, rather than with literature. Which brings us back to critical literacy.

English in the version proposed here takes a more investigative and analytical approach to the whole question of literature. It assumes the existence of literatures and canons and questions what it is about particular texts that has led particular groups to privilege them in this way. The point is not to contest one particular canon and seek to replace it with another: that way lies endless sterile contention. Nor does it seek to impose adherence to any one selection. Students must be free to make their own cultural and literary affiliations; our responsibility is to help them to a greater under-standing of the implications of their own and others' choices. They need opportunities to see texts in their full social contexts and histories, to understand the assumptions underlying both the texts and the valuations put upon them by particular groups.

So what counts as literature? There can be no fixed answer. But the questions of whether, why, how and to whom any text counts as literature are what much of the English curriculum has to be about.

WHAT ARE THE EDUCATIONAL BENEFITS CLAIMED FOR LITERATURE?

No government yet, within a mass public education system, has argued for pleasure as the educational benefit to be derived from literature. The justifi-cations for the place of literature in education have always tended to be more solemn, and increasingly so as we proceed up the age range. Politically, no doubt, this is realistic but it is also regrettable. Pleasure – whether from literature or any of the arts – is a benefit and one we could usefully be more confident about. Both history and experience demonstrate what is generally overlooked by the zealots of prescription: that without pleasure few of the other supposed benefits accrue.

In thinking about the benefits to be derived from the reading or study of literature, we need to clarify whose benefits we are discussing, the students' or those who are responsible for the system as a whole. One of the main criticisms to be levelled at the cultural heritage model of English, whether in its Newbolt or 1990s version, is that by and large the benefits in mind were largely assumed to accrue to the dominant social order. The induction of the masses into the literary heritage would serve to heal social discord and increase understanding as to why things were as they were and had to remain so. Literature would enable individuals to locate themselves in history and identify with it. It is easy now to mock such conscious attempts at manipu-lation, and right to reject it. But it is important to recognise that it is the attempted manipulation or imposition of a tradition that is objectionable, not the fact of making one. For one undeniable benefit of literature is just that process of locating oneself in history, putting together a selection of texts for which particularly resonant meanings have been made by individuals and groups. Opening up for discussion and analysis our students' experience of that process in their encounters with significant texts is an important part of critical literacy. This entails taking our students' literary affiliations as seriously as our own.

The educational benefits claimed for literature in the personal growth version of English are very different. They were summarised some time ago by Yorke (1979), on the basis of a survey of English teachers, as follows:

> Literature helps the pupil to develop personally and socially. It helps him [sic] to be tolerant of others' views and ways and offers insights into their personalities and motives, needs, problems and behaviours and enables them to understand what is involved in social and group relationships and in situations of conflict and choice. It helps him to seek moral standards, to love nature and to understand his physical environment. Literature also offers the chance to face safely the ideas of war, death, loss and the problems of adult life. The pupils might also gain a wider perspective on the world and an understanding of the state of affairs in other countries and at different periods.

Despite sceptical voices that the scream in the novel may prove more real for the reader than the cry in the room next door (Steiner 1978), this view commands widespread adherence, partly no doubt because that it is what we wish to believe, and partly because it may well be true so far as our own or some of our students' experiences are concerned. But there are major theoretical problems with these claims for the transformative power of literature, not least that they are unverifiable. It is also 'difficult to account for the failure of some readers to derive these benefits without recourse to damagingly negative explanations in which deficiencies, social, linguistic or personal, are attributed to either teachers or to students' (West 1987).

The approach to texts which I have designated *critical literacy* offers other modes of relating to texts which are less intimidating to students, because less prescriptive in the responses to them which are allowed or expected. In essence such an approach would look to the range of possible meanings that could be made from a text, who had made them, what was at stake in their differences, how they had changed over time and why.

WHAT IS LITERATURE CENTRAL TO?

Years ago, Thompson claimed that literature was central to English teaching when he asserted that literature was *the only thing worth teaching English for*. The politically radical edge of that view – the purpose of English teaching being *to unfit students for the workplace* – dissolved into damagingly elitist and negative approaches that were hostile to the cultural experiences of the majority of students (Mulhern 1979). This is likely to be the inevitable consequence of any approach taking such a narrow view of what constitutes literature.

If literature is to be central in an English teaching that is appropriate for a multilingual and multiethnic society, then we have to start with the processes of language and with all aspects of the making of meaning. In arguing for a view of English as critical literacy, I take the business of English

> to be the production, reproduction of and critical interpretation of texts, both verbal and visual, spoken and written. It requires activities which enable students to make meaning; develop their understanding of the process whereby meanings are made, and of the processes whereby meanings conflict and change.
>
> (West and Dickey 1990)

This view is most similar to the cultural analysis model mentioned, but not developed or discussed in any detail, in the English Working Group Report. There are, however, significant differences. The cultural analysis view

> emphasises the role of English in helping children towards a critical understanding of the world and cultural environment in which they live. Children should know about the processes by which meanings are conveyed, and about the ways in which print and other media carry values.
>
> (DES 1989)

There is much here with which to agree, but

> it is inadequate in at least two respects. Meanings are made and contested as well as simply conveyed and in a democratic society students are entitled to participate in as well as understand those processes. What is missing here and elsewhere in the report is an adequately detailed or explicit social dimension.
>
> (West and Dickey 1990)

This highlights a major problem with the current legislation for English: a political imperative which allows language to be seen as a social phenomenon, but which precludes any recourse to explicit social theory. Official silence on these matters is understandable, but that should not deter us from making good the gap as best we can. We need to tease out the implications of Tomkins' insight that

> contemporary critical theory has come to occupy a position very similar to that of the Greek rhetoricians for whom the mastery of language meant mastery of the state . . . . The similarity lies in the common perception of language as a form of power.
>
> (Tomkins 1980)

REFERENCES

Ahmad, A. (1993) *In Theory: Classes, Nations, Literatures*. Verso.

Barnes, D., Barnes, D. and Clarke, S. (1984) *Versions of English*. Heinemann.

Bolton, E. (1992) Vision of Chaos. *Times Educational Supplement*, 31 August.

Cox, B. (1992) Politicians and Professionals. In *Made Tongue Tied by Authority: New Orders for English*? NATE, Sheffield.

DES (1989) *Report of the English Working Group* (The Cox Report). HMSO.

Freire, P. and Macedo, D. (1987) *Literacy: Reading the Word and the World*. Routledge.

Mulhern, F. (1979) *The Moment of Scrutiny*. Verso.

NATE (1989) *Learning to be Literate in a Democratic Society*. NATE, Sheffield.

Steiner, G. (1978) *On Difficulty*. Penguin.

Tomkins, J. (1980) *Reader-response Criticism: from Formalism to Poststructuralism*. Johns Hopkins University Press.

West, A. (1987) The Limits of a Discourse. *English Magazine*, No. 18.

West, A. and Dickey, A. (1990) *Redbridge High School English Department Handbook*. NATE, Sheffield.

Williams, R. (1965) *The Long Revolution*. Penguin.

Yorke, M. (1979) *English in Education*, Vol. 13, No. 1.

Chapter 15

Teaching black literature

Suzanne Scafe

In the process of contextualising Black texts, we must be aware – and ensure that our students are aware – that contexts need to be provided for all literary texts. In other words, we consciously need to acknowledge that we place all texts in the world, and that in our classification of literary production and our approaches to teaching we signal the historical, social and cultural context of its making. No teacher would approach Shakespeare without some reference to the historical context of his work and its means of production, yet we still speak of its timelessness and 'truths' as though the writing had been an idealised rather than a concrete activity.

Although Black literature represents a powerful challenge to those claims, we cannot assume that it will automatically reveal basic 'human truths'; opposition to its existence as 'literature' is continuous, changing and powerful. The task for teachers and educationalists is to ensure that Black writing is valued critically; that it is read as it defines itself, as a cultural and artistic whole reflecting and a reflection of the political and cultural struggles which are its context. The reading should not be used to confirm its status as 'other' but to 'change the perceptions' of the minority who are the gate-keepers of the canon and who have defined 'human' in terms of their own image.

(from Suzanne Scafe, *Teaching Black Literature*)

The practice of using literature by black writers in schools and colleges because teachers think that the students can more easily 'relate' to it, as it mirrors their experience, still persists. As a result, the literature is still, by and large, ghettoised; it is used in schools where a significant number of the students are black. And when these texts are read, the focus is too often on the content; they tend to be read as a sociological or political testament which can explain events in history, provide examples of poverty and deprivation, or explain racism and race relations here or in North America.

TEXT AND CONTEXT

One of the reasons that the context becomes more important than the text itself is that readers and teachers do not experience a tradition of black literature; therefore the content, the subject of that writing within a literary context, is new. More importantly, however, I think that we read the writing as overtly political, partly because it is often expressed as such, partly because the form of the writing, the language for example, suggests a history and a relationship to writing and literature which is political, and partly because when the subject is black people or black people's lives, it is interpreted as 'problematic'; the text is seen as a means of illuminating a social or political problem.

All texts have a political context but they are not necessarily read as problematic, however controversial or alienating the context or background to the writing may be. Literature is not traditionally read or used as social commentary; on the contrary, when reading texts by white European writers, students are usually asked to focus on the interior of the characters; the individual and emotional dimensions are emphasised. On the whole, however, black texts are read in entirely the opposite way. The issue of social relevance, that is whether a student can 'identify' with a text, becomes of prime importance and is used to include narrowly, or to exclude.

What I'd like to consider here is an approach to reading and teaching literature by black writers where the cultural, historical context of the writing informs rather than replaces the text.

LANGUAGE

I would like to suggest that an approach to reading and teaching black texts would be one which includes an examination of the linguistic features of the text and encourages students to look at the way in which the writer uses oral speech structures in the narrative, the dialogue, and in relation to both dialogue and narrative. I have chosen works by Caribbean women writers, Louise Bennett, Olive Senior, Lorna Goodison and Jean Breeze, all of which are examples of effective use of Jamaican Creole.

The reading of a poem written in Creole would in itself generate some discussion about its history and identity. I would point to the idea that language is a human creation, produced in historical, political and social contexts. Any discussion of the use of Creole would also illustrate the relative status of language and language variety. It was not, until quite recently, even after political independence in Jamaica in the early 1960s, considered an appropriate written form. Louise Bennett writes:

I have been set apart by other creative writers a long time ago because of the language I speak and work in . . . . From the beginning nobody recognised me as a writer.

(*Caribbean Quarterly*, 1968)

Increasingly, however, writers in the Caribbean use and have extended and developed Creole in their writing, using the oral quality of the language form and other aspects of oral culture, to shape their work.

Edward Brathwaite describes the significance of oral culture to the writing of poetry:

> The poetry, the culture itself, exists not in a dictionary but in the tradition of the spoken word. It is based as much on sound as it is on song. That is to say, the noise that it makes is part of the meaning, and if you ignore the noise (or what you think of as noise, shall I say) then you lose part of the meaning . . . . The oral tradition on the other hand demands not only the noise but the audience to complete the community: the noise and sounds that the maker makes are responded to by the audience and are returned to him.

The poems which follow provide examples of the participatory aspect of oral culture; they also echo the rhythm and musicality of oral speech. The language used is not a linguistically accurate reproduction of Creole; rather it is a creative impression of the language where some Creole structures are used; lexical items might be changed, though not always consistently. The significant feature of the writing is the poet's use of metaphor and idiom to create a sense of the language.

Louise Bennett's poetry provides excellent examples of literature which is about language. In themselves, of course, their very presence in the classroom is a statement about literary language, and one which challenges an accepted definition of the language used in literary texts. Her poems are about the social relationships which are reflected in language and about the historical circumstances that go into the making of language.

In *No Lickle Twang*, for example, she describes a mother's disappointment when her son returns from a visit to the United States, without a 'twang' – an American accent. In the poem, she shows the predominance of American culture over Caribbean cultural forms and it becomes clear that varieties of English or dialects of English do not have equal status and that their relative status is related to their position of power and dominance in the world. The inferior status of a poorer, black ex-colonial culture is keenly felt by the mother who sees any transformation of the boy's language as an example of his increased sophistication. It is also a poem about immigration and the desire to migrate in order to escape from a culture which is perceived of as one without true value, status or identity:

An yuh sister what work ongle
One week wid Merican
She talk so nice now dat we have
De jooce fi understan?

Boy, yuh couldn improve yuhself!
An yuh get so much pay?
Yuh spen six mont a foreign
Come back ugly same way?

It is because the language has such grave social, political historical ramifications that writers in the Caribbean and black writers in the United States and in Africa use the language to speak of the content. Another of her poems *Speechify*, in which she portrays a Master of Ceremonies at a wedding struggling for the correct register in which to conduct a wedding, is an example of this. He begins by searching for standard English, thereby signalling that he is addressing a formal occasion:

Let I takes in hand wine glasses
Let I full it to de tip
While Miss Clemmy share de cakeses
.Let I rise and let I sip

The errors that he makes in attempting to conjugate his verbs correctly add to the humour of the poem. As his speech progresses, however, he is reminded of a woman who is clearly putting pressure on a man to marry her and who might have taken heart from his speech, which celebrates May, the bride who has sustained 'Tirty years' of courtship before marrying Tom. In his indignation he forgets all attempts at grammatically correct standard English, forgets to impress with his use of words of three or more syllables, and bursts out with:

One warning wud: Young gals, no force
No man fi married yuh . . .

RHYTHM

Jean Breeze, a contemporary Jamaican poet, incorporates reggae and jazz rhythms into her writing and uses powerful but simple imagery to evoke the spoken language.

Ordinary Morning:
. . .
wasn't a hangover headache
mawning
or a worry rising mawning

. . .

no
it wasn't de day dat did start out bad
wasn't even pre m t
or post m t
was just anadda ordinary get up
get di children ready fi school
mawning
anadda what to cook fah dinna dis evening
mawning
anadda wish me never did breed but Lawd
mi love dem mawning
jus anadda wanda if ah should a
tek up back wid dis man it would a
ease de situation mawning

The rhythm emphasised by the use of Creole reflects the daily, humdrum 'ordinariness' of this woman's life. The language used in the poem also describes the subject – an ordinary working-class woman whose concerns are centred around her home, the children, her relationships. Her mornings are marked by these routine considerations. The poignancy is in the simplicity of the language and the imagery, in the creation of a giving and forgiving 'loving' woman.

'LIKE I READ ONCE ...'

I want to include an example of Lorna Goodison's work to illustrate the variety of ways in which Creole is represented in literature. The title of one of her collections *Heartease* (a modification of Heartsease) reflects the simple structural changes which she makes to suggest an emphasis on oral language forms. Often in her work Creole is used to signal a conversational tone, such as in *Some Nights I Dont Sleep*. The ideas in the poem are linked conversationally with such phrases as:

Like I read once
in a woman's magazine . . .

. . .

And maybe she did not know

Towards the end of the poem, the echoes of Creole in her writing draw the reader and writer into an intimate relationship; the tone is protective, and very woman-like; there is a strong nurturing quality to the spirituality of the last lines:

So to wake now don't really matter
for some nights is not for sleep

is to use collective light
as laser beams
to clear the home stretch
to Heartease

A stark contrast is created between these lines and earlier phrases which echo the news or a kind of written history, and are expressed in standard English:

. . . about bodies floating
in the water system
and shocking stadiums
running with blood
and live men
cemented into silence . . .

The participatory quality of the writing is created, as we have seen in the examples above, by the conversational tone or by having the subject address an audience. In prose, oral storytelling structures are used, particularly in stories written by women. The writers re-create an oral storytelling style, in a conscious attempt to link the literature to black oral narrative traditions. The use of this form also provides a context for the use of Creole, by linking the language of the narrative to the language of the speaker.

THE VILLAGE CHRONICLER

Olive Senior's *Real Old Time 'Ting* opens with the narrator, who is, as in other stories in this collection, presented as the village chronicler, criticising Pauline, a 'returnee' from England who has come back to Jamaica to live after spending many years in England. The story is, among other things, about 'naming'; a constant source of irritation for the narrator is Pauline's renaming of their culture, using imported English phrases. At the same time, however, she wants to collect as ornaments or antiques the things that they still use in the village, and preserve their original names, while distancing herself both from the objects and their names. We see her actions as those of the anthropologist who transforms, for the cultural voyeur, real lives into curiosities.

> Is the one name Patricia did start up about how Papa Sterling need a new house or it look bad how their father living in this old board house it dont even have sanitary convenience. Sanitary convenience! So it dont name bath house any more? Then if she so hot on sanitary convenience why she down here a buy up all the old water goblet and china basin she can find a talk say is real country things and how she just finding her roots.

A discussion of language and of structure therefore necessitates an examination of the historical context that shapes the writing. However, in addressing this context we should be looking at ways of furthering students' understanding of the texts. In looking at language, for example, we would need to consider its effectiveness in relation to characterisation, narrative, dialogue, and the images used. Similarly, when discussing structure students should be led to consider whether or not the narrative is made more effective by the use of oral structures.

PROCESS AND PRACTICE

I would like to suggest that in practice, teachers do contextualise all texts. Additional material is used to help students imagine visually, or 'relate' to Jane Austen, to James Joyce, and so on. Stories with either unfamiliar or significant settings are contextualised. It is important that this process should continue, and that readers are pointed to the idea that literature is an actual rather than an idealised activity. Experienced readers create a context from the text but even then might look at the sleeve notes or read reviews, in order to place the writing historically, geographically, socially. The process or the reason for contextualising is the same as for all literature: it informs the text.

Whether or not a student can 'relate' to a text – has experienced the experiences described there – should not be the criterion for the inclusion of literature by black writers. While the social and political content might resonate forcefully, and this should be addressed, the text is a product of the writer's imagination. The writing is informed by its cultural, social and economic context, but is mediated by the imagination and particular experiences of writers and readers.

Chapter 16

Teaching Shakespeare in schools

Rex Gibson

In this chapter, I shall address the two questions most frequently asked by teachers and students:

1 Why teach Shakespeare?
2 How should Shakespeare be taught?

To answer those vital questions I shall draw on the evidence collected by the Shakespeare and Schools Project (Gibson 1986–93): a research and development project concerned to improve the quality of school students' experience of Shakespeare. All that follows is based on the views and practice of successful classroom teachers, and their students.

WHY TEACH SHAKESPEARE?

I must begin with a necessary and yet trivial reason: it is a statutory requirement. The National Curriculum in English requires that all students in Key Stages 3 and 4 have 'some experience of the works of Shakespeare'. That requirement is in the process of being given more precise specification by virtue of the compulsory tests (SATs) pupils will undergo at 14 and 16. At the time of writing, for example, the majority of 14-year-olds (Year 9) will be tested on one of three Shakespeare plays: *Romeo and Juliet, A Midsummer Night's Dream*, or *Julius Caesar*. So Shakespeare is taught in the secondary schools of England and Wales because 'some experience' of his works is compulsory. Shakespeare, like everything to do with the English curriculum, has become in the 1990s an intensely political issue (Cox 1992). But there are other, essentially educational reasons.

Language

Shakespeare's language is both a model and a resource for students: powerfully energetic, vivid, sinewy, active, physical, robust, sensuous, volatile, immediate and reflective.

Relevance

Shakespeare's characters, stories and themes offer virtually endless opportunities for interpretation and reformulation. They treat of human relationships and passions which are immediately recognisable and personal: wives, fathers, sons, daughters . . . jealousy, love, hate, sexuality, loyalty, friendship, envy . . . . They also exemplify more distant levels of social relationships: power, authority, politics, conquest, colonialism, war, wealth. Distinctively, and with unparalleled skill, they show the interconnections between these personal and public levels.

Cultural heritage

Shakespeare has played a highly significant part in British social and cultural history. Every pupil therefore is entitled to knowledge and understanding of the many ways in which Shakespeare has affected (and still does influence) so many aspects of our society. He is used to define meaning in British society (Hawkes 1992). Students should be enabled to understand how Shakespeare has become a cultural icon of great power – and to grasp how that power operates.

Shakespeare offers emancipatory possibilities

Education must open up emancipatory possibilities. It must show there are worlds elsewhere; other ways of living, other sets of values and belief; other ways of defining oneself. Education is concerned that individuals should not be imprisoned in a single point of view. Shakespeare's plays have this quality supremely. They offer an inexhaustible resource of alternatives of what it is to be human, and of what societies are or might be.

Feeding students' imaginations

Shakespeare's plays evoke open, multilayered responses. They therefore give opportunities for students of all ages and abilities to encounter them imaginatively in a wide variety of ways. Rich in imagery, thought and feeling, they contain 'an invitation to infer' on every page. Such an invitation is enormously productive of pupils' imaginative responses as they speculate, reason, argue and reach their own conclusions, on meanings, motivations, absences and silences in each play.

Shakespeare resources students' writing

Because every play has its own unique language characteristics, Shakespeare provides pupils with rich models for study, imitation and expressive, personal re-creation. Shakespeare himself worked within the dialectic of discipline and freedom, convention and originality, formality and flexibility. The discipline of English is based on a similar dialectic. Students can learn from Shakespeare how form resources freedom.

Shakespeare requires demystification

There is a pressing need to remove the aura of bardolatry, overromantic mystification, sentimental and uncritical adulation that distances Shakespeare from many students. Shakespeare should be made accessible to all, not reserved for a minority of students. Many adults (and students) reject Shakespeare even though they have never encountered him at school. Enjoyable, successful encounters can demystify the elitist, obscure image that negatively colours students' attitudes.

To empower pupils

Cultural materialists (Sinfield 1992) argue that Shakespeare has been used, culturally and educationally, as a major instrument of social control. Here, the alleged reason for teaching his works is to maintain the status quo, to inhibit social change. In contrast, cultural materialists register 'a commitment to the transformation of a social order that exploits people on grounds of race, gender and class' (Dollimore and Sinfield 1985: vii). Thus, argue the cultural materialists, students are taught that Shakespeare displays the unchangingness and unchangeability of human nature and human society. From this standpoint, injustice is simply a fact of life; fate and nature conspire to make change or amelioration impossible. Such a view is profoundly conservative and repressive. Students who accept this viewpoint become, unwittingly, agents of a dominant elite as they are incorporated into the values (if not the material circumstances) of that elite. To counter such a passive, ahistorical, asocial view, Shakespeare should be taught to enable pupils to challenge the assumption that social injustice is inevitable. One example is to teach that a corrupt society, rather than the supernatural power of the witches, produces Macbeth's ambition and tyranny.

All the above suggest a further powerful reason for teaching Shakespeare. School students should be given the opportunity to make the acquaintance of Shakespeare so that they can make up their own minds as to his value and relevance.

HOW SHOULD SHAKESPEARE BE TAUGHT?

There is no doubt that, through appropriate pedagogy, students' attitudes to Shakespeare can be improved, enjoyment and understanding increased, and more imaginative, more genuinely personal responses evoked. There is strong evidence of increased motivation, of students seeing relevance, coherence and meaning, when they encounter Shakespeare through suitable methods. The remainder of this chapter describes the characteristics of such methods.

Students and teachers express strong preferences for varied experience. All evidence points to the need for variety and balance of method. There is no 'one way' into Shakespeare at any level; no single method that works for all. There is major agreement on the need for theatre visits, video and film (Gibson 1992c), and a great deal of discussion. Further, the Shakespeare teacher of the 1990s is aware that historical, political, social and cultural factors have shaped 'Shakespeare'. *Hamlet* is not simply confined to the literary or aesthetic dimensions of experience (Holderness 1988).

But the key, necessary ingredients of successful teaching and learning are *active methods* which open up the dramatic and imaginative possibilities of Shakespeare's plays. The great majority of students enjoy active methods. And active approaches are within the compass of all teachers, not just those with dramatic training or skill. These approaches, 'research lessons', treat Shakespeare less as a 'text' or 'book' than as a 'script', for dramatic exploration. They empower imaginative enactment in modes which blend respect and irreverence. The script is something to be 'made', not simply 'taken'. It yields to, invites and demands inference and interpretation. And it is something that requires readers and performers to make it live.

Thinking of Shakespeare as a script invites any number of possible starting points, a word or a line, a stage direction, even an 'absence'. A well-tried but invariably successful example of an 'absent scene' is when students enact the incident that set the Montagues and Capulets at each others' throats. Ambiguity and openness are accepted as necessary and desirable characteristics. The notion of 'the right answer' is put in hazard (most right answers in Shakespeare are trivial anyway).

Students readily accept that Shakespeare's plays are *plays*: to be acted and seen. They welcome the opportunity to try out their own versions of Shakespeare and are responsive to a wide variety of practical possibilities. Active methods are *learner centred*, acknowledging the active part every reader plays in making meaning. They involve all aspects of students' capacities, not solely intellectual abilities. Based on the premise that 'Shakespeare doesn't stop at the Adam's apple', they assume that students' experience of Shakespeare should not be purely cerebral. Thus, they include physical and emotional involvement. Further, they are social methods: pupils working together with others, sharing ideas and possibilities in collaborative explorations of Shakespeare's language, characters, stories.

'School Shakespeare' is concerned to evoke 'informed personal response', but not under the same conditions as public examinations making the same claim. Thus, examination Shakespeare is typically solitary, silent, individual, competitive, literary. In contrast, active Shakespeare is co-operative, social, a matter for negotiation in groups of various sizes engaged in self-chosen tasks, concerned as much with process as any product.

School Shakespeare is not about producing literary critics. Only a tiny minority of school students go on to read Shakespeare in higher education. Rather, the aim should be to enable students to inhabit the imaginative world of the play. This gives priority to expression, spontaneity, and intuition, recognising that such qualities make important contributions to understanding and insight.

Thus, active methods are concerned to celebrate the imagination, and to avoid becoming trapped in the discourse of literary criticism. They encourage negotiation, co-operation, cross-group and cross-school sharing: there have been many fruitful examples of sixth formers or Year 11 students performing for or working with Year 7 students.

When students have responsibility for a character – or a line or phrase or image – the characteristic response is close, detailed, imaginative exploration of Shakespeare's language. The difficulties of the language can be successfully tackled or overcome when students enact Ariel's story, or Prospero's deposition, or Caliban's subjugation. By acting out the many elements Shakespeare inserts into every such account, the language springs vividly to life.

A huge variety of activities fall under the heading of active approaches. Here there is only room to mention a few. All seek to give imaginative experience a local habitation: the familiar (but infinitely variable) acting out of scenes; tableaux; all varieties of choral speaking; improvisations; Companies; parodies; trials; missing scenes; short versions; confessions; hot seating; intercutting; dreams; sequencing; insults; greetings, partings, commands, and oaths; games of all types; directing; designing; mimes; casting; role playing; inquests; interior monologues; alter egos; voices off; blocking; director's notes; brainstorming; echoes and whispers.

If such a catalogue (only a fraction of what is possible) sounds daunting, you will find that the various editions of Cambridge School Shakespeare (Gibson 1992a) contain literally hundreds of practical examples, all closely tied to Shakespeare's language. The series arose from a special difficulty for students: the nature of many editions of Shakespeare used in school. Nearly all have been watered-down versions of prestigious scholarly editions (Arden, New Cambridge, Oxford).

The impression such conventional editions convey to students and to teachers is that 'Notes' are more important than the script. Students and teachers feel themselves trapped in the discourse of literary criticism. Yet curiously, for all the critical interpretation offered, the script appears to pupils as fixed, objective, determinate. Indeed, it is turned into the all-powerful, authoritative 'text'. Implicitly and explicitly, most editions of

Shakespeare used in schools imply that the pupils' role is simply to soak up and regurgitate the meanings of others.

Most editions used in schools explicitly and implicitly reinforce the pupils' view of Shakespeare as a 'translation' enterprise, rather than as an imaginative, re-creative, intelligence-expanding endeavour. It was to remedy such limiting experience that the Cambridge School Shakespeare series grew out of the Shakespeare and Schools Project. Each edition embodies, in very practical form, the principles discussed above.

How to begin school Shakespeare? There is much variation in teachers' views about how to start students off on a Shakespeare play. Some teachers favour the 'initial read through' with students or teachers reading the whole play over four to six lessons, virtually without pause, before working in detail on particular scenes. Others favour working steadily through the play a scene at a time, letting the plot unfold slowly, aiming to arrive at the last scene at the end of the allotted time. Others favour the teacher telling the story at the start, sketching the plot and characters. Some adopt this method but leave the conclusion hanging in the air for pupils to discover later (most typically the statue in *Winter's Tale*).

Use of video is another practice that produces strong differences of opinion among teachers. Some favour a video at the start of a Shakespeare course. Others strongly condemn the practice. Others prefer to plunge the pupils into one or two scenes, encouraging pupils to speculate about the story and characters, to build up their own picture of what events and dilemmas engage these characters. There is, quite simply, great variation. There is evidence of all types of approach working successfully. When teachers believe strongly in a particular approach, most pupils accept its validity.

My own view is first to recall that there is no *one way* to teach Shakespeare in schools. But the students' desire to know the story must be satisfied. This can be done in teacher-prepared brief versions (the play in ten lines which students enact). With *Romeo and Juliet* an excellent starting point is for students to act out each of the Chorus' opening fourteen lines, with small groups taking responsibility for one or more lines each. Or it can be done by initial detailed, imaginative, dramatic work on one or two key scenes which raise vital questions of the play: the initial brawl; Capulet's raging at Juliet; the lovers' first meeting. Here, students will speculate and hypothesise. This should be encouraged as it develops motivation to find out 'what really happens'.

Much depends on the age of the pupils and the time available. Younger pupils may be best served by a sketch of the story with encouragement to participate in speculation – and detailed work on a number of key scenes. Older pupils (most GCSE, all A Level) will probably have time to read, in a variety of ways, the whole play. Much will depend on the teacher's 'feel for the class' but a combination of teacher reading, active group work, pupil reading in class, in small groups, privately, is appropriate.

Whatever you include, go full-bloodedly for the 'big moments' of Shakespeare (which may be very quiet ones). Seek to create moments of theatre that put some of the most powerful words of the play into the mouths of the pupils and which spur them to a range of imaginative encounters: drama, mime, painting, drawing, craft, writing, and so on.

It is extremely valuable for pupils to keep a diary or journal in which they build up their growing knowledge of the play. And the first entry is probably – what happens next? But it is vital to develop as many types of writing as possible. If 'lit crit' essays are done, don't have them written as instant one-offs. It's best if they are the product of other writing recorded in the journals: character diaries, reviews, genre changes, etc. Provisional work, drafts and redrafts, reworking should be valued and encouraged. Traditional writing stresses narrative, exposition, critical analysis and appreciation. Encourage also re-creative writing, imaginative transposition and reconstructions.

One necessary practice for written work is to set 'you' tasks, not simply pseudo-objective 'we', 'the audience', etc., type questions (which promote the myth of the single right answer). Students should define the audience for their writing (and for other 'performances' that arise from active methods). Also, don't think everything has to go on A4. Use a variety of paper sizes. Large sheets and felt tips are excellent for group work.

'Shakespeare' is remarkably resilient. It has a long history of surviving all assaults, adaptations, interpretations, and can obviously take care of itself. So don't worry about fracturing the Shakespeare script. Don't be afraid to intercut or rearrange, to *play* with Shakespeare, to adopt an irreverent attitude, cutting or transposing the language. This implies setting tasks which enable students to improvise and adapt freely. Don't be afraid to demystify Shakespeare. He'll survive because of his intrinsic strengths.

Three final recapitulatory paragraphs. First, remember that teachers' attitudes are all important. They are the key to successful school Shakespeare. If *you* don't enjoy Shakespeare, neither will your pupils. That doesn't mean you have to be a Shakespeare 'expert'. But as your career develops and your own experience of Shakespeare grows, remember that, however many times you've seen *Macbeth*'s witches, or the mechanicals' *Pyramus and Thisbe*, remember it's the first time for *these* students. Don't let your familiarity with Shakespeare dull the freshness with which students can approach the plays.

Second, it's crucial to stand up for the principle that Shakespeare is for all. Shakespeare is for *everyone* – not an elite minority. Never underestimate pupils. All pupils can have access to Shakespeare in some valid form. Don't give up hope for a pupil. Acquiring an intellectual grasp of Shakespeare is often a slow, recursive process. For most pupils the teacher must be prepared for flaws, halts, omissions, and misunderstandings of what seem to be the simplest matters. But appropriate methods can and do achieve remarkable results with students of all abilities.

Finally, a reminder of the characteristics of active approaches:

- *Learner-centred*: acknowledging that reader actively makes meaning.
- *Social*, collaborative, participatory. Encouraging sharing, negotiation, co-operation.
- *Physically active* to promote imaginative, intellectual and emotional involvement.
- *According choice and responsibility* to pupils.
- *Encouraging a wide range of response*: dramatic, theatrical, written, discussion, artistic, and so on.
- *Involving a wide range of resources*: video, film, programmes, photographs, posters, reviews . . . and some traditional criticism.
- *Celebrating imagination and understanding* – avoiding becoming trapped solely in the discourse of literary criticism. The aim is to enable students to inhabit the imaginative world of the play.
- *Exploratory*, open, unpredictable, non-judgemental, celebrating dialectic of pupil–teacher–text context.
- *Setting appropriate tasks*: task setting is crucial in school Shakespeare.
- *Using varied size groups.*
- *Remember, there's no one way to teach Shakespeare.*
- *Forget 'Shakespeare', think of 'Shakespeares'.* There isn't *one* interpretation, *one* definitive production, *one* way into the plays, *one* method.
- Treat each play as a SCRIPT to be brought to imaginative life through action.
- Above all, remember Shakespeare is to be enjoyed!

BIBLIOGRAPHY

Aers, Lesley and Wheale, Nigel (1991) *Shakespeare in the Changing Curriculum*, Routledge.

Cox, Brian (1992) *The Great Betrayal*, Cohen Chapman.

Dollimore, Jonathan and Sinfield, Alan (eds) (1985) *Political Shakespeare*, Manchester University Press.

Gibson, Rex (1990) *Secondary School Shakespeare*, University of Cambridge, Institute of Education.

Gibson, Rex (ed.) (1992a) *Cambridge School Shakespeare series*, Cambridge University Press.

Gibson, Rex (ed.) (1992b) *Romeo and Juliet*, Cambridge University Press.

Gibson, Rex (ed.) (1992c) 'Teaching Shakespeare using film and video' in *As You Like It*, British Universities Film and Video Council.

Gibson, Rex (ed.) (1986–93) *Shakespeare and Schools Magazine*, 1–20, Jaggard and Blount.

Hawkes, Terry (1992) *Meaning by Shakespeare*, Routledge.

Holderness, Graham (1988) *The Shakespeare Myth*, Manchester University Press.

Leach, Susan (1991) *Shakespeare in the Classroom*, Open University Press.

Reynolds, Peter (1990) *Practical Approaches to Teaching Shakespeare*, Oxford University Press.

Sinfield, Alan (1992) *Faultlines: Cultural Materialism and the Politics of Dissident Reading*, Oxford University Press.

Chapter 17

Balancing the books
Modes of assessment in A level English literature

Stella Canwell and Jane Ogborn

The phrase 'fitness for purpose', once as essential a slogan in relation to assessment as 'know, understand and can do' was to the definition of the purpose of GCSE, seems to have dropped out of use recently. Yet it is crucial to the design of effective assessment systems. From the very beginning, Peter Buckroyd, the first Chief Examiner and Moderator for AEB 660, made it very clear that the content and the mode of assessment of each of its papers should be closely related. Thus *Paper 1: Comprehension & Practical Criticism* gives candidates 2½ hours to answer two questions on unseen material, poetry and prose – adequate time to tackle unfamiliar texts, always provided students have the necessary skills and reading experience, developed through their coursework, and thus know how to set about the task. *Paper 2: Prescribed Texts* is an 'open book' examination, giving 3 hours 15 minutes for four questions. In the words of the syllabus:

> Candidates will have access to their set texts in the examination, enabling them to provide a critical response in depth with close reference to the texts. The texts may contain the student's own notes in any blank space or page, but the use of other materials such as critical works, dictionaries and critical notes is not allowed.

Papers 1 and 2 are externally assessed. *Paper 3: Coursework* is assessed by the teacher and externally moderated. In order to observe the weighting of a maximum of 20 per cent coursework assessment the revised syllabus for AEB 660 will have to extend Paper 1 and reduce the coursework requirements. However, even if the quantity has to be limited, the intention is to preserve freedom in the choice of coursework texts and maximum flexibility in the ways the folder can be organised. By preserving these features of A level literature coursework, as well as the opportunities it offers for student autonomy, it can continue to provide the arena in which reading and writing skills can be developed and where all the assessment objectives of the examination may be tested. These look for:

- the student's first-hand knowledge and understanding of a range of texts, and awareness of the contexts in which they were written;
- appreciation of a writer's craft and style;
- the ability to express a well-informed personal response.

Apart from 'sustained wider reading', which is tested in the coursework through the Extended Essay, all the assessment objectives are also tested by the examination papers. It seems sensible, therefore, that, rather than seeing certain assessment objectives as being tied *either* to the exam, *or* to the coursework, teachers should recognise the value of developing integrated courses where the process and experience of the coursework teaches and fine-tunes those skills which will be assessed in the examination – skills such as summarising, contextualising, selecting and ordering their material; constructing, illustrating, developing and sustaining a line of argument; speculating and hypothesising on the basis of evidence, for example. Such an approach might start from 'content', from the texts chosen for study, but, rather than selecting individual texts according to personal preference or expertise, teachers might try planning their course so that coherent connections are forged between coursework and examination texts. It will be important to pay explicit attention to the skills candidates need in order to succeed in the examinations and to use the coursework as the vehicle through which candidates can be enabled to practise and refine these. For example, teachers often resist the idea of the notional word limit for the coursework essays, arguing that the coursework is the place where candidates can take their own approach to a piece of work and that a word limit constricts this. While there may be some truth in this, the main feature which seems to characterise work gaining grades of D and below is an inability to address a topic clearly and directly and move firmly into the essay's argument. If candidates cannot sharpen their introduction to a coursework essay through redrafting, but need to write themselves in over a side of A4, what hope have they got of producing an essay under examination conditions which makes a range of relevant points in 45 minutes?

As well as clarifying how opportunities can be provided through the coursework to develop the skills needed in the examinations, it is important to be more analytical about exactly what it is that distinguishes coursework from end-of-course examination work. Both are intended to present evidence that candidates have first-hand knowledge of the texts which have been read, and to give opportunities for them to demonstrate their understanding and express their views. However, in addition, coursework offers the opportunity for students to set their own tasks and goals, in negotiation with the teacher, and so develop independence as learners. The terminal examination inevitably puts the candidate in the position of responding to someone else's task, and to approaching a text through someone else's question about it, no matter how inviting. Second, because coursework is not subject to rigid time constraints, it allows students to present a planned and considered response to a task. Opportunities need to be provided for making explicit to the student the ways in which what she or he has learned from redrafting an essay can be transferred to the examination process. Finally, and with a view to possible progression into higher education, coursework offers opportunities for original research and wider reading, and provides evidence of the ability to sustain work over a period of time, and at length. If teachers agree that these are valuable aspects of coursework, they need to think about how they can plan a course which makes the maximum use of whatever weighting is permitted to them for this kind of work, and will at the same time help students to develop and practise the skills required for success in the examinations – tackling unfamiliar texts, contextualising an answer economically, constructing and illustrating an argument, working within a time constraint, and so on.

The assessment systems in place in 1993 for AEB 660 – a set of descriptors for the use of teachers and moderators and similar guidance for assistant examiners – are based on the demonstration of skills. The marking grid (Table 17.1) for Papers 1 and 2 is based on the skills that examiners look for within the three categories:

- textual grasp and appreciation;
- conveying the text and answering relevantly;
- quality of expression.

The guidance for coursework assessment, although structured differently, is very similar to the criteria on the marking grid. Compare the description of work of E quality, from the Coursework guidance, with the features of work worth 11 or 12 within the examination grid:

> *The candidate has fulfilled the minimum demands of writing on chosen material, but treatment may be mainly narrative, pedestrian and not well presented. This work may show some understanding and insight, despite possible defects in organisation, argument and expression. Textual reference may be incomplete, and/or irrelevant to an argument, and/or given without explanation, but provides enough evidence of reading and reflection.*

(Coursework)

and:

> *Response to surface features of text . . . basic and generalised but usually accurate . . . some awareness of effect of text on self . . . paraphrase with some embedded ideas.*

(Examination)

Table 17.1 English literature marking grid

Level	Marks	Textual grasp and appreciation	Conveying the text (and answering relevantly)	Quality of expression
Level 1	1–5	Narrative approach with frequent misreadings.	Mere assertion of points of view. Often irrelevant answer.	Frequent weaknesses of expression. Excessive, aimless quotation. Misunderstood technical terms.
	6–11	Merely accurate storytelling, skimpy reading.	Difficulty in engaging with question. Assertive comments largely undeveloped and unsupported.	Simple expression. Flawed, but conveying basic ideas. Paraphrase plus lengthy quotation. Unassimilated notes.
Level 2	12–16	Response to surface features of text. Basic and generalised but usually accurate response.	Some awareness of effect of text on selves. An attempt to use specific details to support points made.	Expression generally able to convey ideas. Greater variety of vocabulary and sentence structure. Paraphrase with some embedded ideas. Quotation often overlong. Technical terms or unassimilated notes may be intrusive.
	17–21	Some awareness of implicit meaning. Straightforward approach. Response to obvious contrasts and comparisons.	Can explain moods and feelings in text. Becoming aware of effect on writer of scene or events. At least implicit relevance to question.	Adequate expression matching understanding. More sophisticated vocabulary, structure of response. Quotation probably overlong but sometimes analysed. Fair grasp of technical terms and some ability to use notes.
Level 3	22–31	Beginnings of appreciation of language and style. Secure knowledge and understanding of text. Awareness of subtlety. Closer reading becomes obvious.	Can see alternative interpretations and/or pursue strong personal response. Analysing. Exploring. Clearly aware of effect on writer of scene or event. Coherent, shaped and relevant response.	Expression clear and controlled. Paraphrase rare. Well structured with links between sentences and paragraphs. Wide vocabulary. Neat and purposeful use of short quotation as part of structured argument. Technical terms and assimilated notes become integral part of informed personal response.
Level 4	32–40	*Answers in this category will have some of the following characteristics in addition to all of those in Level 3* Insight. Conceptualised response. Confident exploration of ideas, language, style. Autonomy as reader.	Overview. Mastery of detail of text. Originality.	Mastery of structure. Confidence in expression. Rarely at a loss for the right word. Skilful use of quotation and close analysis of it. Technical terms and secondary sources enhance response to text.

Additionally, the description of work of A standard has its parallel on the grid between the marks of 32 and 40:

Coherent, fluent organisation of material and argument; accurate textual awareness and sharp insights revealed. Exploratory and thorough work, not pedantic or unnecessarily lengthy. Evidence of free use of text to achieve affective connections of ideas and themes; an individual 'voice', confident, sensitive and thoughtful.

(Coursework)

and:

Insight . . . conceptualised response. Confident exploration of ideas, language and style. Autonomy as reader. Skilful use of quotation and close analysis of it.

(Examination)

The relationship between the systems of assessment for candidates' coursework and their examination scripts points to the necessity for teachers to adopt an approach to course planning and teaching which sees the coursework and the written papers as parts of a whole. Colleagues who act as assistant examiners – and AEB 660 has always aimed to recruit examiners from its teachers – will have recognised the similarities between the guidance given to them as assessors of their own students' coursework and examiners of other students' scripts. The syllabus revision undertaken at the AEB in 1993 as a result of the work on common cores for the subject has brought these two separate systems even closer together. The relationships between them are more explicit, and this provides even greater impetus for teachers to ensure that they develop A level literature courses which will combine content and process in order to encourage the development of students' skills throughout all the components of the examination.

Chapter 18

How do they know it's worth it?
The untaught reading lessons

Margaret Meek

TEACHING READING IN SECONDARY SCHOOL

Secondary school teachers of English in Britain have, traditionally, little experience in the teaching of reading which, in our training institutions, has been the purview of educational psychologists and primary school teachers. A great deal of the research has passed unnoticed by those who could profit from it. But after the publication of the Bullock Report in 1975 no teacher was exempt from the concerns that cling to the promotion of universal literacy and the extension to all pupils of the type of literacy that was once the privilege of the few.[1] Research reports continue to insist, although I believe that pragmatic evidence is against them, that too many children do not read and write well enough to participate in the life of a literate community. For teachers of English (as mother tongue or as second or other language) this is a special kind of challenge. As our awareness of children's language development grows, as literature written for children becomes more and more the material by which they can learn to read, as we see the growth of understanding that, despite the proliferation of information retrieval systems and 'non-paper' materials in libraries, there will still be a kind of reading one must do for oneself,[2] so we need to enter more fully into the business of how children learn to make prose mean. This is central in any coherent rationale for English studies in the context of our changing culture.

THE READER AND THE TEXT

Our responsibilities situate us between two reservoirs of perceptions with access to both. On the one hand are the literary theorists whose writings promote the idea that 'a theory of literature is a theory of reading'.[3] By opening up the questions related to interactions between the reader and the text, critics have shown how reading as an activity has none of the literary or ideological innocence that is still generally assumed in the teaching of it, whatever the age of the learner. Questions as to the extent individuals perform the same operations or how far these operations are confined to a tiny community of professional critics cannot really be answered until we are rather better at describing the operations in question, says Culler.[4] I want to ask: who can best describe the operations in question? Must they be 'only a tiny community of critics'? Agreed, they read more, but is it not possible that in teaching children to read, to relearning to look at reading, or in helping those for whom the operation is still stubbornly a mystery, teachers might uncover what could count as evidence of the development of literary competences? Have not teachers in school promoted much of the data on which studies in children's language development have been founded?

If we enter this field we need our second reservoir of insights, drawn this time from the reading experts, notably those, like Smith and Goodman, in the psycholinguistic tradition.[5] By moving the model of reading away from behaviourist hierarchies of learned skills to the interpretative understanding of written language they emphasise the reader's role in the *production* of a text. Their central pivot in articulating the reading process is the learner's proven ability to make text mean, so they investigate the relationship of language and thought.

We are apt to glide over our ignorance of what kinds of literary experience generate and nourish reading competences and how development proceeds. Individual case studies of how readers (and, for that matter, writers) are made are rare. My guess, not yet dignified as a hypothesis but in the process of investigation, is that children develop literary competences by interaction with what they find to be significant texts and literacy develops as they learn to *produce* texts, by reading and writing. The teacher's role – whatever the experts say it should also include – is to help the writing to happen and the texts to be read, not just as classroom exercises, but so that the young become independently responsive to both what they read and how they write.

It is fashionable now to talk of teaching as 'facilitating', in which lurks an implied meaning, 'to make easy' (but they may learn more easily without us). I don't think helping children to learn to read is easy, but when it is explorative and collaborative it is exciting. Long before they can write critical essays for examinations good readers practise reading, as James Britton says, as doctors practise medicine.[6] Readers are made when they discover the activity is 'worth it'. Poor, inadequate, inexperienced readers lack literary competence because they have too little idea of what is 'in' reading for them. We, their teachers, are to blame not because we didn't give them reading lessons, but, as I hope to show, because too often we kept the essential reading secrets to ourselves in the mistaken belief that they are common knowledge.

THREE LEARNING SITUATIONS

I propose to take you into three learning situations and to adopt the narrative mode.

First, a large group of postgraduates in training, most of whom have no background in literary criticism, are having their introductory lesson in the teaching of reading. Of the sixty or so, only three can remember their own childhood reading lessons and they are the ones who experienced difficulty, chiefly in understanding their teachers' instructions (e.g. 'sound it out'). The rest are mildly surprised by the suggestion that the very fact that they take their reading skills so much for granted may prove a hindrance to their teaching. The tutor's concern is to make ordinary reading anthropologically strange so that practised readers can inspect what they do without thinking.

The class is to read the first page of a novel without knowing where it comes from.[7] This situation is common in school when children are given similar typed sheets to work from 'new text'.[8]

> Behind the smokehouse *that* summer, Ringo and I had a *living* map. Although Vicksburg was just a handful of chips from the woodpile and the River a trench scraped into the packed earth with the point of a hoe, it (river, city, and terrain) lived, possessing even in miniature that ponderable though passive recalcitrance of topography which outweighs artillery against which the most brilliant of victories and the most tragic of defeats are but the loud noises of a moment. To Ringo and me it lived, *if only because* of the fact that the sunimpacted ground drank water faster than we could fetch it from the well, the very setting of the stage for conflict a prolonged and wellnigh hopeless ordeal in which we ran, panting and interminable, with the leaking bucket between wellhouse and battlefield, the two of us needing first to join forces and spend ourselves against a common enemy, time, before we could engender between us and hold intact the pattern of *recapitulant* mimic furious victory like a cloth, a shield between ourselves and reality, *between us and fact and doom*. This afternoon it seemed as if we would never get it filled, wet enough, since there had not even been dew in three weeks. But at last it was damp enough, damp-coloured enough at least, and we could begin. We were just about to begin. Then suddenly Loosh was standing there, watching us. He was Joby's son and Ringo's uncle; he stood there (we did not know where he had come from; we had not seen him appear, emerge) in the fierce full early afternoon sunlight, bareheaded, his head slanted a little, tilted a little yet firm and not askew, like a cannonball (which it resembled) bedded hurriedly and carelessly in concrete, his eyes a little red at the inner corners as Negroes' eyes get when they have been drinking, looking down at what Ringo and I called *Vicksburg*. Then I saw Philadelphy his wife, over at the woodpile, stooped, with an armful of

wood already gathered into the crook of her elbow, watching Loosh's back.

'What's that?' Loosh said.

'Vicksburg', I said.

Loosh laughed. He stood there laughing, not loud, looking at the chips.

'Come on here, Loosh', Philadelphy said from the woodpile.

There was something curious in her voice too – urgent, perhaps frightened. 'If you wants any supper, you better tote me some wood.' But I didn't know which, urgency or fright; I didn't know because suddenly Loosh stooped before Ringo or I could have moved, and with his hand he swept the chips flat.

'There's your Vicksburg', he said.

'Loosh!' Philadelphy said. But Loosh squatted, looking at me with that expression on his face. I was just twelve then: I didn't know triumph; I didn't even know the word.

Without the support of the rest of the book, the cover, blurb, author, the readers have to rely on their experience of how first pages work. Most of them tackle the reading as if it were a test – interesting in itself. On being asked if anything impedes their understanding all are confident that they can 'guess' their way through the passage. With this agreement it is not difficult to establish 'guessing' as acceptable reading behaviour.

Next, they read it again. According to Barthes, this is the habit of the young, the old and professors.[9] Rather, it is read to them by someone who knows the text well and who treats it as a score, tuning it with subtleties of intonation in response to speech marks, commas and paragraph separations and giving it the dynamics of a coherent interpretation. By virtue of inserting a voice into the text, the readers now separate the author from the narrator and the narrator from the child he once was. With no more explanation, the page becomes 'known text' for the readers who thereafter set about their own *readings*, discussing in groups what is happening *as an actuality*, treating the characters as new acquaintances and 'reading between the lines'.[10]

Some of the outcomes are the predictable result of a *prise de conscience*, but as the discussion proceeds the students are surprised that what first seemed obvious in the narrative was no longer so. There is uncertainty about who was involved in and who won the Battle of Vicksburg, whether it matters or not, and whether the author was counting on the reader's knowledge. Assumptions are made and changed about the age and colour, relationships, political stance and affiliations of the characters. The gaps in the text are filled in. There is a fairly general assumption that the author has made this account of a children's game unnecessarily complicated, and on the whole the students are not disposed to do more on their own than draw narrative inferences about 'what is happening'. A secondary school English teacher might recognise this as fairly characteristic behaviour of 15-year-olds in response to an examination 'set book' – the last time most of the class engaged in this kind of activity.

Even at this stage, however, their view of 'being able to read' is changing. At the start of the class they had expected to be instructed in a 'method' or 'approach' to teaching reading that bypassed this systematic investigation of their underlying assumption of what reading is. They have now to see how speech and written language differ by being asked about the way dialogue is written. They realise that events are ordered by the author in a significant sequence that is not necessarily chronological and somehow the reader sorts this out (or doesn't). That 'narrative events have not only a logic of connection but a logic of hierarchy'[11] is the reason they eventually adduce for the clarification of this particular page. Everyone agreed that before the passage seemed complicated it had appeared straightforward, so clearly being able to read was connected with expecting to understand.

Two further questions were asked: What does Loosh *know*? Vicksburg is again the problem. If only we *knew* what *actually* happened! Why a *living* map? Ah, metaphor. They invent the answers and neglect the phrase beginning 'if only . . .' so that they miss the secret of the omitted 'but also'. Then another look at these unlikely sentences, ending with 'between us and fact and doom'. Is that how you expect an adult narrator to remember an ordinary day, or an extraordinary one? So we go back to the beginning, to the fourth word that we scarcely noticed even at each re-reading, '*that* summer'. What was so special about it?

By now the students have realised that a writer takes infinite trouble with an opening paragraph while a reader, with a whole novel to sort things out in, rushes ahead. Then they can understand that the author is making them read *against* the text. (It is very difficult, in fact, to read it aloud.) So the next possibility unfolds. So used are they to the past tense of narrative that they sacrifice the symbolic for the sequential (as Genette explains, they do not recognise *seeds* and *snares*).[12] Very few students propose, even after several readings, that the boys are playing their game at the same time as the battle is being fought. Once this is suggested, the page can be read again, quite differently, and with the additional element of *surprise*, another aspect of reading that we take for granted.

As a reading lesson this discussion dispels the idea that reading is 'decoding' words to speech. Guessing, anticipating, predicting, drawing on life experience, reading experiences are readerly activities and collaborative moves are helpful.

The problem is still, how does the reader learn? Yet many, many novel readers clearly do, without the benefit of literature lessons, or even in spite of them. More certainly, children are now learning from texts most of us haven't read. At one point, when the class was marvelling at how easily they did something as complicated as reading, a student suddenly asked about children: how do they know it's worth it? – the critical question.

THE INSIGHTS OF 'UNTAUGHT' LESSONS

The second lesson involves a group of teachers who are caught up in what they see as the problem of 'to have read'. They 'have read' a significant proportion of touchstone texts in English and are persuaded that children who are not initiated into the high literary culture are somehow 'deprived'. The children's cry of 'Oh, Miss, it's *boring*' in response to *The Wind in the Willows, David Copperfield, Alice*, to say nothing of poems and the Carnegie prize-winning novels, cuts them like a knife because they really believe that what Barthes calls '*les desinvoltures de lire*' in their pupils are somehow their fault.[13]

So we agreed to work at what the difficulties are for a young reader of reasonable disposition and moderate skill to tackle a 'classic' text. I confessed an ulterior motive. Given that English is a world-wide literary language, that our educational tradition has been, until recently, insular, I wondered if the lessons to be learned in reading a text of non-English provenance, of earlier age, would apply to reading, say, Caribbean, African and Australian writing in English. So we chose *Huckleberry Finn* as the classic book 'to have read', and concentrated on the problems of 'getting into' the story up to the end of the third chapter:

Huckleberry Finn

We played robbers now and then about a month, and then I resigned. All the boys did. We hadn't robbed nobody, we hadn't killed any people, but only just pretended. We used to hop out of the woods and go charging down on hog-drovers and women in carts taking garden stuff to market, but we never hived any of them. Tom Sawyer called the hogs 'ingots', and he called the turnips and stuff 'julery', and we would go to the cave and pow-wow over what we had done and how many people we had killed and marked. But I couldn't see no profit in it. One time Tom sent a boy to run about town with a blazing stick, which he called a slogan (which was the sign for the Gang to get together), and then he said he had got secret news by his spies that next day a whole parcel of Spanish merchants and rich A-rabs was going to camp in Cave Hollow with two hundred elephants, and six hundred camels, and over a thousand 'sumter' mules, all loaded down with di'monds, and they didn't have only a guard of four hundred soldiers, and so we would lay in ambuscade, as he called it, and kill the lot and scoop the things. He said we must slick up our swords and guns, and get ready. He never could go after even a turnip-cart but he must have the swords and guns all scoured up for it; though they was only lath and broom-sticks, and you might scour at them till you rotted, and then they warn't worth a mouthful of ashes more than what they was before. I

didn't believe we could lick such a crowd of Spaniards and A-rabs, but I
wanted to see the camels and elephants, so I was on hand next day,
Saturday, in the ambuscade; and when we got the word, we rushed out of
the woods and down the hill. But there warn't no Spaniards and A-rabs,
and there warn't no camels nor no elephants. It warn't anything but a
Sunday-school picnic, and only a primer-class at that. We busted it up,
and chased the children up the hollow: but we never got anything but
some doughnuts and jam, though Ben Rogers got a rag doll, and Jo
Harper got a hymn-book and a tract; and then the teacher charged in and
made us drop everything and cut. I didn't see no di'monds, and I told
Tom Sawyer so. He said there was loads of them there, anyway; and he
said there was A-rabs there, too, and elephants and things. I said, why
couldn't we see them, then? He said if I warn't so ignorant, but had read a
book called *Don Quixote*, I would know without asking. He said it was
all done by enchantment. He said there was hundreds of soldiers there,
and elephants and treasure, and so on, but we had enemies which he
called magicians, and they had turned the whole thing into an infant
Sunday-school, just out of spite. I said all right, then the thing for us to do
was to go for the magicians. Tom Sawyer said I was a numskull.

You know, of course, what emerges; another series of untaught lessons.
Again the problem: how do children learn to 'tune' the voice on the page? A
child I knew well once asked me to read the first paragraph aloud for her
('and no more') as she 'couldn't make it come right'. After I had added a
nasal note to my reading voice she said, 'That's it' and went on.
Understanding, it seems, in the sense of taking on the world the author has
made, is linked to the creation of the illusion which is, again, an act of
collaborative communion. My young reader tuned into Mark Twain by
means of cowboy films she'd seen on television. Lesson one: Don't assume
ignorance, find connections.

Potentially successful readers tolerate uncertainty because at some time
someone has made the narrative connections come quickly enough to make
the story 'interesting'. Dialogue keeps action moving, or seems to. In
Chapter 3 of *Huckleberry Finn* are two pages of close type that proved a
stumbling block for the pupils in our experiment. Here the readers' tolerance of Huck, sympathetically extended to his spelling problems with Miss
Watson, and the formation of Tom Sawyer's gang with its bloodthirsty
proposals, falters on the game of robbers. This passage is written as a report.
We looked at it in detail, for it is on just such text that the teacher's most
frequent, authoritative interpolations and commentaries occur. This is
school reading of the classics, with yawning accompaniment. The teacher
wants enjoyment of what is, for him or her, clearly humour; the class
announces boredom.

It is not difficult for experienced readers to list what can here be learned:

how Huck Finn needs a shared sense of humour between reader and author and an agreed tolerance and sympathy. Wandering *inside* the text to see both Huck's and Tom's view of the game, we see the camel train and the Sunday-school class in a kind of double vision by means of the interconnecting narrative perspectives; we are both in the game and out of it. When Tom says that Huck would have seen the A-rabs if he read *Don Quixote* we know the rules that let an author refer to the whole pantheon of literature in the way that football experts cite teams and games and chess players read classic moves.

We are wont to say that these questions are answered by the close reading experience. But what, exactly, constitutes this experience? At first my student colleagues thought that only books of a certain 'density' offered this kind of textual awareness. A more honest inspection of our own reading habits and a closer look at our pupils brought other notions. First, we realised exactly how little we re-read the books we were so pleased to have read until we shared them with our pupils. We were revisiting memories; they were reading new text. Our concern to let nothing of the resavouring escape the young often blocked what they could have done for themselves. Successful readers 'press on regardless' leaving the gaps in the text as adults' business. But our 13-year-olds read *Huckleberry Finn* with sensibilities refined not by books but by events in the streets of the inner city. So we, the teachers, learned that what we really had to look at is not what young readers don't understand, but how they ignore what does not make the story work for them. This is literary competence of a kind we are too practised to recognise.

In traditional reading lessons, literature teachers tend to be the leaders. But group work, collaborative learning, children choosing texts all offer opportunities for understanding what our very experience may shut out. This is in no way to undervalue the teacher's competences, but simply to say that we must guard against living on a diminishing capital. We shall not discover the growth of literary competences in children if we invite them into literature only on our terms. As has always happened, they will simply behave well (or not) in class, and read other books under the desk.

We still have to understand more about the ideological hinterland of 'to have read' (Raymond Williams' *The Country and the City* was a good starting point for us).[14] Our most pressing current reading problem with regard to adolescents is not to make the classics readable but to deepen and extend reading skills developed on a range of narrative texts we know nothing or too little about – new comic strips, films, video images and the mental images that go with them.

HELPING INEXPERIENCED READERS

The third learning situation involved five London teachers and the same number of adolescent pupils whose reading was too unpractised to let them function adequately in ordinary lessons. These teachers decided to offer the pupils the chance to become readers by inviting them to take on that role in as normal a situation as could be devised: to learn to read by reading real texts instead of specially constructed materials.

Our concern was to help our inexperienced readers to read a book with confidence and pleasure and to see what was involved in the teaching and learning of this process. What, we asked, could the competent readers do that the less successful do not know they had to learn?

Our ignorance proved more than a little shaming. Videotape recordings of lessons showed us how even the most caring, insightful, well-read teachers can unwittingly take from a pupil what little competence he or she has. In sharing a book, for instance, who turns the pages, smooths them down, looks back at the pictures? As a colleague said: 'Some lessons you do not even know you teach. When I turn these pages over I'm really saying "you are such a poor reader I even have to find the place for you" when he or she could certainly do it on his own.' No one who has taught or seen 'remedial' lessons given to inexperienced readers can fail to be struck by the apparent distance between the halting, word-by-word deciphering of those whose concern is 'to get it right' and the rhythmic patterning and apparently effortless command of narrative conventions of the practised readers of the same age. The poor reader is seen as the victim of his or her background and experience, despite the fact that there is plenty of evidence that middle-class children have the same problems. The pupils we taught were content to go through any motions as long as we would collude with their belief that they would never really be able to master this puzzle. They could not understand why we persistently refused to do so.[15]

From the significant lessons these pupils taught us I offer two for inspection. The first concerns the way the learner's view of the task maintains or inhibits real reading competence.

Trevor certainly had no idea that he was a natural disciple of Todorov in the way he dismantled the system of texts.[16] When his teacher read to him he would demand: 'Why does it say that . . .?' 'Doesn't this stupid writer know that . . .?' and proceed with systematic commentary on the words and the plot. The teaching problem was to keep this activity intact in the face of Trevor's insistence that reading was 'saying the words right', a lesson that had been fiercely driven home in his first years in school. When he was finally aware that he could read, three-and-a-half years later, the elusive joy of his earlier approach was gone.[17] He learned to read by means of a compromise between his desire, the excitement stories awoke in him, and what he mistakenly believed, against all evidence, was what a teacher wanted. Trevor taught us how high the wall is for inexperienced readers to climb into the enchanted garden, a wall, I feel, we build.

Throughout this, often painful, learning time with these pupils we discovered more about why they didn't think reading was 'worth it'. We strove to help them to predict and guess their way through narrative texts outside the remedial reading schemes, we discovered how 'readability', the measurement of text, vocabulary and sentence length, is not what makes text difficult. Instead, we studied the significance of what the author doesn't say, about the world inside the story and the world outside it, with the scores of unexplained textual conventions that the reader has to learn. That they *can* learn them is evident; they have little trouble with comics which are equally rule governed and which they read out without difficulty.

Gradually our pupils discovered that there was more to be gained than reading skill. We argued that if there was no text they could enjoy and make sense of, then they must help to produce one. Thus we became the scribes of their stories. They dictated to us and we wrote and in so doing we discovered they already had the competences we imagined were lacking as the result of their inexperience. They related one incident to another; they tagged dialogue or not as the occasion demanded. One boy dictated 4,000 words in narrative chunks and in prose rhetoric. They needed our educational skills when the gaps in the text were too wide for another reader and in sorting out the cohesion within the sentences, but the narrative conventions were generally firm. We learned what we had always known: you don't teach children to tell stories; you let them, and then help them to know that's how other authors – the ones who write books – do it too. Their stories were both fantastic and everyday, informed by both poetic and common sense. They were drawing on a storehouse of narrative structure that psychoanalysts have long since known to be common property.[18]

CHILDREN'S DEEP RESPONSES

We learned most from these pupils where we expected to learn least, from their interaction with narrative texts. The slow oral production that they believe is reading is a kind of gripping grief to the well-practised listener. As we had laid on each other the obligation to inspect all the evidence we collected we listened, painfully, to many hours of this. We learned again, as in literary criticism, to *overread* what we so usually underread – books written for children. We discovered what Frank Kermode calls 'secrets' which resist 'all but abnormally attentive scrutiny, reading so minute, so intense, and slow that it seems to run counter to one's "natural" sense of what a novel is'.[19] Kermode is describing hermeneutic criticism; it applies perfectly to what our pupils made us do.

We discovered the deep structures of some children's novelists, the construct of childhood latent in the writings of Dahl and Philippa Pearce, and the way 'popular' texts transform the motivations of authors. Our most successful book was *The Iron Man* about which its author, Ted Hughes, has written a persuasive analysis of myth in education.[20] As we read it again and again we saw how our inexperienced readers had more than enough of the common understanding of the clash of technology and nature to match the workings of the poet's imagination with their own. They had learned the conventions from Batman and Superman. They could make the story work as a metaphor of their own convention. They were the little boy who befriended the Iron man, and the Iron man who saved the world. As for us, we had to learn again the history of literature, the creation myths, St George and the Dragon, *Pilgrim's Progress*, the reconciliation of man and nature. Unlikely? Reading as slowly as our pupils did, we discovered with them how we moved inside a literary text and gained 'the moving viewpoint which travels along *inside* that which it has to apprehend'. As our pupils learned, so we came to understand what they were learning. 'This mode of grasping', says Iser, 'is unique to literature.'[21] That was the lesson for us all.

These are some of the untaught lessons. But my opening question – my students' insight – still stands. How *do* they know it's worth it? What gets in the way is, I believe, our view of the task. We are so keen to make our readers competent, lettered, skilled, that we foreground what is *not* our joy in reading and background the fact that we have been secretly playing games. Storytelling can be a kind of lifelong play. As Vygotsky tells us, play can give the child a new form of desire and teach him or her to relate this 'to a fictitious "I" – to his role in the game and its rules. Therefore, a child's greatest achievements are possible in play-achievements which tomorrow will become his average level of real action and morality.'[22] We have to be more hospitable to new texts and new conventions of writing, and must nurture the latent competences of storytelling that children learn without our teaching, if we are to enlarge the 'tiny' community of those who read with desire.

NOTES AND REFERENCES

1 See D.P. and L.B. Resnick, 'The Nature of Literacy' in *Harvard Educational Review* 47, 3, 1977, pp. 370–85.
2 See Louise M. Rosenblatt, *The Reader, the Text, the Poem*, Southern Illinois University Press, 1978.
3 The phrase comes from Jonathan Culler, *Structuralist Poetics*, Routledge and Kegan Paul, 1978, which not only makes clear the links literary theory has with the linguistic studies of Saussure, but also relates this general statement to the diversity of the writings in this field.
4 J. Culler, 'Prolegomena to a Theory of Reading' in S. Sulieman and I. Crossman (eds), *The Reader in the Text*, Princeton University Press, 1980.
5 See Frank Smith, *Reading*, Cambridge University Press, 1978, Frederick U. Gollasch, *Language and Literacy: the selected writings of Kenneth S. Goodman*, Routledge and Kegan Paul, 1982.

6 James Britton, *Language and Learning*, Allen Lane, 1970.
7 It is *The Unvanquished* by William Faulkner. The passage was chosen by Harold Rosen for the first conference of the London Association for the Teaching of English in 1949 when the topic was 'comprehension'.
8 See Resnick.
9 R. Barthes, *Le Plaisir du Texte*, Sevil, 1973.
10 See Seymour Chatman, 'Story and Discourse' in *Narrative Structure in Fiction and Film*, Cornell University Press, 1978.
11 *Ibid*.
12 G. Genette, *Narrative Discourse*, Blackwell, 1980.
13 R. Barthes, 'Sur la lecture' in *Le français aujourd'hui*, 32, 1976.
14 Raymond Williams, *The Country and the City*, Chatto and Windus, 1973.
15 M. Meek *et al.*, *Achieving Literacy: a kind of evidence*, Routledge and Kegan Paul, 1983.
16 Zuetan T. Todorov, *The Poetics of Prose*, Blackwell, 1977.
17 The words are those of my colleague, Judith Graham.
18 Roy Schafer, 'Narration in the Psychoanalytic Dialogue' in W.T. Wilson (ed.), *On Narrative*, University of Chicago Press, 1981.
19 See Kermode in Schafer.
20 Ted Hughes, 'Myth in Education' in *Children's Literature* in *Education* I, 1970, pp. 55–70.
21 Wolfgang Iser, *The Act of Reading*, Routledge and Kegan Paul, 1978.
22 L.S. Vygotsky, 'Play and its role in the mental development of the child' from *Soviet Psychology* 12, 6, 1966, reprinted in J.S. Bruner, H. Jolly and K. Sylva (eds), *Play*, Penguin Books, 1976, p. 549.

Part IV

Writing

Brian Cox's account of the English Working Group's recommendations which informed the National Curriculum contains some clear thinking on the processes of writing. The sections contained there, including the relationship between spoken and written language, are useful frameworks for considering effective teaching of writing. ('The best writing', he says, 'is vigorous, committed, honest and interesting.')

Brian Cox's last sentence refers to whole-school language policy. The National Writing Project was set up with the aim of promoting writing competences across the curriculum. Pam Czerniewska, Director of the Project, outlines the aims of the NWP in the next chapter, which includes an account by Richard Landy, then a Head of English in Mid Glamorgan, of his school's experiences of developing a whole-school language policy. Initially, other subjects had different expectations of writing. These differing perceptions on writing have their roots in a debate about teaching writing explored in Janet Maybin's chapter 'Teaching writing: process or genre?' The process approach, drawing on the work of Donald Graves and Donald Murray, takes as its basis that the pupil is a real writer, and thus has a sense of ownership of and commitment to that writing. The genre approach, based on the work of Michael Halliday, relates writing to specific language purposes. Thus, Janet Maybin writes, 'Learning about a particular subject discipline, therefore, involves also learning about specific ways of using language.' She explores these theoretical positions with examples of classroom practice, and addresses three fundamental questions: What is involved in the process of becoming a writer? What are our criteria for good writing, and when and how should teachers intervene in pupils' writing?

These questions are taken up in Michael Rosen's chapter 'School students' writing: some principles'. Although he does not identify his theoretical position as such, the ideas of the process theory are clear here. He writes: 'to promote form as the starting point of writing denies the existential, cultural and ideological purposes of writing'. As a well-known writer himself, Michael Rosen is clear about the principles of writing teachers of English should be promoting in the classroom.

In contrast, Jonothan Neelands in 'Writing in imagined contexts' looks at the genre approach to language, but works through drama techniques in the promotion of writing. The powerful medium of drama in English is shown through the study of a class responding to the stimulus of an imagined situation, a derelict piece of land, and the plans of the community living around it. Jonothan Neelands describes the strategies available to the teacher, and explains how each of these worked in the project.

'Teaching poetry in the secondary school' by John Taylor, HMI, also deals with a powerful writing experience. He quotes Seamus Heaney:

> In practice you hear it coming from somebody else, you hear something in another writer's sounds that flows in through your ear and enters the echo chamber of your head and delights your whole nervous system in such a way that your reaction will be 'Ah, I wish I had said that in that particular way' . . . . And your first steps as a writer will be to imitate, consciously or unconsciously, those sounds that flowed in, that influence.

The work of a 15-year-old following his reading Ted Hughes' *Hawk Roosting* is proof of this:

> . . .
> Power is behind me.
> Only money has changed since I began.
> My pen has permitted that change.
> I am going to keep things like this.

The final chapter in this part looks at grammar and is co-written by two members of the LINC (Language In the National Curriculum) Project. This DES- (now DFE-) funded project was designed to develop the model of language recommended in the Kingman Report that is a descriptive and analytical model. The project, which explored knowledge about language (KAL), had publication of its materials refused by the secretary of state, but was allowed to use the materials for in-service training. The perspective of the LINC Project has remained popular with teachers, and Frances Smith and Mike Taylor investigate grammar using the LINC model. 'Grammar', they say, 'is important. Language . . . is a rule-bound system. Exploring these rules is an exciting and challenging part of learning about language.' The chapter addresses principles and strategies in teaching grammar, and demonstrates that grammar is significantly more than verb-spotting exercises.

Chapter 19

Writing

Brian Cox

The evidence gathered from successive surveys of pupils' attitudes to reading and writing suggests that the language experience of many pupils is concentrated in a relatively narrow range of types of writing.

(*APU*, Pupils' Attitudes to Writing, *1987*)

OUR RATIONALE

The term 'writing' is ambiguous: in the first place, it can refer either to the process of writing or to the written product. The term is also ambiguous between the composing aspects of writing and the secretarial aspects, such as good handwriting and spelling. For example, it is possible now for word processors with spelling checkers to take over some of the proof-reading aspects of writing and to produce impeccable printout.

Attainment targets and programmes of study must therefore cover both these aspects of writing, here called for convenience 'composing' and 'secretarial'. Our main principle was that the secretarial aspect should not be allowed to predominate in the assessment while the more complex aspects of composition are ignored. It is evident that a child may be a poor speller, but write well-structured and interesting stories, or be a good speller, but write badly structured and boring stories.

FUNCTIONS OF WRITTEN LANGUAGE

Written language serves many purposes both for individuals and for society as a whole, and is not limited to the communication of information. For the individual author, writing can have cognitive functions in clarifying and supporting thought. (Spoken language also allows thoughts to be formulated in one's own words, but written language has the added advantage of making a detached reflection on them possible.) Such writing is essentially private. At the level of whole societies, written language serves the functions of record keeping and of storing both information and literary works. It therefore supports and transmits the culture. Such writing is essentially public and intended for an audience.

These points are relevant both to the programmes of study and to assessment, since they show that linguistic forms cannot be corrected or assessed independently of their purpose. The nature of the assessment should be geared to the purpose of the writing. For example, it is perfectly appropriate to demand neatness, correct spelling, and features of standard English in work which has a public purpose. But this may be less appropriate for work with essentially private purposes. The different functions of written language are an important topic for knowledge about language and part of an understanding of how society works.

THE RELATIONS BETWEEN SPOKEN AND WRITTEN LANGUAGE

There is no simple transition from spoken to written language. In the development of their writing, children have to move from casual to formal language, from spontaneous to planned language; and from a known to an unknown audience. Further, some children have to add the forms of standard English to their own non-standard forms, and others have to move from their mother tongue to English. In each case, the language competence acquired is additive: it does not replace earlier competences. Children also have to acquire forms of written language which are rarely or never used in spoken English, since written language is not just spoken language written down. Children cannot be expected to learn everything at once. A measure of tolerance of errors in different language tasks is essential.

Spoken and written language are closely related both developmentally and theoretically. Spoken language tends to be informal, spontaneous and interactive with the speakers face to face, whereas written language tends to be formal, edited and non-interactive, with writer and reader separated. But these are only the most typical configurations. All combinations are possible. For example, a letter to a friend may be informal; a telephone conversation is not face to face; interactive written communication is possible via computer terminals; a speech may be a carefully edited and rehearsed monologue; etc. Even so, the various features characteristically associated with casual conversation and with formal writing provide a way of organising programmes of study. The basic principle is so to organise teaching that children have experience of producing written language across these various forms. Language experiences which will ensure this are set out in the programmes of study.

ASSUMPTIONS

When children first come to school they have a large body of language experience to draw on. This will differ according to the richness of the environment provided by the home and the wider community, but all children live and grow up in a print-rich world full of writing and people who write.

Just as many young children come to school believing that they can read, so they will come willing to try to be writers. The very youngest children, given the opportunity to use what they know, are able to demonstrate considerable knowledge of the forms and purposes of writing. This may at first be simple 'draw writing', but as they develop and learn more about how written language works, their writing comes increasingly close to standard adult systems. It is normal for their early attempts to consist of strings of letters, with words represent by the initial letter or by clusters of consonants. Children's early invented spellings often demonstrate logical consistency; this grasp of regularity should be recognised as an initial achievement and children should be helped to be confident in attempting to spell words for themselves without undue dependence on the teacher.

In early writing we see errors of letter formation, spelling and composition occurring as children make hypotheses about the rules that govern the writing system. Teachers provide the greatest encouragement for children to communicate in writing when they respond more to the content of what is written than to such errors, and when they share a child's writing with other children.

Through increasing encounters with a range of examples children make sense of literary experiences and it is the responsibility of the teacher to provide and foster that range in the classroom. Teachers will have diverse roles to play in the development of young writers: they will be observers, facilitators, modellers, readers and supporters. Through these roles the teacher intervenes in the child's learning, most often by a careful structuring of the contexts for writing.

During the early years of the secondary school, and as they grow into adolescence, pupils will increasingly be able to take a more objective view and develop greater understanding of the writing process. In so doing they will be building on their earlier writing experiences, which should have given them a positive view of themselves as writers who are capable of making and receiving meanings using a variety of forms depending on audience and purpose.

The programmes of study should, above all, enable pupils to exercise more conscious and critical control over the writing process. It is possible to identify a number of strands which should feature in their development as writers during these years. These are to do with an increasing ability to:

• write in different forms for different purposes and audiences;

- write coherently about a wide range of topics, issues, ideas, incidents, etc., organising different kinds of text in ways which help the reader;
- craft writing which is significantly different from speech, showing a developing control of grammatical structure and of a differentiated vocabulary; and write in a style which is appropriate for the purpose, audience and subject matter;
- know when and how to plan, draft, redraft, revise and proof-read their work;
- understand the nature and functions of written language.

It is important that teachers should help pupils in this process by recognising the interrelatedness of writing, reading and speaking and listening. I have already stressed the need for younger pupils to have increasing encounters with a range of examples through which they make sense of literary experiences, and this should continue into the secondary stages. By careful planning of schemes of work to integrate programmes of study for speaking and listening, reading and writing, teachers should be able to foster the writing development of their pupils, helping them to develop an ear for language through reading or listening to works in a wide variety of styles written by really fine authors. Both literary and non-literary writing will often develop from the interaction between the pupils' own insights and what they have read (or heard read) in the classroom.

An essential aspect of development in the secondary stages is that pupils should increasingly make their own decisions about their writing – what it is about, what form it should take and to whom it is addressed. The written essay – usually 400–500 words long – has dominated the English language and literature curriculum for many years because it has been seen as the main vehicle for the transmission of knowledge in written examinations. The advent of GCSE and the more widespread development of continuous assessment of coursework in all English examination syllabuses have provided opportunities for pupils in secondary schools to use writing for a much wider range of purposes and audiences. This is a development to be welcomed and encouraged.

All pupils should be expected to keep a file containing work in progress, as well as completed pieces, which may need to be selected and filed separately for the purposes of moderation and final assessment. It is most important that teacher assessment should take account of the way pupils tackle writing tasks – that is, it should be sensitive to the writing process as well as to the finished product. Consequently, pupils should keep in their files the necessary range and variety of types of writing, including where appropriate any rough notes, plans or early drafts. They should play an active part in assessing their own progress through discussion with those who read their writing – their peers, teachers or other adults.

Much writing in English will be attempted by pupils to record their thoughts on topics of personal or public importance. Through discussion or role play, teachers should seek to provide frequent opportunities for this type of writing to occur, and should respond to the meanings that their pupils strive to convey.

Pupils should know that their writing need not always be formal or follow literary models; it can also effectively capture and record first thoughts and immediate responses and can be used for note making, collecting and shaping information, etc. Equally, however, it should be recognised that some writing is about communicating with the outside world and having a say in that world. In the Kingman Report we wrote:

> *People need expertise in language to be able to participate effectively in a democracy. There is no point in having access to information that you cannot understand, or having the opportunity to propose policies which you cannot formulate. People receive information and misinformation in varying proportions from, among others, family and friends, work mates, advertisers, journalists, priests, politicians and pressure groups. A democratic society needs people who have the linguistic abilities which will enable them to discuss, evaluate and make sense of what they are told, as well as to take effective action on the basis of their understanding. The working of a democracy depends on the discriminating use of language on the part of all its people. Otherwise there can be no genuine participation, but only the imposition of the ideas of those who are linguistically capable. As individuals, as well as members of constituencies, people need the resources of language both to defend their rights and to fulfil their obligations.*
>
> (chapter 2, paragraph 2)

Teachers should both create and respond to opportunities to focus on aspects of knowledge about written language and about some of the differences between speech and writing.

The full development of both reading and writing in the secondary years requires a broad definition of text to encompass both literary and non-literary forms. Pupils should continue to develop in their dual roles as makers of meanings in their own texts and as receivers and makers of meaning in the texts of others.

STRANDS WITHIN LEVELS OF ATTAINMENT

If proposals for assessment are to have coherence, they must be based on a theory of difficulty. Bearing in mind some caveats below, it is possible to predict the relative difficulty of a writing task (and of a language task more generally). Other things being equal, a writing task is easier if the organisation is chronological; if the subject matter is drawn from personal experience; if the subject matter is concrete rather than abstract; and if the audience is known to the writer. The first distinction is usually clear cut: the organisation is either chronological or not. (Texts which are typically chronological are narratives and reports; texts which are typically non-chronological are descriptions and arguments for a point of view.) The other distinctions are relative rather than absolute; for example, the subject matter may be more or less abstract, the audience may be very well known or less well known.

As I have already pointed out, children do not learn particular features of written language once and for all at a particular stage. Development is recursive. This means that writing development must be defined in broad terms and cannot be measured solely by one-off tests at particular ages. Language competence is dependent on the task: children will show different ability on tasks of different kinds. Therefore only a relatively broad range of tasks can hope to assess children's performance. The general line of development extends from emergent writing, through the early stages of composition, towards growing fluency and control and finally to full independence. We share the view of the National Writing Project that 'To try to put ages against these expectations produces great problems.' However, bearing these caveats in mind, it is still reasonable to expect children to have made demonstrable progress along the developmental path when they reach key stages in the education system.

One aspect of development as a writer is the growing ability to handle successfully different forms such as stories, poems, accounts, reports, instructions, essays, etc. In order to learn the conventional ways in which subject matter is organised and presented in these different forms, it is necessary for children to have plenty of opportunities to read or hear read good examples of a range of different types of texts. Young children hear stories either told or read from a very early age and, as soon as they have the skill, they read them themselves. In this way, they internalise the elements of story structure – the opening, setting, characters, events and resolution. Similarly, they come to realise that, in satisfying, well-structured stories, things that are lost will be found, problems will be solved, mysteries will be explained, and so on. It is partly because of this early extensive experience of stories that so much writing in primary schools is in story form. In responding to children's writing, teachers are well able to distinguish between an embryonic attempt at a story and a more developed example; indeed, there is substantial research available on the stages of story-writing through which young writers progress. So, because children know and use the story form and because it is possible to discern a sequence of development, we specified various aspects of story structure in the statements of attainment from Level 2 to Level 4. From the beginning, though, children should be learning to write in other forms and for other purposes. In the early stages we distinguished between 'other chronological writing' and 'non-chronological writing'. We have not continued the story strand in the statements of attainment beyond Level 4, although many pupils will continue to write stories of increasing complexity throughout the secondary school, because by then it will be just one of the many types of writing that pupils might undertake.

Throughout the school years, all children should have ample opportunities to write poetry, either singly or in groups; this is made explicit in the programmes of study. However, we did not include a poetry strand in the statements of attainment because we did not feel that any pupil should be required to write a poem in order to achieve a particular level of attainment.

An important part of the composing process is the choice of appropriate and lively vocabulary. Nevertheless, we have not included vocabulary in our statements of attainment until Level 7. This is partly because vocabulary is the most individualistic part of a person's knowledge of language, and continues to develop throughout life, although its growth is clearly fastest in the early years. It is also because the choice of vocabulary is determined by the subject matter. It can be assessed only by its appropriateness, but this depends entirely on what the pupil is writing about and for what purpose (and so has a cross-curricular dimension). The main line of development is that vocabulary becomes increasingly differentiated according to the purpose of the writing (e.g. whether it is everyday or technical) and to its style (e.g. formal or informal). There is also growing differentiation between colloquial and literary vocabulary. This aspect of writing development is one in which it is relatively easy to specify the direction of development, and achievements at higher levels, but where the precise specification of intermediate levels is much more difficult. It makes little sense, for example, to require that children have a command of formal vocabulary before they are competent in technical vocabulary or vice versa.

The best writing is vigorous, committed, honest and interesting. We did not include these qualities in our statements of attainment because they cannot be mapped onto levels. Even so, all good classroom practice will be geared to encouraging and fostering these vital qualities. In their revisions the NCC tried to include these qualities, but everyone agrees this is very difficult.

Development in attainment target 3 is marked by:

- increasing control over the structure and organisation of different types of text;
- a growing ability to handle complex or demanding subject matter;
- a widening range of syntactic structures and an expanding vocabulary, as the pupil begins to use language that is characteristic of writing rather than speech and to strive for a style that is appropriate to the subject matter and the readership;
- a growing capacity to write independently and at length;
- an increasing proficiency in re-reading and revising or redrafting the text, taking into account the needs of the audience;

- a developing ability to reflect on and talk about the writing process.

Punctuation is included in this attainment target because it helps the reader to identify the units of structure and meaning that the writer has constructed.

With regard to spelling, the aim should be that by the end of compulsory schooling pupils should be able to spell confidently most of the words that they are likely to need to use frequently in their writing; to recognise those aspects of English spelling that are systematic; to make a sensible attempt to spell words that they have not seen before; to check their work for mis-spellings and to use a dictionary appropriately. The aim cannot be the correct unaided spelling of any English word – there are too many words in English that can catch out even the best speller.

ASSESSMENT

General

The attainment targets suggested above should be assessed through a variety of writing, using a combination of internal and external assessment. Those aspects of the targets which relate to the writing process, as distinct from the product, should be covered by mainly internal assessment – for example, probing pupils' ability to reflect upon and discuss the organisation of their own writing. For these purposes teachers will need to keep samples of children's writing in order to monitor its range and development over the course of a key stage; and they will need systematic means of recording and appraising the ways in which pupils approach writing tasks, including talking about what they are doing and why. As part of the internal assessment process, some self-assessment should be involved, through children's discussing a piece of writing with the teacher or with their peers, and then redrafting it. The children could use a standard pro forma to assess their own performance against the relevant parts of the attainment targets. We therefore recommended the development by SEAC of a national format and guidelines for internal assessment of these aspects of writing, to parallel our similar recommendation in the case of reading.

Extended tasks in external assessment SATs may also, however, be capable of monitoring aspects of the writing process, as well as the product of composition and its physical presentation: we recommended that SEAC should commission development work with this in mind.

Assessment in secondary school

Internal assessment and recording in the secondary school should build on that of the primary school. More particularly, pupils should compile a folder of coursework containing writing of a range of types on a variety of topics for different and clearly specified audiences. In both Key Stages 3 and 4 they should have the opportunity to present an extended piece of work that has been planned, drafted, revised and polished over a period of time.

The SATs at ages 14 and 16 should provide pupils with a wide choice, but should require them to produce a number of contrasting pieces of writing within both long- and short-timed tasks and spanning the range from imaginative literary uses of language to the clear and orderly presentation of information and argument. As in the earlier key stages, we recommended that where the 'secretarial' aspects (presentation, spelling, handwriting) apply, they should not be assessed in isolation, but through purposeful writing activities.

Marking policy

I have discussed the process of continuous assessment and the function of the samples of children's work in providing a basis for further development. In this context it may be helpful to include a section here on the teacher's response to children's written work, and in particular to the marking policy adopted. As James Britton and his colleagues put it:

> very close reading of children's writing is essential, because that is the best means we have of understanding their writing processes. Children value perceptive comments, responses and questions on their writing, but they quickly see through perfunctory approval and generalised faint praise. And it's worth remembering that for very many children, for many years, their teachers are the only readers of the bulk of their work.[1]

It is axiomatic that the context of children's learning is significant. The teacher's ability to react sympathetically, to welcome a pupil's contribution, written or spoken, in a supportive manner, is especially important. Such a response nurtures trust in the relationship.

> The encouraging comment, sincerely meant, however brief, is the English teacher's most powerful weapon. It is utterly at variance with this to adopt what Andrew Wilkinson has nicely described as the role of 'the teacher as self-appointed proof reader . . . GRowling and SPitting and hiSSing from the margin'.[2]

Negative methods of responding in marking are likely to produce sterile, cumulative consequences in a child's writing: pupils quickly discern what is acceptable to the teacher and merely aim to fulfil those expectations.

The teacher's response to written work should aim to foster a child's confidence in the exploration of ideas and the manner of their presentation. Pupils benefit from the opportunity to shape and reformulate their thinking in a helpful, non-threatening atmosphere, where experiments in language are not only acceptable, but encouraged. The marking response can play a vital part in promoting this linguistic growth through establishing a dialogue, and not merely concerning itself with surface features of the writing, or the routine correction of technical errors. 'Assessment is not in question; it is when it becomes an automatic and unvaried process that it loses its value for both teacher and pupil.'[3] The process should encourage the pupils to play an active role in learning.

Schools should formulate marking guidelines, as one feature of a cross-curricular language policy. These might establish:

- the purpose, style and tone of written comments;
- the basis for pointing out technical errors, and the manner of their correction;
- the techniques to encourage successful examples of language use;
- the part played by discussion with individual pupils in marking their work;
- the way marking will be used in connection with further learning, and hence as a crucial link in a coherent programme of study;
- the contribution of the assessment to a pupil's record of achievement.

Such guidelines can help to clarify aims and objectives in setting, and responding to, written work, for the benefit of pupils, staff and parents. Pupils, especially, might increase their understanding of how they learn. In addition, the clarification of such issues could well provide the initial stimulus for a whole-school language policy.

NOTES

1 James Britton *et al.*, *The Development of Writing Abilities. 11 to 18* (Macmillan, 1975), p. 44.
2 Anthony Adams and John Pearce, *Every English Teacher* (Oxford University Press, 1974), p. 92.
3 Bullock Report, paragraph 11.10.

Chapter 20

The National Writing Project

Pam Czerniewska and Richard Landy

INTRODUCTION – PAM CZERNIEWSKA

In 1985, the School Curriculum Development Committee (later replaced by the National Curriculum Council) set up the National Writing Project with the aim:

> to develop and extend the competence and confidence of young adults to write for a range of purposes and a variety of audiences, in a manner that enhances their growth as individuals, their powers of self-expression, their skill as communicators and their facility as learners.

The project was funded for four years by a national grant plus some LEA support. While the project was about writing development in schools, it was also about curriculum development, exploring means of effecting change in classrooms. To this end, it began by asking twenty-four LEAs to form teacher groups who would look at different aspects of the curriculum for ages 3–18. Between them they covered issues such as writing in the early years; community involvement in writing; bilingual writers; writing development in different subject areas; writing and work; children's perceptions of writing; the use of micros for writing development and the assessment of writing. The project was organised centrally by a small team and locally by LEA-appointed co-ordinators.

The work represented one of the most extensive investigations ever made into children's writing experiences in school. It resulted in a major rethink about:

- how we view writing: what and who it is for; what it is about;
- how we organise the learning context so that it provides a range of experiences in literacy processes and products;
- how we view learners; their development and their role within the learning process;
- how curriculum change is best achieved.

No curriculum development project of this size is without the uncertainties and tensions that sit alongside successes and agreements. After four years, we had as many questions as answers. Richard Landy's account of his school's investigations represents well some of the lessons learned about writing and curriculum development. Richard was seconded to the Mid Glamorgan National Writing Project for two years and developed the work reported here in his own secondary school as well as setting up other groups in his LEA. The initial focus of the Mid Glamorgan project was writing in different subject areas and writing and work. Like many project groups, the teachers began by observing writing practices in their own classrooms and finding out children's perceptions of writing. This served as the catalyst for experiments with the writing curriculum, many of them innovative and highly successful.

Reading between the lines, it is clear that the success of the work resulted from the teachers' commitment to improving the curriculum (obvious in the extra hours they found to meet and plan) and from the support they received from their co-ordinator. It helped, too, that, as part of a national project, their work was disseminated widely through conferences and publications; the teachers found themselves 'going public' early on in their thinking. Above all, though, the teachers saw themselves as the agents of change.

REWRITING THE SYLLABUS – RICHARD LANDY

Looking back on it all, I can see where I went wrong. As head of an English department in a typical secondary school, I dutifully spent six years, off and on, talking to colleagues (or, more probably, at them) about the urgent need for a school policy for language across the curriculum. I addressed meetings. I wrote documents. I manoeuvred subtly and I made outright demands. I argued, confronted and sulked. I don't think it got me very far. There were some simple truths about curriculum development which I hadn't learned. Perhaps I still tended to consider policy in an abstract rather than a practical sense? As teachers, we have a healthy distrust of sterile documentation, but we do enjoy doing things together, particularly when they work. It's practice that makes policy, not paper.

Some eighteen months into the National Writing Project, my diary contained the following entries relating to project activities at one secondary school in Mid Glamorgan:

2nd March: World of Work group: joint meeting with local employers
4th March: Visit by Liz V. from Hampshire
11th March: Pupils collating material for 'Caerphilly Campaign' special issue
14th March: Llanbradach bypass project group meeting
22nd March: World of Work group: planning response to employers
24th March: Meeting Olwyn H. and pupils at 'Campaign' offices

28th March: Llanbradach bypass: presentation to other pupils
29th March: Planning meeting for years 1/2 'Our School' project
30th March: 'Home Front' presentation for senior citizens

Now here's a writing policy in action! It's worth considering how and why all this activity – involving teachers from almost all curriculum areas and pupils of all ages – came about.

Working groups can be difficult. I can remember the first meeting of our group quite vividly. It was a very tentative occasion. Olwyn, who had recently been given responsibility for language across the curriculum, had convened the group by asking for volunteers, twisting a few arms in the process. All of us were willing but unsure of each other and, perhaps, ourselves. We broke the ice by talking about the kinds of writing demands we made of pupils in our different subject areas, taking, as a starting point, a list of very straightforward but fundamental questions, such as: 'Who are they writing for?' 'Where are they writing?' 'What do we do with what they've written?'

On looking back at the notes of that meeting, it's interesting to see the general conclusions which we reached. We commented that much of the pupils' writing was done with the intention (our intention, that is!) of collating information into a usable form which would itself become a learning resource. We noted that our pupils often seemed to perceive writing as a necessary proof that learning had taken place. Invariably, we felt, our pupils were asked to write in an impersonal way. (One of us commented that he always told his pupils to *'leave out the "I"'*.) We conceded that, generally, our pupils were given little opportunity to work on their writing for more than a very brief period of time, that the vast majority of tasks were one-off writing assignments, and that the idea of reworking writing through a process was one which, for a variety of reasons, was largely ignored. When we came to discuss what we actually did with the writing our pupils undertook for us, we all admitted to assessment, but very little else. We talked about the reasons for all this: the constraints under which we felt we operated in our different subject areas and the pressures of time caused by syllabus content and requirements.

Aware of the dangers of generalisation, we agreed to begin our investigation by trying to obtain some sort of snapshot of our pupils' writing diet, first by looking at some examples of written work that pupils had recently done, and second, by persuading two classes of pupils to keep writing diaries in which they recorded: what they wrote, the nature of the task, the amount of writing done, the time available, the audience and any further comments they wished to add.

The diaries, rough and ready blunt instruments that they were, turned out to be a good place to start – particularly in a secondary school where, of course, there is a real danger that nobody is taking an overall view of the writing that pupils are asked to undertake during the course of a day, a week or a year. Those dividing walls of the secondary curriculum can be very high and rigid at times. When we peered over, I think we were all genuinely surprised, even in the light of our earlier comments, by: the sheer quantity of 'end product' writing pupils were expected to produce, the limited opportunities available for redrafting or editing, the lack of choice of task or format, and the 'teacher-centredness' of an activity for which the teacher was, invariably, the only audience. It was a picture which didn't seem to vary much from subject to subject. In a way it deflated us, but at least the diaries had identified some aspects of writing which clearly needed further investigation and development.

Looking at each other's examples was much more difficult. In retrospect, perhaps this was the wrong time to do this. Even though the members of the group knew each other very well, because we were all from different subject areas we weren't necessarily used to working with each other. We hadn't had the time to develop, for example, a shared vocabulary, and we didn't yet have that sense of collective enterprise which is so necessary for groups such as this. Consequently, we were all very wary of asking each other the very basic questions that we needed to ask about pupils' work. We remained polite. Trust takes time to establish. Good friends in the secondary staff-room can remain very distant professionally!

Meanwhile, I was quietly beginning to panic. Where on earth were we going? How were we going to get our investigations started while everybody was being so very careful about what they shared and said? Who was going to take the plunge?

Ed did. Ed is head of the Geography department. In our first discussions about the writing demands made of pupils in our different subjects, Ed had talked about what he saw as the difficulty of reconciling a more open approach to writing with his concerns for subject content and methodology. He said that he'd considered trying out such approaches in the past but had always ended up asking himself, '*But is it really Geography?*' Unbeknown to the rest of the group, Ed decided to see for himself what might happen when a more open approach to writing tasks was adopted. He experimented by encouraging a class of first-year pupils to write freely about a set of contrasting landscapes/cityscapes. Surprised not only by the empathetic quality of their writing but also by their willingness to speculate about what was shown in the pictures, he decided to extend his investigation by inviting groups of fifth-year pupils to write, in role, as various interested parties in an inquiry concerning the proposed closure of a local colliery. Finding that such an approach could produce writing that most certainly was Geography, and effective Geography at that, Ed came to our next meeting with examples of the pupils' work to show us.

That first investigative work of Ed's was the crucial moment in our group's development. Until that point we'd been on safe if unfamiliar ground, in that we were still just talking rather than doing. The fact that Ed was prepared to try something different in his classroom and return to share what had happened with a group of 'curricular strangers' made, I think, all the difference. His example certainly encouraged us to begin to undertake classroom work ourselves. A series of after-school meetings followed during the next few months, as members of the group took it in turn to describe and show to the rest of us what they'd been doing to investigate those issues about writing which our first discussions and then our diary survey had raised. Different members of the group took up different issues in different ways. In Maths, John investigated ways of helping his pupils in the reporting of their investigative work for GCSE. In French, Olwyn's pupils worked in groups to make information sheets for other, younger pupils. Cory experimented by allowing her RE pupils to determine their own mode and format for reporting their discussions. Fay looked at ways of using writing to foster empathy in her History pupils. Alan's less confident pupils discovered the potential of the microcomputer to help with the writing and production of storybooks for younger pupils.

I sometimes wondered whether this was really the right approach. Shouldn't we be tackling one issue at a time – and tackling it as a group? Was there a danger of the work losing its coherence and sense of direction? With hindsight, I think that in the case of our group we were probably right to proceed in the way we did. Dealing with all the issues one at a time would not have been a realistic option for a group which was meeting voluntarily, out of school hours. The way in which we worked also allowed different members of the group to identify their own priorities for investigation – necessary in a group containing teachers from such a wide range of curriculum backgrounds. The variety also helped us to keep our momentum. Often, one teacher's activity sparked off another's, and we found ourselves continually asking new questions and identifying further issues.

The synthesis began to emerge with time. It became clearer and clearer that most of our subject-based concerns with writing were, in fact, shared concerns about the role of writing in learning. When Fay observed that Cory's pupils' reports of their findings on the subject of prejudice had a direct relevance to the work her pupils were doing on the rise of Fascism, it sparked off the idea of tackling the writing issues we wanted to investigate through a genuinely cross-curricular collaboration. For all of us, this seemed a logical extension of the work we'd been developing in the project so far. However, agreeing on a topic or theme for collaboration was a more difficult matter. Experience with another working group in a secondary school where some of the teachers had decided to work together in this way had suggested to me that, in a cross-curricular project, it's quite important to try to move away from the usual syllabus content. One of the difficulties that the other group had experienced in an otherwise successful investigation was that, for all sorts of reasons, teachers sometimes tend to come to familiar material with a predetermined approach. We tried to build on that group's experience by choosing topics for our investigations which would involve new content for the classes concerned. Eventually, we settled on a subdivision of our (now extended!) working group into two parallel groups, both concerned with the planning of a programme of work which would cross curricular boundaries and, we hoped, generate a more open and balanced diet of writing for the pupils concerned. One group worked on a programme for a specific third-year class on the theme of the 'Home Front' in English, French, History, Home Economics and RE. The other group, involving teachers of English, Geography, Maths and Science, brought a variety of fourth-year classes into collaboration on the topic of plans for a local bypass. Both groups planned to work to a tight schedule, involving pupils in roughly six weeks' work. In the event, the collaboration took months rather than weeks, as the pupils' work developed in ways which the groups hadn't anticipated. A major learning outcome for the teachers concerned was the need to plan such collaborative enterprises on a more flexible basis. It takes only an unforeseen spin-off or a staff absence for the best laid plans to go awry! In the case of the 'Home Front' work this occurred when the third-year class decided that the most appropriate way for them to communicate the learning that had taken place would be to stage a massive end-of-term presentation for other pupils and parents, involving a range of displays and activities including an hour-long musical production written and performed by the pupils. One teacher from outside the group commented that their presentation demonstrated more learning than several exercise books full of notes ever could.

The group working on the theme of the local bypass demonstrated that GCSE coursework requirements in different subject areas could be satisfied more coherently for the pupils through cross-curricular collaboration. For example, a survey of local residents' feelings was designed during English lessons, went through a process of data analysis and graphical representation in Maths, and found its way into pupils' Geography folders as part of their GCSE submission on the topic. At this level, cross-curricular collaboration can not only expand and broaden the writing diet, but also rationalise the sometimes burdensome demands which are made of pupils.

As the extracts from my diary for March demonstrate, development has continued. Further cross-curricular programmes, gradually involving more and more members of staff, have evolved from that initial work. First- and second-year pupils have been working with teachers from different subject areas on the production of an information pack about 'Our School' for next year's intake. Pupils in the fifth and sixth years have been making their own newspaper about the world of work. Discussions about writing inside and outside school have been broadened through the involvement of ex-pupils and employers. As I said at the beginning, this seems to me to be the best kind of writing (or language) policy – one which is driven by the notion of teachers working at shared concerns by investigating them together.

Of course, this isn't the only possible approach to that vexed question of how to get at the writing and learning issue with colleagues from different curriculum areas. Where it's possible to bring teachers of, for example, Maths or Science together to look at the role of writing in learning in a particular area of the curriculum, much can be achieved. However, within the context of a typical secondary school, such as the one referred to here, there exists additional potential for collective investigation – a resource too rich to be ignored.

What conclusions might be drawn from our experience in Mid Glamorgan, as typified by the case of this particular school? I would identify four major ones. The first is that the development of a school writing policy should not be English led. In the school in question, the English department was certainly involved, but, sensibly, never attempted to dominate discussion or determine direction. If it is to be successful in practice, a writing policy needs to be commonly owned.

The second conclusion is that the best way of developing a policy is through a programme of practical investigation, rather than through planning on paper.

The third is that in the context of a secondary school, cross-curricular collaboration is a very effective way of bringing shared concerns about writing and learning into the open, and of generating the necessary dynamic for change.

The fourth and final conclusion is inescapable. It is that if genuine development is to occur, it is vital that provision is made for teachers from different curriculum backgrounds to meet, talk and reflect together, and that those teachers are supported effectively in their enterprise.

ENDNOTE – PAM CZERNIEWSKA

I'm sure that all teachers involved in the National Writing Project would agree with Richard Landy's conclusions. It takes courage to mount a critique of a curriculum area as large as writing. It was successful because it was based on actual classroom practice, and because the teachers involved could support each other through their explorations and reflections. The pressure to change current practices came from within the classrooms – and with it came an enormous amount of hard work and a compensating quantity of satisfaction.

Chapter 21

Teaching writing
Process or genre?

Janet Maybin

INTRODUCTION

During the 1970s and 1980s an approach to teaching literacy, usually referred to as *process writing*, became influential in North America. Drawing on the work of Donald Graves and Donald Murray, this approach spread to Australia. Many ideas were taken up by the British National Writing Project and have now been incorporated into the National Curriculum. Process writing shifts the focus from the finished product to the processes which pupils need to go through as writers. It aims to give pupils a greater sense of ownership and enhance pupils' commitment to their work. This approach has been a major influence on policy and classroom practice in many schools. Since the mid-1980s, however, an alternative writing pedagogy has been gathering strength in Australia, and, at least in that country, looks set to replace process writing as the main teaching orthodoxy. The *genre approach* developed from the work of Michael Halliday and draws heavily on his theory of functional linguistics. Halliday argues that we have developed very specific ways of using language in relation to how certain things are accomplished within our culture, and that different contexts and language purposes are associated with different registers, or genres of language. Genres encode knowledge and relationships in particular ways through the use of different language structures. Learning about a particular subject discipline, therefore, involves also learning about specific ways of using language. We expect pupils to write in a number of different specific ways in school, and we assess them according to how well they manage to reproduce these different genres, but we never actually tell them how to do it. Proponents of the genre approach argue that making the genres explicit and showing how to write them will enable pupils to understand more fully how knowledge is constructed in different academic disciplines. It will also empower pupils to deal with the various written genres used in the adult world.

These two approaches suggest different responses to fundamental questions about teaching writing in school:

- What is involved in the process of becoming a writer?
- What are our criteria for good writing, and how are these communicated to pupils?
- When and how should teachers intervene in students' writing?

PROCESS WRITING

Graves' initial premise, and the first sentence of his 1983 book *Writing: teachers and children at work*, is 'Children want to write'. He suggests that the writing process can be divided into a number of distinct stages, from the initial discussion of ideas through drafting, conferencing, revising and editing to publishing. The teacher plays a vital supportive role in each of these stages, but it is important that the writing topic is chosen by the pupils, and that they retain ownership of the writing throughout. Thereby, Graves suggests, students can find their own authentic writing voice and development of the craft of writing will come naturally, including attention to surface features like spelling and handwriting.

Graves suggests that teachers can support and check on pupils' progress through writing 'conferences'. Below is an example of a conference on 'working with the main idea' (conferences can be about any aspect of writing, from choosing a topic to punctuation, and can be held with groups of pupils as well as individuals). According to Graves, Mr Sitka suggests how Anton might move on in his writing while still leaving him in control of the piece through asking 'questions that teach'.

MR SITKA: Where are you now in the draft?

ANTON: Oh, I've just got the part down about when we won in overtime.

MR SITKA: So, you've just got started then. Well, it's probably too early to tell what it's about. What did you figure to do next with the draft, then?

ANTON: I don't know. I don't want to just write and wander around. I've written about when we've won but it sort of just has me stuck at that point.

MR SITKA: Tell me about that coach of yours.

ANTON: God, how I hated him! I almost quit three or four times maybe. I thought he couldn't stand me. He'd yell, catch every little thing I did wrong. We'd run and run until we couldn't stand up. Have some passing drills, then he'd run us some more. He'd just stand there yellin' and puffin' on his cigar. Course he was right. When we won the championship, I think it went way back to those early practices.

MR SITKA: The way you tell it sounds as though you have quite a live beginning to your story. Try just writing about early practices, then see what your piece is about.

In process writing pupils are seen as apprentice authors writing for real audiences. Their writing is published and put into the class library for other pupils to read. Classrooms become workshops and communities of writers, where teachers are also writing and encouraging pupils to develop particular kinds of behaviours for each stage in the writing process rather than focusing on specific skills in isolation. For many teachers associated with the British National Writing Project (1985–8), Graves' work seemed to provide a structured way to support pupils' writing in accordance with the English curriculum model of personal creativity and growth through language (see Dixon 1967, Barnes *et al.* 1969).

In addition to assimilating ideas from process writing, the NWP tried to follow through some of the implications from recent research by anthropologists and cultural psychologists. This suggests that reading and writing should be seen as social practices rather than as collections of decontextualised skills, and that classroom methods should take account of the meaning and function of writing practices outside the school (e.g. Heath 1983, Street 1984, Scribner and Cole 1988). NWP teachers tried to build a range of real purposes and audiences into pupils' work, and to develop more explicit links with the outside world; for example pupils might be writing for senior citizens or to a newspaper, or exchanging stories and journals with pupils in other parts of the country.

CONTENT AND VOICE

There are many accounts by teachers of how an emphasis on process, ownership and real purposes can produce outstanding pupil writing and high levels of enthusiasm and commitment. A number of critics, however, have questioned how absolute students' control over the content of their writing should be, whether the notion of students developing a personal writing voice through process writing is sustainable, and whether students should not be receiving more direct help with the structure of their writing.

Pam Gilbert (1988, quoted in Czerniewska 1992) suggests that sometimes the content of students' writing needs challenging, for example where they are uncritically reproducing sexist or racist stereotypes. She quotes a story written collaboratively in a process writing classroom by some 10-year-old boys in which most children in their class appear as characters who are attacked by maurading Efa Bunnies. In 'Bloodbath Efa Bunnies' the boys are represented as Rambo-like heroes while the girls are either killed or married off, with one exception. This girl, who was the largest in the class, jumps on the bunnies and the boys' text reads ' "AAAA! My God! Super Blubber!" they said as they got up. "Run!" ' Gilbert suggests 'No need to kill off this female: her size and aggression have effectively excluded her anyway. (What worse fate for a girl than to be called Super Blubber?)' This story was duly typed, bound and added to the class library without any criticism or questioning. Particularily at a time when teachers are checking school resources for instances of sexism and racism, Gilbert suggests that we should be encouraging students to interrogate the social stereotypes they reproduce in their own writing, perhaps in the case of these boys through encouraging more consideration of the audience for whom the story is intended. (Interestingly, two days after 'Bloodbath Efa Bunnies' was placed in the class library, it mysteriously disappeared . . . .) Janet White also criticises process writing for ignoring the cultural construction of writing practices within which pupils are differently positioned according to, for instance, their sex and ethnic background. 'Giving pupils power over the writing process does not necessarily mean that they are writing more powerful texts . . . (perhaps) all we have helped pupils to own are versions of cultural clichés' (in National Writing Project 1990).

Reproducing their own experience may also mean that students cover only a limited range of topics over a year, and produce an even narrower range of written genres. Martin *et al.* (1987) quote an aboriginal classroom where children's writing covered only four topics in the year: visiting friends and relatives, going hunting for bush tucker, sporting events and movies or TV shows they have seen. These events were all written about in the 'recount' genre – a simple sequential retelling of events. Rather than giving pupils freedom, Martin *et al.* suggest that this approach is actually restricting children's development, and denying them access to the writing skills which would provide them with power in the real world.

Graves' notion of how students develop a personal writing voice is also questioned by Gilbert. She suggests there are unacknowledged criteria that determine which 'voices' are acceptable to the teacher but that these criteria (which privilege a particular kind of class and literary experience) are never made explicit to pupils. Gilbert argues that, although the criteria become particularily important in relation to the assessment of students' work at secondary level, most students still have just to guess at what they think individual teachers will like.

Gilbert uses two examples of 16-year-olds' writing to explain why framing the purpose and audience for a writing task and providing resources and discussion still does not necessarily give students enough help with the style and structure required for the piece. Susan and Ken's class were asked to write a magazine article on the topic 'Are creative writers always abnormal?' They had a class discussion about what was abnormal and were given information sheets about various authors from which they could draw evidence. Their teacher also read them extracts from published magazine articles. The openings of Susan and Ken's pieces are given in Figures 21.1 and 21.2.

The teacher was disappointed that out of all the class only Susan had

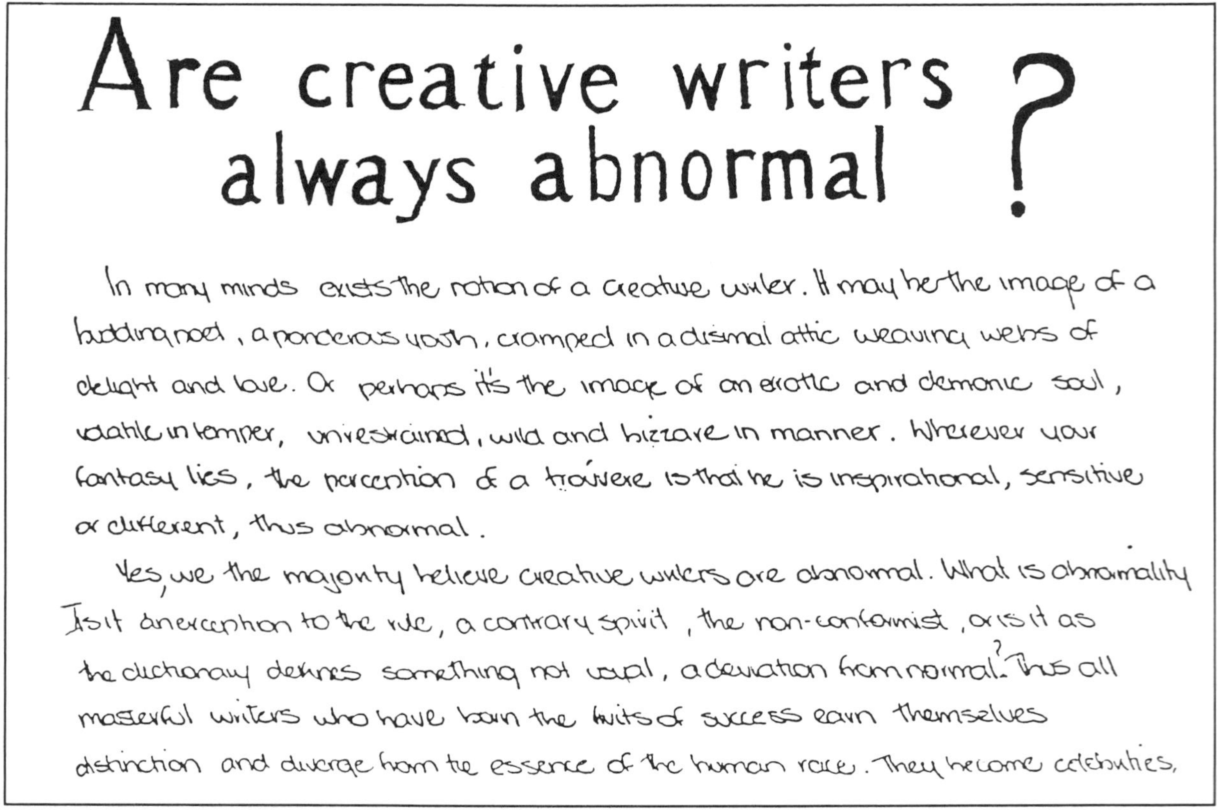

Are creative writers always abnormal ?

In many minds exists the notion of a creative writer. It may be the image of a budding poet, a ponderous youth, cramped in a dismal attic weaving webs of delight and love. Or perhaps it's the image of an erotic and demonic soul, volatile in temper, undisciplined, wild and bizarre in manner. Whatever your fantasy lies, the perception of a true writer is that he is inspirational, sensitive or different, thus abnormal.

Yes, we the majority believe creative writers are abnormal. What is abnormally? Is it a deviation to the rule, a contrary spirit, the non-conformist, or is it as the dictionary defines something not usual, a deviation from normal? Thus all masterful writers who have born the traits of success earn themselves distinction and diverge from the essence of the human race. They become celebrities.

Figure 21.1 Extract from English assignment by 'good' student (reduced size)

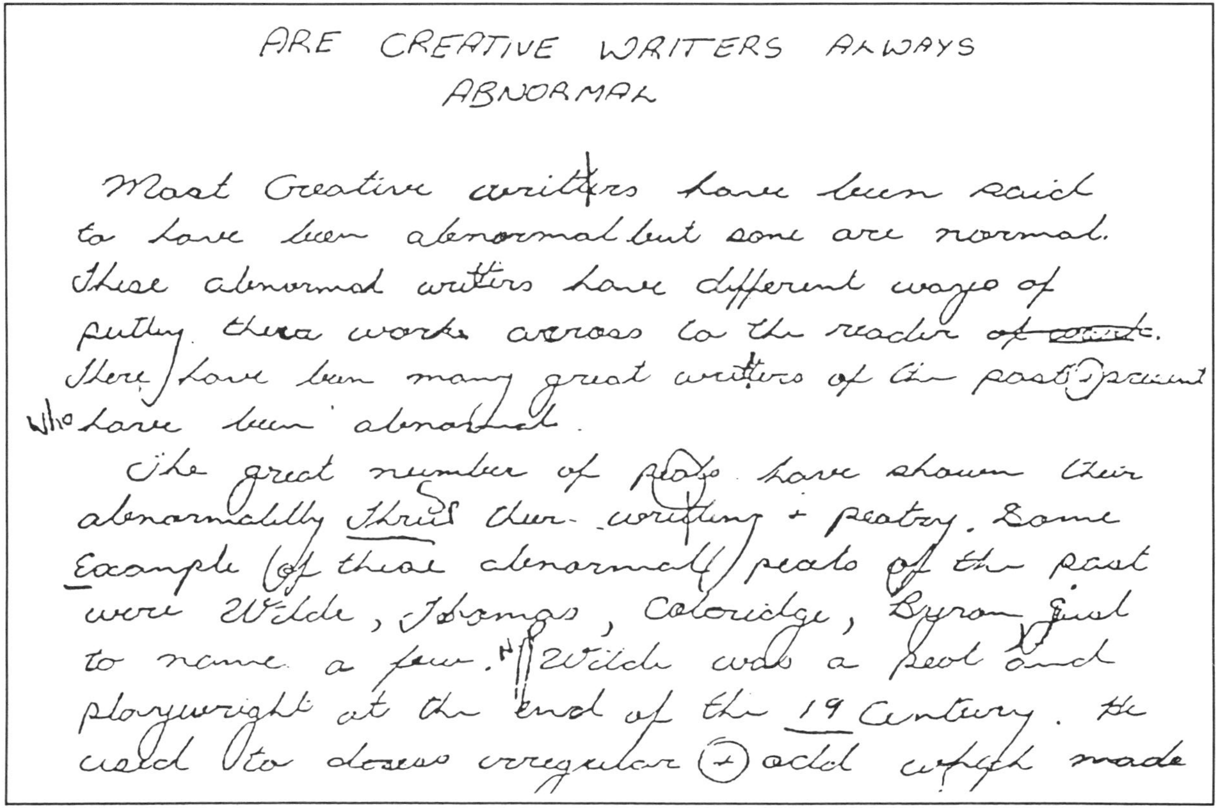

ARE CREATIVE WRITERS ALWAYS
ABNORMAL

Most Creative writers have been said
to have been abnormal but some are normal.
These abnormal writers have different ways of
putting their works across to the reader of ~~~~~.
They have been many great writers of the past/present
who have been abnormal.

Like great number of ~~~~~ have shown their
abnormality through their own writing + poetry. Some
Example (s) of that abnormal poets of the past
were Wilde, Johonsgo, Coloridge, Byron and
to name a few. Which was a poet and
playwright at the end of the 19 Century. the
world [+] also made

Figure 21.2 Extract from English assignment by less competent student (reduced size)
Source: Gilbert 1992

managed to produce 'that funny blend between personal writing and yet impersonal writing because it's in a newspaper', and she felt at a loss about how to help the other students organise pieces of information into an acceptable journalistic format, and take on the particular linguistic features which identify a journalistic style. Susan creates the effect her teacher was looking for through using first person plural pronouns, rhetorical questions and pairs of juxtaposed sentences, but Ken's assignment reads like a school essay and is based on the notes the teacher gave the class. In her comments on Ken's work, the teacher focuses on the surface features of his writing: 'Ken, you must proof-read *much* more carefully. A magazine article cannot have such basic errors.' While these are undeniably a problem, Gilbert suggests that he also needs to be taught how to reproduce a specific written genre.

THE GENRE APPROACH

'Learning the genres of one's culture is both part of entering into it with understanding, and part of developing the necessary ability to change it . . . . Capacity to recognise, interpret and write genre is capacity to exercise choice' (Martin *et al*. 1987). Proponents of the genre approach argue that writing is very different from talk, and pupils cannot simply pick up the specialist linguistic structures involved: they need to be taught. Written genres tend to be more condensed and abstract, frequently involving the use of nominal forms, for example 'the *failure* of the crusades', 'the *precipitation* of the solid', 'the *betrayal* of Macbeth'. Our culture also requires that pupils learn to use genres which are differently structured depending on the purposes and audiences for their writing. For example, they need to be able to reproduce procedures, descriptions, reports, explanations, arguments and various kinds of narratives. These all have distinctive overall structures (for instance, a simple narrative structure involves an initial orientation, a complication, a resolution and a coda), and particular kinds of grammatical uses and vocabulary. To teach a specific genre the teacher is advised first to provide exemplars and discuss their particular features with the students. The teacher then jointly negotiates a piece of writing in this genre with the class, and after this the students research and draft a piece of writing in the chosen genre. There is further consultation with the teacher and finally the piece may be published for the class library.

The genre approach focuses strongly on how to construct particular kinds of texts. Unlike process writing, the teacher has a strong directional input at the beginning and explicitly scaffolds students' writing structures. Martin *et al*. (1987) perceive the example quoted above where Mr Sitka is helping Anton as an example of poor and unfocused conferencing which will not help Anton to shape the structure of his narrative, or to avoid 'just writing and wandering about'.

It may even be that a narrative is not the appropriate genre for Anton's piece. The Australian genre teachers argue that the emphasis on narrative rather than expository genres in many primary schools leaves children inadequately prepared for writing in secondary school, and unable to engage with knowledge in the different subject areas. Denying pupils access to the genre means denying them access to the subject. They are left, Martin *et al.* suggest, stranded in their own words, cut off from what history, science and so on are really about. (This is an almost directly opposite argument to the one mounted in Britain in the 1970s by Britton and Rosen, who advocated allowing students to use more personal and expressive language across the curriculum. For them, subject genres could set up artificial and unnecessary barriers which *prevented* students from engaging with subject knowledge.)

A number of criticisms have been made of the genre approach. First, although genre theorists claim to be treating texts as socially constructed out of particular contexts and relationships, proponents often make rather naive claims about empowering pupils through teaching them to reproduce particular genres of texts. As Barrs (1991–2) points out, it's not just knowing how to write that matters in this world, but

> being in a position to ensure that your writing reaches an audience, and then is noticed and read. We could all learn how to write certain powerful genres – such as high level memos – but this wouldn't increase our access to power by one jot.

Second, teaching about genre sometimes offers a rather impoverished model of learning, with little sense of process or development. Knowledge about genres is transmitted from teachers to students, with little opportunity for active student-led learning or collaborative work. Third, there is the question of who determines the genres which are to be taught in school and whether the values and power relationships which are encoded in dominant cultural forms and their associated genres should be accepted as 'given' by teachers and uncritically transmitted to their students.

CONCLUSION

The process writing and genre approaches derive from different theoretical models: the first treats language as a personal resource, and the second, language as a social construct. In the first, learning to write is seen as a natural process supported by the teacher who creates a motivating working context with real purposes and audiences. In the second, the teacher's responsibility is to equip students with linguistic skills so that they can read and reproduce the genres which will give access to subject knowledge and power in the outside world. Criteria for good writing in the process model emphasise personal creativity and effectiveness in terms of audience and purpose while genre teachers, although also wanting to ensure effectiveness, assess this through how successfully students have managed to reproduce particular genres of writing.

Both approaches claim to 'empower' students, the first through giving them ownership of their writing and the second through equipping them with important linguistic skills. Taking both these approaches together suggests that they could be seen as complementary rather than oppositional. There is a need to build motivation and learning opportunities into the process of writing, but also to ensure that students understand and can work with the linguistic structures needed for specific genres. In addition, we need to look at how writing practices in the classroom relate to those used outside the school, and at whether there is scope for extending the range of activities used with students. Finally, one of the distinctive qualities of writing in relation to oral language is that it enables one to stand back from and reflect on one's own ideas and understanding. This kind of metalinguistic activity is central to intellectual development and work with pupils on writing should include critical reflection, not only about process and structural aspects of their writing but also about its content – the values it expresses and how far it constitutes an engagement with real and important issues of learning and understanding.

REFERENCES

Barnes, D., Britton, J. and Rosen, H. (1969) *Language, the learner and the school.* London: Penguin.
Barrs, M. (1991–2) 'Genre theory: what's it all about?' in *Language Matters* No. 1.
Czerniewska, P. (1992) *Learning about writing: the early years.* Oxford: Blackwell.
Dixon, J. (1967) *Growth through English.* Oxford: Oxford University Press.
Gilbert, P. (1992) 'Authorizing disadvantage: authorship and creativity in the language classroom' in Christie, F. (ed.) *Literacy for a changing world.* Victoria: The Australian Council for Educational Research.
Graves, D. (1983) *Writing: teachers and children at work.* Portsmouth, New Hampshire: Heinemann Educational Books.
Heath, S.B. (1983) *Ways with words: language, life and work in communities and classrooms.* Cambridge: Cambridge University Press.
Martin, J.R., Christie, F. and Rothery, J. (1987) 'Social processes in education: a reply to Sawyer and Watson (and others)' in Reid, I. (ed.) *The place of genre in learning: current debates.* Centre for Studies in Literary Education, Deakin University.
National Writing Project (1990) *What are writers made of? Issues of gender and writing.* Walton-on-Thames: Thomas Nelson.
Scribner, S. and Cole, M. (1988) 'Unpacking literacy' in Mercer, N. (ed.) *Language and literacy from an educational perspective*, Vol. 1. Milton Keynes: Open University Press.
Street, B. (1984) *Literacy in theory and practice.* Cambridge: Cambridge University Press.

Chapter 22

School students' writing

Some principles

Michael Rosen

In this chapter I want to look at the place of creative writing in the secondary English curriculum.

The 'liberal humanistic' basis for creative writing lay in the following kind of statements:

- Narrative is a primary act of mind. It is a seemingly genetic characteristic or at least common to all cultures. We deduce from this that we all need to be narrators in our daily lives. English studies can, in short, help students become better narrators.

- Narratives of all kinds help situate ourselves in relation to friends, enemies, parents, genders, institutions, other cultures, other classes. They help us to do this through such characteristics of reader response as identification and projection whereby we try out various actions and emotions through the safety of the reading situation. One way to understand these narratives, their structures and their objectives is to write narratives oneself. Writing narratives is a way of critiquing all narrative.

- In writing of any kind we are forced to impose a certain order on experience. Writing is in essence linear – we cannot make two statements at the same time – and 'non-expressive' in the sense that apart from a few limited signs such as underlining it has no extralingual apparatus. No gestures, tones of voice or raised eyebrows. Communicative writing has to be learnt, and the best teachers are an 'audience', to tell the writer whether meanings have been made.

- As one example of ordering of experience, writing has the advantages of externalising, preserving and sharing. Externalising is psychologically important in that it enables the writer to witness him- or herself, to stand in judgement on statements concerning self. Preserving is a way of validating self, rather as a photo album does. Self-respect is difficult when people are deprived of means of establishing identity. The preservation of important events, feelings, attitudes and cultural practices in the form of writing is therefore important in respect of identity. Writing is a cultural form that is easily and quickly produced (unlike, say, sculpture), easily and quickly shared and so holds out the possibility of writers and readers comparing experiences and interpretations. Again, psychologically this is important as a way of overcoming isolation and self-blame.

Within that humanistic framework, there have been many variations of emphasis and method. One would only have to compare, say, the work of Chris Searle as shown through such books as *Stepney Words, The World in a Classroom, Classrooms of Resistance* and, say, Jill Pirrie in *On Common Ground*. Or for that matter, the work I've outlined in *Did I Hear You Write?* and, say, Sandy Brownjohn in *Does It Have to Rhyme?* Some of these variations are in fact oppositions and it does no one any favours to ignore this. I would like to focus on one in particular.

There is a school of thought as evidenced both in theoretical statements in such places as *Signal*, a magazine concerned with children's literature, and in practice, in the hosts of books designed to teach children to write poetry, that states that children cannot run before they can walk. They must be shown poetic and narrative forms, inducted into learning them and imitating them. In this way they can interpret their experience in a satisfying and powerful way. The poetic and narrative forms talked about here are those that poets and writers have created and used over the last thousand years or so – ballads, haiku, sonnets, short stories, and so on.

In opposition to this, I, amongst others, have said this: to promote form as the starting point of writing denies the existential, cultural and ideological purposes of writing. Writing is only important if there are things you want to write about. The primary task of a teacher of writing for children (and inexperienced writers) is not to induct into form, but to help students discover the purposes and uses of writing: as satisfying ways of interpreting, preserving and sharing experience and imagination. Connecting with students' lives as led and their actual dreams and fantasies (1); creating an atmosphere of generosity to others' feelings and performances (2); fostering curiosity about all kinds of writing (3); creating appropriate audiences for students' work – peers, parents, younger children or whoever (4) – are all more important processes to gear up than introducing literary forms.

It is my experience that students will use, find, create and share forms of their own accord provided these other processes are in place (see *Did I Hear You Write?*). This is, of course, quite threatening to many teachers who thought that their role in encouraging writing was to *teach* writing. After all, what were all those college hours spent doing, if it wasn't learning how great writers write? I am suggesting that this approach denies the creative base of writing. Writers need to find both the 'what' and the 'how' of writing at the same time.

There is also an ideological question surrounding form. That is, in short, which forms? Most, but not all, of the formalists privilege certain forms over others. High on the list of poetry is the metaphor. In fact, implicit in most poetic practice, criticism and teaching of the last fifty years has been that to be poetic is to be metaphorical. However, this is not how poetry needs to be or for that matter always was. Anecdotal, polemic, imagist and much narrative poetry has worked on other principles. Again, various 'high art' forms such as the sonnet have been held out as summits of a hierarchy. In reply, I would say that there is no school student who is without a repertoire of forms from jokes, comics, TV soaps, pop songs, scurrilous and obscene rhyme, greetings cards, autograph book aphorisms, stand-up comic dramatic monologues, and advertising's ruthless plundering of all forms of discourse. Unless you as teacher have an ideological objection to these popular and public forms, then there is no artistic reason why students shouldn't feel free to use them in their writing. In other words, though I prioritise experience as the starting point for writing, I don't dismiss form. Rather, I ask the question, which forms and why?

Implicit in my argument is the vexed word 'creative'. All human linguistic performance is creative, in the sense that every statement we make involves taking from 'langue' and making 'parole', taking from the shared cultural base of language and making an individual utterance. But that said, it is clear that we can be more or less creative. In general usage, we mean this when we say that something is really 'original' or conversely 'old hat', 'corny' or 'derivative'. But there is another sense in which writing can be more or less creative: in the degree to which it is transformative for the writer. And this is the nub of the matter. For me, writing is important because it changes people.

Leaving aside the question of audience, writing changes writers. In shaping experience, externalising it and sharing it, I stand the chance of becoming more aware of what I was, what I am and what I might be. In making anything, I am no longer the same person. Making is itself an experience that goes into memory, but will also have effects on all future acts of making. By sharing what I make with an audience engaged in the same practice, we foster an idea that language, culture, fantasy, plot, form and a lot more besides are not 'givens'. They are all humanly made, changeable and variable practices. We live in a world that emphasises its 'givens'. Film and TV are high-level technological products that our students are unable to match or change. They live through many social institutions that seem beyond their control: TV, school, even family life. Writing holds out the prospect of being an activity that challenges the givens, or even challenges the right for there to be givens in the first place. In a world where the institutions we live and work in are clearly so unsatisfactory, that seems to me to be a highly worthwhile activity. On the other hand, if, at the very moment we offer students a practice that contains this active, transformative potential, we say, in effect, don't do it like that, do it like this, we snatch from them a large part of this creative potential.

Earlier, I outlined four principles of practice for writing: connecting with students' lives as led and their actual dreams and fantasies (1); creating an atmosphere of generosity to others' feelings and performances (2); fostering curiosity about all kinds of writing (3); creating appropriate audiences for students' work – peers, parents, younger children or whoever (4).

(1) In practice, this means that we have to overcome adult prejudices about youth culture, adolescence and childhood. These may revolve around concepts of young people as being in some sense incomplete human beings. Most educational and sociological theory treats children as on a developmental slope. This encourages us to treat children's lived experience as if it was on the way to being something else, rather than valid on its own terms for the child concerned. If we are serious about asking children to write, it has to be serious about accepting their world picture, their interests, their outlook, their cultures. These may reflect a child-dominated world, where children appear almost to be their own ethnic group with their own games, language, customs and the like, or it may reflect an adult-dominated world with children as people responding to adult constructions, rules, domination and nurture. We must be prepared to be open to both and listen to what students have to say about all this, if we want them to write about things that matter to them.

(2) One of the ways we can become interested in being writers is to find out more about how other people have written. 'Other people' should be taken here as both peer group, teacher and 'literature'. Part of becoming better writers is listening to how other people are doing it and have done it. As a teacher with some experience of reading, we are in a good position as a researcher and provider of appropriate reading, reading that connects. For example, anyone who has worked with black children knows of the excitement that can be generated when students come across black writing by someone like Benjamin Zephaniah or Grace Nichols. I remember listening to a 14-year-old girl complaining that there weren't any books in the library that were interesting. Having talked to her for about half an hour or so, I found out that her parents came from Spain after the Civil War, so I suggested she read Hemingway's *Farewell to Arms* which she gobbled up and asked for more. Boys of 12 and 13 often seem drawn to a kind of science fiction fantasy narrative but find it difficult to measure up to the massive dimensions of the books or films they read. Paul Jennings is a fantasy writer whose stories have young people as heroes. They start out in realist situations, become bizarre and weird and then resolve themselves in quite challenging ways. The stories are very short and written in a breathless, almost film-script form. They offer up possibilities to otherwise quite alienated students.

(3) and (4) Writing has to live on fertile ground. It has to be wanted and loved for it to survive. It cannot survive in an atmosphere of indifference, cynicism, and harsh judgement. This means that amongst the best things that a teacher can 'do' with students' writing is to discuss with them ways of sharing and distributing their work. Sometimes it may be appropriate for

them to work on word processors, produce wall displays, fanzines, play-scripts and so on. Anyone committed to this approach will soon find how writing and reading can become a kind of self-perpetuating motion with writers being critics, editors and readers at the same time. Where possible, you can widen that audience to other classes, parents and community. A teacher is no better a critic than these other groups but simply an equal to them and weighing up opposing critical views is a valuable component in writing.

I would add to these comments a few thoughts:

1 Drafting and redrafting are not virtues in themselves. If we ask students to redraft then we should be very clear on what the criteria are, and whether those criteria are valid. Most redrafting I see is in order for students to satisfy fairly conventional and stereotypical views by teachers of what 'good writing' is, usually involving metaphors and adjectives. Features of 'good writing' can also be economy, good dialogue, clear individual voice, wit, surprise, irony and so on. The point of redrafting is for the writer to internalise the audience's need to re-create the pictures, emotions and motives of a text. How will I help the reader get hold of what I want to say? Some of the best critiques of writing that I've heard are: 'I don't get that' and 'What did you mean by that?' They are 'best' not because they are accurate critiques but because they generate better writing.

2 Writing privileges the 'written mode'. That is to say, when we think of writing we think of certain constructions that belong entirely to writing and not to speaking. The division is in many cases becoming blurred. Anyone reading the *Sun* knows consciously or not that its text is often written as if it was someone speaking. The spoken word has in the past been regarded variously by the powerful as inferior, dangerous, subversive, ugly, inaccurate, wrong, sloppy and so on. These are political value judgements made about ordinary people's lives. My own view of the spoken word is that it is the main source of creative invention in the language, it is the way we make meanings out of experience and ideas whether these are transmitted orally or in writing, it is a major way in which people express their identities and cultures, it is the major way in which we are all social beings.

Rather than turn our backs on the oral as inferior, inaccurate or at least unsatisfactory, we should use it as a foundation. Storytelling, play-scripts, dramatic monologues, speeches, eavesdroppings, proverbs, favourite sayings, modes of verbal punishment, boasting, teasing, commentating, interrogating are all areas that can provide tremendous scope for students to talk/write/perform in the voices they know well.

3 Poetry is no longer the rule-bound discourse that it used to be. It no longer has to obey rules decided by academic conventions of rhythm and

rhyme. In fact, it is no longer possible to define poetry using an external observation. Poets define poetry by saying, this is a poem. In fact, what has happened is that some poets say 'this is a poem' simply because it adopts the rhetorical devices, tones of voice, and page layout that previous poets have used. Others say they are poets because they stand up in public spaces and use oral devices that previous poets have used like chanting or even dancing. Others have described their work as poetry but it seems to belong to other forms of discourse: political speeches, advertising, transcriptions of gossip, jokes, proverbs, riddles and so on. It is almost as if the totality of what is now offered to us as poetry is a form that is defined as without any specific form other than it has permission to borrow and scavenge from anywhere else: previous poetry, legal submissions, letters, broadcasts, sermons, graffiti and so on. This makes it particularly valuable in schools. For whatever psychological reasons, we all know that adolescents in particular enjoy parody, mockery, demolition of pomposity, privilege, authority and power. There are many examples of modern poetry that do this at the level of discourse itself (see *Culture Shock* (Puffin) edited by M.R.). Students may be unaware that such a poetry exists, that so ties in with their own desires and linguistic activity. They may actively resist calling it poetry. No matter. For them to attempt the equivalent on, say, parents, teachers, TV personalities, characters in charge of running local amenities, situations in sport would be to use writing in one of its most powerful functions. After all, it was the very same ex-Secretary of State who introduced the National Curriculum, Kenneth Baker, who edited a splendid little poetry anthology called, *I have no gun but I can spit*!

SOME USEFUL RESOURCES

Emotional Terrorism by Joolz (Bloodaxe). (Her books and records are available from 31 Rushton Terrace, Thornbury, W. Yorks.)

Gifted Wreckage by Roger McGough, Brian Patten and Adrian Henri (Talking Tape).

The Dread Affair by Benjamin Zephaniah (Arena). (His books and tapes are available from BZ Associates, PO Box 673, East Ham, London E6 3QD.)

Glad to Wear Glasses by John Hegley (André Deutsch).

Poetry Jump Up edited by Grace Nichols (Puffin).

Now Then Davos by Ian McMillan and Martyn Wiley (Amazing Collosal Press).

Standpoints edited by John L. Foster (Harrap).

New Angles edited by John Foster (Oxford).

Apples and Snakes (Pluto).

Talking Blues (Centerprise, 136/8 Kingsland High Street, London E8 2NS).

City Lights (English Centre, distributed by NATE).

In the Pink edited by 'The Raving Beauties' (The Women's Press).
No Holds Barred edited by 'The Raving Beauties' (The Women's Press).
Life Doesn't Frighten Me At All edited by John Agard (Heinemann).
Down to Earth and on its Feet – anthology (Bristol Broadsides).
The Popular Front of Contemporary Poetry (Apples and Snakes).

Michael Rosen (relevant material)

Poetry

Mind the Gap (Scholastic).
When Did You Last Wash Your Feet? (Collins).
You Tell Me (with Roger McGough) (Puffin).

Anthologies

Culture Shock (Puffin).
Action Replay (Puffin).
Speaking to You (with David Jackson) (Macmillan Educational).
The Chatto Book of Dissent (with David Widgery) (Chatto).

On writing

I See a Voice (Stanley Thornes).
Did I Hear You Write? (Scholastic).

Stories

The Deadman Tapes.

Video pack

Why Poetry? (six ten-minute performances by different poets on video +
   70 pp. set of photocopiable lesson notes and guidelines for writing
   activities) (Team Video, 105 Canalot, 222 Kensal Road, London W10
   5BN).

Chapter 23

Writing in imagined contexts

Jonothan Neelands

THE SOCIAL CONTEXT OF LANGUAGE USE

Learning to use language effectively involves recognising that what we say, what we hear, what we read, and what we write is in response to the social situation that we find ourselves in and our particular communication needs within that situation. The meanings that we exchange with each other through language are embedded in whatever social situation has produced them. The choices we make in selecting or decoding language are determined by our social position (status/culture) within the situation; the social position of our audience; and by our need and purpose in seeking to change or develop the situation we find ourselves in.

Learning to use language appropriately involves recognising that different social situations will produce different uses of language. The language of the courtroom is different from the language of the dance floor. We learn through experience to match the register and vocabulary of our speech to the particular requirements of the situation that we find ourselves in – we speak with respect and attention to grandparents, we avoid slang and non-standard English when we are applying for a job.

We also learn to recognise that certain kinds of social situations will share common linguistic characteristics. These groups, or genres of situation, will tend to produce similar forms and selections of language (a disagreement is a disagreement in whatever situation it might occur!). We begin to discover that more often than not these similarities of form and selection comply with shared cultural traditions in our uses of language. The language in which a trial is conducted is in part a response to the particular situation of the courtroom and those involved in it; but the language of the courtroom is also the result of a long historical process in which certain linguistic choices have become institutionalised. We learn to expect lawyers, judges and others to speak in a particular way.

In our culture we frequently adopt distinctive forms and selections of language when we find ourselves needing to report events (journalism); justify a point of view (deductive reasoning); collect evidence in order to develop a theory (research work). To use language effectively, and appropriately, we need to assess the situation we find ourselves in; our roles and need within that situation; the role of the audience within that situation. But we also need, as the courtroom example shows, to be aware of whatever cultural 'laws' (traditions) we may have learnt about the uses of language in situations that are similar to the one we find ourselves in – the genres of language.

It follows that the more that we can discover about the situation that has produced, or demands, a particular example of language use (spoken or written) the more we can know about the meanings and linguistic choices, including the choice of genre, which constitute the language found in the example.

For some young people simply being alive and open to the experience of language in their day-to-day lives teaches more about the relationships between language and situation than any textbook can; they are fortunate to live in the social and cultural conditions that provide a very broad range of different kinds of social situations – they have been read to, travel abroad, encouraged to discuss and negotiate their needs and desires; they are exposed to a wide range of literature and social experiences. But many young people are socially and culturally restricted, often for economic reasons, from experiencing the same rich diversity of situations and uses of language. How can the classroom provide all young people with the *experience* of language?

The classroom can only offer a distanced and once-removed experience of 'out-of-school' language uses. Language and situation can be talked about, but that's not the same thing as really experiencing a situation and discovering the language it will produce. The language experience offered in the classroom is usually restricted to teacher–pupil and pupil–pupil talk related to the classroom situation, unless the teacher decides to provide alternative language experiences by transforming the classroom situation into a different one through the use of drama.

DRAMATISING THE SOCIAL CONTEXT

To do any form of drama we need to create and agree on the characteristics of a particular situation – we need to decide who we are, where we are, when it's happening; what has just happened; what are we trying to make happen next? In drama we recognise that what we mean and the way in which we say it will be determined by the situation we have created – we 'role-play' language and actions in response to our imagined position within the situation that is being improvised. Through this process of building a situation and trying to behave 'realistically' within it we escape, in terms of our use of language at least, from the roles of teacher/pupil in the classroom. Young people can invent any situation or role they like and as a result have a different experience of language use, an experience that is freed from the usual language restrictions of the classroom.

Drama also offers other advantages as a medium for developing language awareness. It is practical, often fun, it allows young people to use their bodies as well as language in order to express themselves; everyday objects and clothing are used to represent different places, people and times. Drama is 'interactive' so part of the discovery of language in drama will be a result of speaking from a particular point of view and hearing others speak from a different point of view according to their perspective on the situation. This opportunity to look at how language is produced out of the interactions of people who have different relationships to the situation they find themselves in is not an abstract one. In drama, situations are improvised, or acted out, 'as if' they were actually happening – the students are involved as participants, feeling, discovering, thinking, manoeuvring through 'acting', and 'reacting', in response to the situation as it unfolds around them. The 'characters' in the drama appear before us behaving as we would expect them to if we were to meet them in life itself.

Through drama we create the conditions to explore language in the same way we explore it in life – through cultural experience, interaction and representation.

THE PROBLEM OF CONTEXTUALISING WRITING

The relationships between language and situation may be particularly difficult to understand when the language is provided in a written form. When we communicate our needs through writing we need to abstract language *from* the situation that produces it; we are no longer using language as participants but as spectators or recorders. The author writes in a particular situation, the audience reads it in another and the meanings embedded in the writing may refer to some other hypothetical situation or idea. A simple letter between friends will bridge the writer's context with the reader's but often by referring to all kinds of other situations in the form of news, gossip, reminiscences, theory. The genre of the writing must correspond to the communicative needs and purposes of the writer and readers who do not, generally, expect to be present at the same time in the same place. The choices about the genre of writing – is it to be a story, a newspaper article, a legal disposition, a set of instructions? – will also be determined by the content and by the nature of the social relationship between writer and readers.

WRITING IN RESPONSE TO DRAMA

In the following example drama is used to provide students with the experience they need to produce writing in response to a particular need and purpose. The example shows that the teacher is trying to overcome some of the difficulties of the writing task by giving the students the opportunity to build an appropriate context, discover the needs and concerns of the writer, meet and talk with the intended audience and select a mode of writing that is appropriate to audience, purpose and context.

The Toronto School Board in Canada uses a particular task as part of its battery of 'benchmark tests' which are assessed tasks (like SATs) used to establish levels of ability within its school population. One of the tasks is as follows: 'Following a one hour discussion each student should write a letter to a local newspaper raising an important environmental issue'. Not surprisingly children who come from homes where newspapers are read and discussed, where there is the luxury of time to discuss environmental issues and where letters may, from time to time, be written to editors of newspapers will do rather better, in this test, than their friends who don't. A one-hour classroom discussion cannot even out this disadvantage in terms of having previous social experience of the actual use of the genre of language required by the assessment task.

So, as part of a recent research project a class of children, whose experience of different uses of language was likely to be restricted by social and economic factors, were given a one-hour drama session instead of the discussion. They were shown a picture showing a local community of shops and houses surrounding a piece of dangerously derelict wasteland. They were invited to take on the roles of people living and working in this imagined environment, which was not unlike their own neighbourhood. After establishing, through various role-play exercises, the culture and interests of the community, a meeting was held in which the community resolved to use self-help to transform the wasteland into a leisure park; this action became a symbol of the community's desire for regeneration. 'If we can do this together, who knows what we might do next!'

A letter from the local government was introduced which informed the community that the land was to be used for government offices. The teacher asked the outraged 'community' what should be done – *they* suggested 'writing to the local newspaper'. The teacher invited the class to meet the editor of the newspaper so that they could find out how best to get their letter in the newspaper. The teacher, in the role of editor, explained that the newspaper generally supported the policies of the local government and anyway letters had to be balanced and objective in their argument; they also had to be grammatically and syntactically correct to stand any chance of being published. The children, with this advice in mind, went away and wrote, in role, to the newspaper – there was a significant qualitative difference between their handling of the genre of written argument and that of a similar class who were restricted to discussion.

In this example, the students all produced the same required piece of writing. The same situation could have been used to create a variety of other

Table 23.1

Role/point of view	Communicative purpose	Possible audiences	Mode of writing	Mode of social interaction
Elderly shopkeeper	To remind the community of how much change there has been over the years	Young people, newcomers, officials	Letters to an overseas relative written over the years, article for a local history magazine, autobiography	Addressing a public meeting, talking to customers in the shop, telling grandchildren on a visit
Young mother	To argue the need for more facilities for children	Other parents, teachers, officials, her friends/family	Leaflets, letter seeking help from authorities, an accident report for own child	Interview with local radio, talking to other parents outside school, telling child off for playing in an unsafe place
Police officer	To draw attention to the high crime rate in the area	Senior officers, members of the public, local politicians, media	Police notebook, crime report, statistics, witnesses' reports, advice to shopkeepers/ homeowners	Induction for new police officers, door-to-door enquiries, presenting evidence at trial
A girl from a different ethnic/ cultural group	To share her pain and frustration over racial abuse	Peers, family, teachers, relatives in another place	Diary, letters, essay for school, evidence to a tribunal	Talking to friends, reporting incident to the police, challenging racists in the street

examples of language in use. By considering different relationships of role, purpose, audience and mode of language the students could experience, for themselves, the choices, meanings and forms of communication that we find in the world at large. Table 23.1 attempts to map out some of the written and spoken language possibilities offered by the context of the community drama.

The ideas given in the table are all located *within* the situation of the drama; each one of the ideas could result in a dramatic change in the situation for one or more of the people involved. The young mother's appeal to officials may result in improved facilities for children; the girl's recording of her fears in her diary may give her the conviction to report those who attack her. Student writing that is suggested by the drama, and then used as part of the script, or as a crucial 'prop', for the next stage of the drama, enables students to experience for themselves the direct cause and effect of different kinds of language use.

Students are also likely to develop an emotional relationship to the lives and dilemmas of the people they 'role-play' and write as. They will care about the girl because they will have 'met' and talked to her in the drama; she is not an abstract proposition. A dramatic representation of a situation will tend to emphasise the social drama of living – tension is the mainspring of all drama; most young people can be expected to understand the concept of tension and social drama from their experience of drama in film, TV and their own lives!

Because drama offers a representation of the real world, pieces of writing may be worked on so that they are as authentic, in appearance, as possible. If a letter is going to be used as a 'prop' it matters what it's written on, whether it's typed or handwritten, whether it's been carefully kept or thrown away. In considering the appearance of the piece of writing as a dramatic object, the student's attention is drawn to considering every aspect of a text, not just the linguistic choices but the appearance and packaging too.

STRATEGIES FOR DEVELOPING DRAMA

Students are not asked to write 'cold' in drama. Prior to the writing stage of the drama the teacher will use a variety of dramatic strategies to help the students fully understand the living context for their writing. The non-statutory guidance for Drama in the English National Curriculum suggests a number of strategies for creating drama. The purpose of these strategies is to help the students make and believe in the dramatic situation, feel comfortable about getting involved, develop 'characterisation' and think about the implications of the language and actions in the drama. Some of the strategies that are mentioned are described below as they might be used in the context of the community drama described above:

- *Freeze-frame*: students in small groups devise a tableau which demonstrates what they want to say; the rest of the class is asked to interpret:
  - groups work on producing tableaux which represent a collection of old photos kept by the shopkeeper;
  - tableaux are made to represent images of the community in the local press;
  - tableaux of the mother's fears for her small child, the images show the different dangers there are;
  - tableaux to demonstrate the difference between the way the girl is abused by her neighbours and how they treat each other.
- *Improvisation* where a class may separate into small groups each exploring a facet of an overall theme capable of being brought together at some later point.
  - community meeting to discuss the waste land;
  - scenes showing what goes on in the community at different times of the day/night;
  - scenes contrasting the girl's life in the community with scenes from stories her grandmother tells her about life in a far-off land;
  - scenes to show what the class think causes a person to become a racist.
- *Hot-seating* in which either the teacher or a member of the group adopts a role and is questioned by the rest of the class:

–the teacher agrees to take on the role of the elderly shopkeeper, the class ask him about his life in the neighbourhood as he shuts up shop at the end of the day;

–a student in the role of the young mother answers questions about the joys and problems of single parenting;

–a student in the role of the girl's father answers questions from the class in the role as her teachers who are concerned about her absences from school.

- *Forum-theatre*: a scene is acted out, but the audience has the right to intervene and change the scene through questioning and suggesting alternatives:

  –the class improvise what the girl might say to a group of youths who surround her on her way home, the class make suggestions about how she might resolve the situation and take it in turns to play the role of the girl in order to try out their ideas;

  –the class help the police officer to tell a parent their child has been injured in a car accident.

- *Expert roles*: pupils adopt certain expert roles and responsibilities, as detectives, scientists, journalists, archivists, etc.:

  –class in the role as journalists covering the dispute between the council and the local residents;

  –class in the role of a councillors' meeting to decide on planning permission for the new council offices;

  –as health and safety officers, the class prepare a report on the environment of the community.

- *Set design*: the classroom is physically rearranged to represent a place in the drama, the class might add object and props, such as personal possessions, photographs, etc.:

  –the classroom is rearranged into spaces representing the shop, the young mother's flat, the detention room of the police station; the class prepare scenes for each of the spaces and then the class move from 'set' to 'set' to watch the scenes;

  –the classroom is rearranged to represent first the wasteland as it is, then as the community want it to be.

DEVELOPING LANGUAGE THROUGH IMAGINED EXPERIENCE

Drama is a particularly efficient medium for studying impersonal and non-chronological genres of writing. It is difficult to see how to motivate young people to write in ways that might seem strange, artificial and rule bound. When the need for a report, set of instructions, survey or persuasive argument is prompted by a situation, created in drama, the motive for writing becomes personal even if the form or genre is not. Young people have the chance to see that by conforming to the rules of the required genre they can powerfully affect and change their situation in the drama. They are also able to look at the history of a text by representing it in the situation and social networks that produced the text – they can experience how the meaning of a piece of writing will be shaped by the selection of genre.

Dramatising different experiences of language use and genre provides all young people with a bridge between the concreteness of the real world and the abstract remoteness of the classroom. Without drama the experience of language, for many young people, is restricted to and by their daily inter-actions, interactions that may be restricted to a narrower range of genres than those experienced by their better-off peers. Discussion or instruction about unfamiliar uses of language cannot be a substitute for actual experi-ence. The imagined experience of drama, however, can offer a powerful and concrete alternative to actual experience, particularly when the imagined experience heightens the tensions and emotions of real life and makes a connection between the causes and effects of different genres of language.

Chapter 24

Teaching poetry in the secondary school

John Taylor

In practice you hear it coming from somebody else, you hear something in another writer's sounds that flows in through your ear and enters the echo chamber of your head and delights your whole nervous system in such a way that your reaction will be 'Ah, I wish I had said that in that particular way'. This other writer, in fact, has spoken something essential to you, something you recognise instinctively as a true sounding of aspects of yourself and your experience. And your first steps as a writer will be to imitate, consciously or unconsciously, those sounds that flowed in, that influence.

(Seamus Heaney)[1]

I think with a poem, it's very important that you can have it all packed in, full of all the things you wanted to say . . . . I think that's what attracts a reader, what it sounds like, the way it's written, the sort of flow of words.
(Emma, *aged 10, in a Nottinghamshire primary school*)[2]

Poetry matters because it is a central example of the use human beings make of words to explore and understand. Like other forms of writing we value, it lends shape and meaning to our experiences and helps us to move with confidence in the world we know and then to step beyond it, to respond to the generation of meaning through significant, memorable and deliberated kinds of language. It is an activity to which we are drawn because in its range and rigour we feel both the presence and the pressure of human experience. Poetry embodies delight in expression, stretched between thought, feeling and form. As we become aware of the 'true soundings' of poetry so we become aware of what we ourselves might do with language.

Poets work at the frontier of language. They are engaged with the struggle for clarity and meaning and those who wrestle with and refine language in order to be lucid and articulate are, in a crucial sense, the guardians of the accumulated richness of our written and spoken inheritance.

There has never been any serious challenge, since English came to be considered a suitable subject for the classroom, to the view that literature, including poetry, should be at the centre of its preoccupations. However, it is also fair to say that literature has become institutionalised in education and that around the reading of books there has grown a whole structure of secondary activities – glossaries, paraphrases, analyses of plot, character studies, biographies, background studies – which have severed the connections between literature and the language and experience of reading, so that the image of literature in many pupils' minds is of a form of knowledge to be examined, like many others in the curriculum, rather than of a man or woman sitting down with pen and paper and making something in a common human idiom. It is this which provides the context for Adrian Mitchell's refusal to let any of his work be used for the purposes of any examinations whatsoever and Shaw's 'eternal curse' on anyone who should make his plays hated as Shakespeare is hated.

The sharp severance that often exists in schools between the study of language and the study of literature suggests that literature is a special and select activity carried out by a few established writers which has few connections with the uses made of language by pupils or with the language of home, community and ordinary living. When reading is set apart from writing, or everyday speech from literature, pupils do not see literature as part of the universal uses of language, more subtle and deliberate perhaps than everyday expression but essentially hand in hand with it. The roots of what we call literature are in everyday stories, dramas, rhythms, songs, rhetoric and the flow of language in relationships. In the shaping and making of their insights to be communicated, it is important that pupils perceive that whenever they write they are sharing the medium with those whom they may regard as writers.

Poetry needs to be at the heart of work in English because of the quality of language at work on experience that it offers to us. If language becomes separated from moral and emotional life – becomes merely a trail of clichés which neither communicate with nor quicken the mind of the reader – then we run the risk of depriving children of the kind of vital resource of language which poetry provides.

As teachers we are concerned not so much with the numbers of words potentially available but with the degree to which the resources of language are put to current use by our pupils. Among other things, literature is, as Ezra Pound argued, a way of keeping words living and accurate. It is the place of poetry in English teaching to help us to restore to pupils a sense of exuberance and vitality in the acquisition of language and in the power and savour of words.

MAKING READERS – THE POOL OF LANGUAGE

> Let (the pupil) read – let him wander with it and
> reflect upon it and bring home to it and prophesy
> upon it and dream upon it.
>
> (Keats, *Letters*)

Ted Hughes in his important and influential book *Poetry in the Making*[3] described two aspects of poetry that seem to him to be central. His first claim is that poetry is possessed of 'a certain wisdom, something special, something that we are very curious to learn'; his second is that the latent talent for self-expression in any child is immeasurable. These recognitions are at the heart of reading and writing poetry in schools and the activities in the classroom need to reflect a desire to promote both, in a collaborative endeavour between teacher and pupils.

However, the current state of the teaching of poetry in many secondary schools does not show much faith either in the wisdom of poetry or in the powers of self-expression of the pupils. Inspection of and visits to secondary schools indicate that there is in many of them very little poetry included regularly in the work in English. The findings of specialist one-day visits and a number of full inspection reports show that poetry was at the centre of work in English for rather less than 5 per cent of the English lessons observed. The evidence is that, in national terms, poetry is frequently neglected and poorly provided for; its treatment is inadequate and super-ficial. Many pupils spend much more time completing language exercises of little value than they do reading, writing or talking about poetry. They are very much more likely to be given a course book for work in English than they are to be given an anthology of poetry or the opportunity to read widely in the work of particular authors.

Some English teachers express great unease about teaching poetry and it appears that there are few genuine enthusiasts who read poetry extensively themselves and communicate that enthusiasm to pupils. The reasons why some teachers seem afraid of poetry are not easily discerned but it is clear that choosing and presenting poetry is not as easy as presenting fiction and that teachers are often aware of a background of hostility to poetry among their pupils. There is the danger of a self-defeating process here and it is notable how few English departments, through their guidelines, meetings or discussion papers, have faced the problem directly. Most English depart-ment documents have little to say about the teaching of poetry. It is recognised in many as being a good thing – 'Poetry should be encouraged wherever possible' – but the resources and methods for that encouragement are not detailed. Some schools see the teaching of poetry as an apparently straightforward task of escorting pupils through a formidable barrier of technical terms – 'In this year metaphor, simile, onomatopoeia, assonance, alliteration, synecdoche and oxymoron will be taught' – and in one school there they were, defined, copied out, learnt for tests, with not a single reference to a complete poem. Many schools have large stocks of old anthologies which are never used, and it is not uncommon for modern anthologies, containing material that would extend and deepen pupils' experiences of poetry, to lie idle in English department stockrooms.

Teachers' attitudes to poetry are crucial in the importance they attach to it; the enthusiasm with which they read it aloud; the extent to which they read it widely themselves; and the way in which they demonstrate a concerned responsibility for it – in short how they give it rank and status. The message children receive about poetry from its placing in most course books is clear enough: it comes a poor third behind the 'For written answers' section and 'Find out more about' demands. Teachers should not themselves reinforce that message by relegating poetry to the end of the day or the week or the term, when resistance is low and all the 'essential business' of English has been completed.

It is dispiriting to note that in general terms the features of the teaching of literature noted in The Bullock Report[4] in 1975 have not changed to any marked degree as far as the teaching of poetry is concerned – 'The explanations and the summaries have expanded to take-over point; the literature has receded'. The treatment of poetry as 'little more than comprehension passages', the proliferation of 'model answers, stereotyped commentaries . . . with no hint of felt response' have persisted in creating unsympathetic attitudes to literature in the minds of many secondary school pupils. There is evidence for this in the statistics of APU's first Secondary Language Survey,[5] where 47 per cent of pupils indicated that they read no poetry out of school; 73 per cent indicated that they did not read poetry to any great extent; and 36 per cent were completely hostile to it. For many pupils, poetry has not been a series of experiences where the young reader could find a mirror of some of his or her own feelings and preoccupations in a common human idiom. If this is to happen it must be recognised that it will not happen by chance (although room should be left for the chance encounter) and that approaches to poetry in the classroom must be at least as clearly structured and provided for as other aspects of English, if they are to impart a sense of pleasure and direction.

The ways in which meaning is established for the reader of poetry in the classroom depend upon the associations and contents of the language of the poem reaching into the reader's mind. So although the initial engagement of the reader with the poem is a private affair proceeding at an area below articulation, it issues finally in language that reflects an active process which has taken place in the reader's mind – a mental travelling, which we can call response, judgement or understanding. Above all, pupils need time to make their own responses, to assimilate and ponder before being plunged into talking and writing about what the poem means. Thereafter this opening up of a poem and the exploration of its meaning depend upon the sensitive direction of a teacher concerned about both the language of the poem and the responses of the pupils as they approach the poem, in George Herbert's phrase, as 'a box where sweets compacted lie' whose unpacking is a process full of pleasure and satisfaction.

DEVELOPING THE AUDITORY IMAGINATION

Poetry is rooted in an oral tradition and poetry in schools can endeavour to restore something of its traditional public and rhetorical voice through performance. Donne's *Songs and Sonnets* and Blake's *Songs of Innocence and Experience* remind us of the connections between poetry and song and activities engendered in the classroom should bring the sound of poetry to pupils' ears. In the first instance teachers need to read poetry aloud well, and to exploit their capacities for doing so, but the pupils' experience should extend to preparations for reading aloud and performance. For a group of pupils to consider how they are going to read a poem aloud means they become closely involved with meaning and the expression of meaning: they experience the power of alliteration, hear assonance, rhyme and rhythm at first hand and absorb in the most obvious and common-sense way what are often taught as remote technical features. If pupils are asked to prepare programmes of poetry for particular audiences the selection of suitable material becomes a critical process which asks questions about suitability and difficulty and can only be answered by students on the basis of their informed reading and perception of occasion and audience. What poems might a fifth-year group choose for a tape-recorded poetry programme for first-year pupils? If a group of pupils prepares material for a live reading for a local old people's home, or for a programme about Christmas for a hospital radio station, what considerations might inform their selection and balance of material?

The dimension of performing poetry gives to pupils an opportunity to experience the operation of those technical and formal devices which have for so long been the subject of irrelevant classification in the classroom. These terms (rhyme, rhythm, alliteration, assonance, metaphor, simile, imagery and many more obscured in the language of Greek prosody) cannot be ignored in the exploration and establishment of meaning, but they must stem naturally from the organic whole of the poem and not be seen as ingredients placed in solemn proportions in the poetic mixing bowl and then stirred.

Poetic rhythm has its roots in the patterns of ordinary speech, more highly and consciously organised, but not applied from outside. The 'auditory imagination', as T.S. Eliot called it, is a feeling for rhythm and syllable 'below the level of conscious thought'. To develop a response to this it is essential for pupils to be given the opportunities to hear the words as a pattern of articulate sounds, to read with the ear as well as the eye and to recognise that rhythmic effects are only part of a number of other subtle and elusive aspects of poetic language. Pupils can apprehend that rhythm sets up a pattern of expectation in the regularity of a pattern of stresses, as part of their experiences of reading. They will sense, too, that rhythm in poetry reinforces meaning and that stress patterns derive from the normal pronunciation of words, with the normal emphasis of everyday speech. Pupils best exercise the auditory imagination by regular reading and listening to whole poems read aloud. In a sixth-form college, each student in turn was expected to spend at least one hour on a prepared reading of a poem of his or her choice, every week. Reading the poem aloud was the introductory part of the lesson which the student conducted, giving thoughts, perceptions and responses to the poem. For one boy, the work on the preparation for reading aloud had given him a key to the poem he had chosen – *View of a Pig* by Ted Hughes:

> As I read this poem aloud the words had the sound of flesh on flesh to me. It seemed to me that Hughes was, in essence, slapping and kicking this inert mound with his words. I couldn't hear this as I read it silently in my head.

The effects of rhyme and rhythm are closely connected with sound and verbal patterns; metaphor by contrast is concerned with the meanings of words and is at the centre of poetic expression. Metaphor has been called 'the swift illumination of an equivalence', a comparison which involves the mind of the reader in a positive act of interpretation between the attributes of the things compared. Living metaphor also shocks and surprises the reader by its audacity, stopping us in our tracks and causing us to delve and explore. Lists of worn similes and metaphors learned by heart lose all this force. Thus pupils can, by their experience of reading, be brought to the point where they are able to enter into the nature of the implied comparison. One approach would be to alert children to the fact that everyday language is full of metaphors – 'You rat', 'Don't be wet', 'You're throwing away your chances', 'Let's float the idea', 'I'm heart-broken', 'There's something in the wind', 'I can't make head or tail of it' – and examples can be collected and displayed. In this way pupils will realise that metaphor is deeply embedded in language: the act of reading metaphor makes them aware of the comparison between familiar things, and this presents a new dimension and precision to feeling and experience. For poetry does not simply make statements. It takes the reader into the re-creation of experience; and metaphor, in a subtle and flexible way, draws the reader into understanding by causing this active and positive response. In this way, pupils can become aware of the special emotional and imaginative control a poet achieves when the familiar and everyday metaphors of ordinary speech no longer suffice, when the pressure of experience creates its own originality:

Life's but a walking shadow; a poor player,
That struts and frets his hour upon the stage,
And then is heard no more: it is a tale
Told by an idiot, full of sound and fury,
Signifying nothing.

(Macbeth Act V, Scene V)

It was argued in the opening paragraphs that poetry is important because it has qualities of utterance pupils need to experience if they are to become more aware of the possibilities of language. Insight into poetry grows with insight into language and the processes are mutually supporting. Approaches to poetry in the classroom can make children aware of the wide range of emotional possibilities each word possesses according to its context, its speaker, its association or its history. Indeed just as it can be pointed out that metaphor – an apparently remote term – is deeply rooted in ordinary speech, so pupils, through looking at the examples around them in advertising and the press, can readily perceive how the emotional reverberations of language and its potency as a purveyor of ideas and images are exploited for particular effect. They will recognise similarly that poets for rather different reasons work with conscious thought and rigour in forming their words into a powerful creative order, which often depends strongly on association and context. It has been argued that reading poetry is a discovery or creation of its meaning and that reading poetry aloud heightens the sense of its unity and organic quality whereby the whole is more than the sum of constituent parts. So if insight into the possibilities of language is a product of the experiencing of it, it is important through the sustained reading and discussion of poetry to give pupils the chance to become more linguistically alert, competent and adventurous, bringing their own experiences, thought and rigour to bear on, and combine with, the poets they read. It is this influence which Seamus Heaney described in his image of 'words entering the echo chamber of your head'.

FINDING A VOICE

In a sense all writing connected with the experience of poetry is creative, when it is the pupils' own, whether it is evaluative and analytic or expressive and poetic. Wherever pupils are themselves involved in placing this word next to that, there can be expressions of freshness of thought and feeling. It is important that pupils' writing is not confined to an unduly narrow framework and that a range of possibilities is seen to be available and to be equally valued for the language and insights which they generate. Children need to experience the placing of words together so that they can become 'makers' for themselves. A girl in a Nottinghamshire school was asked where her words came from in her own complex and luxuriant writing. She replied:

I just pick them up – out of the books I read, really – and I use them every now and then. Everything I read has a good word in it and I fix that word in my mind so that I won't forget it.

It is a function of poetry in school to feed pupils' store of words so that when they write themselves they become absorbed in the 'fascination of what's difficult', in the assembly of what Ted Hughes calls the living parts of language.

The point is illustrated by the writing of a 15-year-old pupil from a Northamptonshire comprehensive school. The class had been reading poetry extensively for half a term and were encouraged, in their responses, to work in a variety of ways, including experiments in the form, but not necessarily using the substance, of a poem they had read which had caught their interest. One pupil took Ted Hughes' *Hawk Roosting* and made of it a striking vision:

A BANK MANAGER[6]

I stand above the rest, watching intensely.
Inaction no falsifying dream
Between my pressed suit and polished shoes:
Or in a sleep rehearse stern looks and nos.

The convenience of house buyers!
The light room and large windows
Are of advantage to me;
And the people look up to me, so nervous

My fists are clenched around leather arms.
It took a Nation of investors
To produce my desk, my each clerk:
Now I hold the Nation in my fist

Or drive and admire it keenly –
I stop where I please, because it is all mine.
There is no laughter on my lips:
My matters are the selling of money –

The allotment of debt
For the one path of my success is direct
Through the pockets of the classes.
No arguments assert my right:

Power is behind me.
Only money has changed since I began.
My pen has permitted that change.
I am going to keep things like this.

Such control over form and idea could not have come about without a prolonged immersion in the reading of the original poetry, whose 'echoes' have given a new dimension to the writing.

The teacher has a vital role to play in helping pupils in all the stages of their writing, in their experiments, tentative formulations, processes of clarifying meaning and expression. There is now general agreement that the unthinking assumptions of 'When in doubt, write a poem' are no longer good enough, although it is still common to find choices for pupils' writing ending with 'Or you may write a poem if you wish' as though it required no special preparation or effort. The close connections between reading and writing poetry demonstrate the proper seriousness of the matter, as ideas and feelings are wrought into expressive form. Though tactful, sensitive and positive, the teacher must not receive pupils' work with easy and sentimental praise. Pupils as writers need the benefit of clear and frank appraisal, an expectation that they will rework ideas in sections of their writing, and plenty of time and encouragement to do so. It follows that teachers need to be sure of their judgements, to be widely read in poetry themselves, and perhaps to be engaged in the business of writing themselves alongside their pupils from time to time. Not least, they must be critically discerning enough to recognise a voice the pupil owns and to be able to distinguish it from one that has been rented for the occasion, and to be alert to those moments in a child's writing when there is an important shift in capability and consciousness.

Teachers have a responsibility to make sure their own models of what is to be valued are not stranded in stale and sterile forms. It is of course true that the outcome of poetry teaching need not be writing at all, and that many poems can be read just for themselves, as an experience of the moment, whose echoes for some will last into the future. But the evidence is that a rich and varied experience of poetry will engender in most pupils the desire to write; to seek to close the gap between their experiences and the words that are available to give them shape.

RUGBY LEAGUE: AS EXPECTED[7]

David Woodhouse (14)

Nocker Norton,
Balding albino tiger,
The Boulevard mud
Does not lust for your body
As expected.

The inevitable massive tackle
Does not spread its muddy, muscled grasp
Around another passive Titan
As expected.

But instead flashes like
A laser beam from
Your tinkling fingertips.
The crowd
Loves you
As expected.

In the work of young writers such as this, the reader feels the pressure of human experience and responds to the presence of such creative energy. But work of such quality and personal and linguistic integrity does not simply happen. In the experience that lies behind writing like this there lie those encounters with books and poems which, in Kafka's words, act 'as an ice-axe to break the sea frozen inside us'. By feeling both closeness and continuity with writers who connect with us across gaps of historical time, children find their own originality in the dignity, resources and uses of language. In this way they can themselves begin to make sense of the world in which we live. If literature is the expression of a human dimension and connection then the experience of it should not be a matter of chance but of entitlement.

NOTES AND REFERENCES

1 The extract is reprinted by permission of Faber and Faber and is taken from Seamus Heaney's book *Preoccupation: selected prose 1968–78*. Faber and Faber, 1980.
2 HMI are indebted to Mr J. Ousby, General Adviser, Nottinghamshire, for this quotation.
3 Hughes, Ted. *Poetry in the making: an anthology of poems and programmes from 'Listening and Writing'*. Faber and Faber, 1969.
4 The Bullock Report. *A language for life*. HMSO, 1975.
5 Assessment of Performance Unit (APU). *Language performance in schools: secondary survey report No. 1*. HMSO, 1982. Details of APU's work and publications are available from APU, Room 4/77a, Elizabeth House, York Road, London SE1 7PH.
6 HMI are grateful to Mrs P. Barnard, curriculum advisory teacher in Northamptonshire, for permission to use this poem.
7 This poem is to be found in *Cadbury's second book of children's poetry*. Beaver, 1984. It is reproduced by permission of Cadbury Ltd.

Chapter 25

Getting into grammar

Frances Smith and Mike Taylor

Many secondary teachers worry about the status of grammar within their own knowledge about language, whether they should teach it or not, and how this is best to be done. There are a number of understandable reasons for such doubts. Some teachers may not have been taught grammar themselves. Uncertain about terminology and appropriate modes of describing and analysing aspects of word and sentence structure, they may feel that without this foundation their own teaching remains on insecure ground. Conversely other teachers who endured as students an arid diet of analysing clauses and identifying parts of speech may remain unwilling to inflict upon their own pupils something which they associate with a regimen of meaningless exercises. Teachers conscious of the higher profile of basic grammar teaching in Modern Languages may feel that its equal status in mother tongue teaching would consolidate children's competence in spoken and written English and that a common understanding of grammatical principles should underpin all language teaching. Others again may be worried by the groundswell of public feeling (inflamed by statements from politicians) that without grammar English has become a *laissez-faire* subject without any moral authority. This kind of argument prescribes grammar as a universal nostrum, guaranteeing students, whatever their geographical, class or ethnic origins, access to the social currency of standard English – grammar as the gateway to a classless society. Add to this the constant backcloth of a baying press and a public rhetoric which links a perceived lack of grammar (as a symbol of inherent orderliness and discipline) with every conceivable social malaise and it is no wonder that some teachers are confused and demoralised.

> The overthrow of grammar coincided with the acceptance of the equivalent of creative writing in social behaviour. As the nice points of grammar were mockingly dismissed as pedantic and irrelevant, so was punctiliousness in such matters as honesty, responsibility, property, gratitude, apology and so on.
>
> (John Rae, *Observer* 1982)

Surrounded by the fog of irrationality which any public debate about grammar seems to provoke, teachers need to keep a clear head. Now, more than ever before, it is important that English departments act to defuse parental confusion and uncertainty and to pre-empt some of the worst backwash effects from the inevitable crudity of national grammar testing. One way of achieving this is to have clear statements of school policy about the place of grammar within the curriculum, and clear guidelines on how to develop students' understandings about those kinds of patterning and regularity within the English language which support their competence in spoken and written English.

The ideas that follow come from a range of professional development activities prepared by the Eastern Region Team of the Language In The National Curriculum (LINC) Project to support teachers' understandings of grammar and its place in classroom practice.[1]

WHAT IS GRAMMAR?

Since grammar means different things to different people, creating a shared language and shared understandings among those with a legitimate interest in the topic is the first challenge. Many commentators on English point their fingers at inadequacies in students' language claiming that all such symptoms could be eradicated by a good dose of grammar. More often than not on closer inspection such confusions and immaturities in pupils' speech and writing are nothing to do with grammar at all. Similar confusions are shared by authors of textbooks. This jolly cartoon (Figure 25.1) supposedly illustrates a letter 'full of grammatical mistakes'. It is certainly a poor letter in terms of layout, spelling and register but there are no strictly grammatical errors in it.[2]

It is useful therefore to recognise and disentangle some of the features of language people have in mind when they talk about grammar, as well as coming to a shared definition amongst ourselves as teachers to guide our practice. The diagram in Figure 25.2 has been used with both staff and parent groups to help to clarify what is and isn't grammar. Many of the attitudes reflected here are deeply felt and have to be recognised as such. Some of the definitions describe grammar in the more neutrally descriptive way that is typical of linguistics.

Correct or incorrect? A way of prescribing usage? Only found in standard English? Unchanging?

This view assumes that the function of grammar is to tell you how you ought to speak and write. It sees the forms of standard English (SE) as correct and all non-standard or informal usages as incorrect. This right/wrong view of grammar fails to allow for the fact that different kinds of language and different levels of formality may be appropriate for different situations. Nor does this view acknowledge that even the rules of SE may change over time.

How can grammar help?

Most of us ignore grammar in our everyday speech and in writing quick messages. It is, however, important to be accurate, clear and formal in certain aspects of life:

1.Jobs

Nowadays it is difficult to find a job. No matter how talented or well qualified you are at something, there always seems to be hundreds of other people just as suitable.

If you apply for a job by sending a letter which is full of grammatical mistakes, the employer will give preference to someone with the same qualifications who has expressed him- or herself correctly.

Figure 25.1

For instance, it is now increasingly acceptable to finish phrases or sentences with a preposition, and the construction 'to whom' is felt to be appropriate only in the most formal types of writing. The writers at the Department for Education who drafted the Parents' Charter clearly shared this view when they wrote '*It will tell you about . . . who to talk to in the school about your child's report*'.

Maintaining standards? 'Proper' English? Closely connected with reinforcing discipline and maintaining social order?

This view has much in common with the previous one. It assumes that there are no stylistic variations in language with regard to more or less formal situations. It sees informal language, slang and non-SE equally as deviations from a fixed standard of 'good English'. In extreme cases, holders of these views can conflate sloppy speaking with an inclination towards anti-social

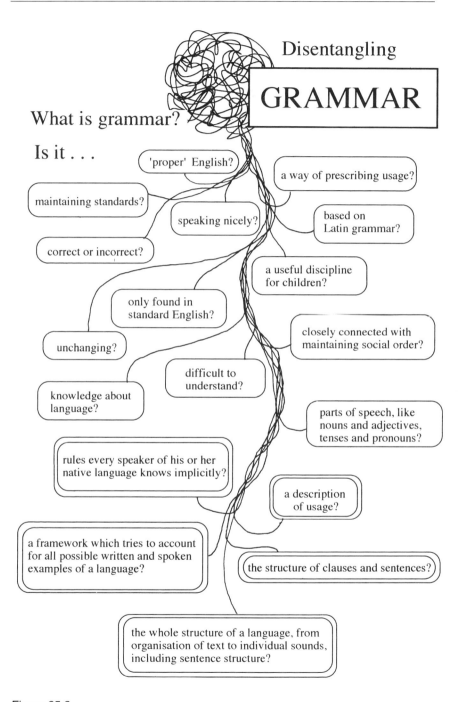

Disentangling

GRAMMAR

What is grammar?

Is it . . .

'proper' English?

a way of prescribing usage?

maintaining standards?

speaking nicely?

based on
Latin grammar?

correct or incorrect?

a useful discipline
for children?

only found in
standard English?

closely connected with
maintaining social order?

unchanging?

difficult to
understand?

knowledge about
language?

parts of speech, like
nouns and adjectives,
tenses and pronouns?

rules every speaker of his or her
native language knows implicitly?

a description
of usage?

a framework which tries to account
for all possible written and spoken
examples of a language?

the structure of clauses and sentences?

the whole structure of a language, from
organisation of text to individual sounds,
including sentence structure?

Figure 25.2

behaviour. Local non-SE forms may be seen as corruptions of 'proper' English, the result of error and lack of care, rather than as rule-bound regional dialects used by a large proportion of English speakers with their own deep-rooted grammatical traditions.

A useful discipline? Parts of speech like nouns and adjectives? Gender and tenses? Based on Latin grammar?

This view may equate grammar with the knowledge of a number of linguistic terms, and the ability to identify language features in traditional exercises. It may also assume that English grammar can best be described in the terms used in Latin grammar. It usually assumes that this analytical ability will lead to improvement in spoken and written language. If parents see grammar as a useful discipline for students we have to be prepared to show how our own teaching about language is equally rigorous, but more useful and applicable to the real world than the ability to label a gerund. Some shared terms for describing language certainly form part of the body of knowledge we might wish students to learn about grammar.

A description of usage? Rules every speaker of a native language knows implicitly? The structure of words, clauses and sentences?

These views reflect some of the ways in which linguists have described grammar. They are interested in describing how language works, not pre-scribing how it *should* work. Specifically they see grammar as the way language is structured. This structure includes the organisation of stretches of speech or writing (discourse structure); sentence structure (syntax); how words are made up (morphology); and patterns of sounds and written symbols (phonology and graphology). Some linguists have focused on the way choices in structure affect the meanings that are made – in particular the use of word order in sentences and word endings (morphology). These are the assumptions about grammar that underpin the National Curriculum for England and Wales. While clearly turning its back on the discredited decon-textualised grammar exercises of the past, this curriculum looks forward to providing students with more opportunities to learn about the structures of the English language and to identify its rules and patterns, this time by reflecting upon examples of speech and writing which have some meaning in their lives and purpose and relevance in their learning.

WHAT DO WE WANT TO TEACH STUDENTS ABOUT GRAMMAR IN TODAY'S SCHOOLS?

Grammar is important. Language in both standard and non-standard vari-eties and in both spoken and written modes is a rule-bound system.

Table 25.1 Teaching grammar: some aspects of grammar that we might want our pupils to learn

1 Knowledge of some **terminology**, e.g. *noun, verb*, but not confined to 'parts of speech'. Terms needed for talking and writing about language, e.g. *paragraph, standard English.*

2 The ability to **write well-constructed and effective prose**, using the grammar of standard English where appropriate.

3 Knowledge of **sentence structure**
   - in children's writing: clauses within sentences, linking words (besides 'and');
   - from children's reading: how sentences are built up, e.g. main clause, subordinate clauses, phrases, etc.

4 Knowledge of **word formation**
   - past tenses, plurals – regular and irregular, e.g. *I goed, bring/brought, mouse/mice* (if necessary!), comparatives and superlatives – -er/-est;
   - prefixes, suffixes, nouns formed from adjectives, and vice versa, etc., e.g. entertain/entertainment, beauty/beautiful.

5 Some knowledge about the **variation in grammar when we write and speak**
   - how the **grammar of standard English may differ from dialect grammars known to the children** and contexts when each may be appropriate, e.g. past tense uses of *did/done* and how each works according to rules;
   - how grammatical choices may vary according to **the speaker's/writer's purpose, audience and context of use,** e.g. when you might or might not use *whom*;
   - how grammatical choices may be shaped by the **demands of different types or genres of writing or speaking,** e.g. grammar of non-fiction books – word order, use of the passive, etc.: 'Because brown bears sometimes killed cattle, they have been hunted and many have been destroyed.'

6 Some knowledge about the ways in which **writers' choices of grammar affect us when we read or listen**
   - This might involve developing ways of talking and writing about language that encourage a critical awareness, leading to an ability to 'see through' language and understand the ways in which messages are mediated or shaped and how grammatical choices can be used to persuade, manipulate or dominate.

Exploring these rules is an exciting and challenging part of learning about language. While children are of course formulating these rules from their earliest years and developing their implicit knowledge about grammar as native speakers, part of this exploration will involve the ability to talk explicitly about the way language works and to use some of the conventional terms in doing so. Table 25.1 summarises some aspects of grammar that we might want our pupils to learn. The most productive contexts for this learning are likely to be:

- discussions where students share their writing with the teacher or each other;
- discussions where the students share their responses to texts written by others;
- investigative projects with a language focus.

Table 25.2 Language terms used in the wording of the English National
Curriculum

Communication and comprehension
• **kinds of meaning:** metaphor, simile, personification, figures of speech; surface
  meaning, subtext, ambiguity, bias, euphemism, stereotype
  Language variation
• accent, dialect, standard English, non-standard variety, regional/social variation,
  home language, first language
• formal language, colloquial language, slang
  Language functions
• **different ways of organising writing or talk:** argument, observation, description,
  report, commentary, narrative, debate
• **the final products:** story, poem, poetry, play, script, anecdote, label, caption,
  diagram, brochure, thesaurus, biography, autobiography, essay, sonnet, ballad,
  haiku, book review
• **during the process:** role play, turn taking, relevance, cause/effect, appropriate-
  (ness); rhetorical techniques, persuasive techniques; chronological, non-
  chronological, fiction, non-fiction; discuss, summarise, hypothesise, classify, compare, contrast, expand, review draft, redraft, revise, proof-read; silent reading,
  'search' reading, skim read, back track, context, phonic cue; character, setting,
  opening, outcome, episode, plot, events, resolution; contents, index, conclusion,
  verse
  Language system
• **structure of texts:** sentence, paragraph, phrase, layout, heading, subheading,
  chapter, coherence
• **sentence grammar:** noun, verb, pronoun, adjective, adverb, preposition, conjunc-
  tion, inflectional ending, singular, plural, *tense*, negative, passive, subordination;
  parenthetical construction, appositional construction
• **words:** word, prefix, suffix, borrowing; vocabulary: specialist, archaic, literary,
  figurative, colloquial, dialect, scientific
• **spelling and writing system:** letter, capital letter, alphabet, lower case; punctuation, full stop, question mark, apostrophe, inverted commas, brackets, dash, colon,
  semi-colon, comma, direct speech; print, typeface
• **sounds:** consonant, vowel, rhythm, rhyme, alliteration, assonance, onomatopoeia

WHAT LANGUAGE TERMS DO WE NEED IN THE
CLASSROOM?

The language terms in Table 25.2 are all drawn from the descriptions of the
programmes of study and attainment targets in the National Curriculum for
English.[3] They are used to describe the work in English that might be
undertaken by pupils from 5 to 16. As you can see, while grammatical terms
are included in the list, many other technical terms are included which
describe language variation and function. This demonstrates that students in
our schools now need to know much more about language than those
previous generations who learned only sentence grammar. It is quite likely
that you will find some terms which you are not sure of yourself, in which case
you could consult one of the glossaries mentioned at the end of this chapter.[4]

Teachers who have shared their ideas about which terms they would use in talking to their students, or which terms they would want their students to learn and use themselves, have found it produces useful exchanges of views about when certain terms might be taught and the contexts which have proved effective in doing so. Of course children will have been using many of these aspects of language in their speech and writing from an early age without needing to know the corresponding terms. However, the ability to talk about language and reflect on its uses and structures helps students to stand back, take stock and sharpen their language achievements. At first they may do this in perceptive and informed ways but without using conventional terminology. Later, as they become members of a community of language users, they will need to share their discussion and reflection further and for this they will need to add to the terms they know already. Part of our responsibility is to decide which terms will be useful to students at different stages of their schooling.

GRAMMAR AND STUDENTS' WRITING

While many English teachers no longer teach grammar through exercises, they still claim to be supporting students' grammatical understanding by doing it 'in context'. Sometimes spoken English may be an appropriate context for discussions of grammar (for instance, in debating the appropriateness of standard or non-standard forms in a specific role play) but more often it is the more consciously reflective process of writing that teachers regard as fertile ground for the discussion of points of grammar. However, in the absence of the punitive red pen, evidence for these processes of grammar teaching and learning remains elusive. How do we make this vital aspect of our teaching more explicit to colleagues and pupils and parents? The following example shows how learning in context can happen. Where meetings for parents and governors are arranged which focus on curriculum issues it would be helpful if examples such as this could sometimes be shared and discussed.

What does the writer know?
About regular patterns of word endings, grammar of spoken English, appropriate styles for different kinds of writing, complex sentence structures using more than *and* and *but*, the needs of a reader, forms of standard English, forms of literary writing, etc.

What does this writer still have to learn?
About appropriate uses of standard English and local dialect, complex sentence structures, word forms, ways of linking sentences, punctuation, awareness of needs of reader, judgement of levels of formality and informality, knowledge of differences of grammar between spoken and written English, etc.

Teacher action: How might you help the writer?
                    What action might be appropriate for a group or the
                    class if other students are at the same stage?

Cosmetic and research testing on animals should not be needed. It is not right that animals should be exploited in this way. Some people may argue that if we don't test these cosmetic products on animals that then they would do us harm. I don't think that this is a fair arguement because if nobody wore any make-up then no one would have anything to complain about because they would all be in the same boat. Animals are sedated so that they cannot fight back or held down also. Different substances are put onto and into the faces, eyes, ears, and other parts of the body of the animal and if they is something wrong with let's say a mascara then the rabbits or other animals eyes might start to go red and bloodshot and they might start to itch but the rabbit won't be able to do anything because it is held down.
(Katie, Year 9. This was her own choice of topic for persuasive writing)

What's happening?

Although Katie is in her third year at secondary school, she struggles to match her strong feelings on the topic with clear argument. We must remember, however, that the demands of organising and expressing written argument are very different from narrative, and students usually have fewer examples of this genre around them, or already in their heads, as models to draw upon. The piece starts with two topic sentences which immediately assert Katie's position. A counter argument is then put forward – *Some people may argue* – which is then refuted. The rest of the extract describes how cosmetics are tested on rabbits.

There are a number of factors which get in the way of the reader's easy comprehension of the piece. First, paragraphing would help in signalling the transition which starts *Animals are sedated*. Here words appear to be omitted and the function of *also* is unclear. If this new paragraph was preceded with a clause such as *When animals are tested they are sedated* then the change of direction would be clearer. Arguably though, the reader requires a stronger signal than this with the inclusion of a new topic sentence such as *The amount of cruelty caused to animals by laboratory testing is clear. Firstly they are sedated, or held down, so that they do not fight back.*

The long sentence which follows this – *Different substances . . .* – also needs to be made clearer, possibly by cutting out some of the connectives and starting new sentences. Beginning the last sentence with the adversative *However* rather than *but* would also help here. Having said this, we must acknowledge Katie's sophisticated use of the comma to guide her reader through the argument at this point. Different tense forms are handled here with some proficiency, though the modals *may* and *would* don't seem to be in agreement. The phrase *in the same boat* seems to break the register of formal argument.

What to do individually

First, it is important to acknowledge briefly what Katie knows about written language. She uses varied and appropriate vocabulary most of which is spelled correctly. She uses standard English. Most of her sentences are demarcated clearly by punctuation. She can handle complex sentences. Oddities in the syntax are products of careless omission rather than flawed grammar. The key weakness in the piece probably lies in Katie's failure to signal the change of direction in a second paragraph. It would be interesting to hear how she reads this extract out loud and whether changes of intonation signal a new topic. Some discussion about topic sentences and 'signal' words and those that might be incorporated here could be helpful too. The last sentence is clearly too long. It would be reasonable to ask Katie to work with a friend to make the meaning crisper and clearer.

What to do with others in the group or class

The teaching and learning of written argument occurs cumulatively over a long period of time. No simple interventions or 'one-off' sessions can achieve skilled and confident persuasive writing overnight. However, some of the following might be helpful.

Modelling Reading more argument aloud to students so that they can internalise its cadences and characteristic rhetorical and grammatical patterns. For example, the generic structure *thesis/preview–argument/elaboration/illustration–recommendation/summary/résumé*; modal tenses and passives; conjunctions expressing logical relationships – *if, like, why* (just as most students have already successfully assimilated the structures and patterns of 'story').

Relevant examples Discussing some of the characteristics of written argument by looking at real-life examples (from campaign leaflets or appeals for instance).

Reflection Shared construction of a text with one student composing the argument while a teacher or partner scribes. This helps to slow down the composition and offers support which is vital in the transition between spoken (interactive) and written (self-sustained) argument.

This commentary has included reference to patterns of written language which exceed the boundaries of sentence grammar. With this in mind we should note the following:

1 There are many reasons for errors in students' writing. Frequently these are not to do with grammar.
2 Texts that do not read well or in which there is ambiguity may contain a range of errors that are not always grammatical. The sequencing and organisation of material may be a major factor.
3 The influence of spoken forms persists in many different ways in students' writing often creating the impression that there are grammatical errors. More often than not the real problem is inappropriate choice of words and expressions.
4 Grammar should not be confused with punctuation, choice of vocabulary or spelling.[5]

GRAMMAR AND STUDENTS' READING

Working on their writing is an obvious context for helping students to make explicit and develop their understandings about the forms and structures of English. However, grammar is also important in developing students' reading. When we read texts we are responding unconsciously to the specific grammatical choices made by the author. These choices predispose us to particular interpretations and meanings – meanings which, once we are aware, we can choose to collude with or distance ourselves from. The examples in Figure 25.3 illustrate ways of helping students to look more closely at the way grammar helps to shape such responses. Simple starting points for this kind of reflection are headlines, tabloid stories, jokes and adverts where the intentions of the writer are often fairly direct and overt. Later, discussions can be extended to more subtle examples from poetry, fiction and non-fiction writing.[6] Students might consider the following questions:

From the reader's point of view what is this extract doing?
For example, evoking an atmosphere, arguing a case, providing a factual report or description, persuading?

What is your initial response to the language of the extract?
For example, tone of voice, kind and range of vocabulary, whether the sentence structure appears simple or complex.

Now look more closely at the grammatical choices. Find some examples of ways in which the author's grammatical choices seem to help shape your response.
For example, paragraph structure, word order, use of voice or tense, compressed or elaborated sentence structures.

> # *PERFUMERY*
> ## THE PERFUME YOU WEAR
> ## SAYS A LOT ABOUT YOU.
>
> *The range we have says something about us.*
>
> What is it that nobody sees yet everybody,
> but everybody notices? It only takes
> a dab of perfume to make you feel like
> a million dollars.
> And feeling good is looking good.
>
> Nothing triggers memories as strongly as scent,
> just a hint of a familiar fragrance brings back
> That Time, That Place, That Person. Names are
> forgettable. Even photos fade. But perfume
> lingers. Whatever the look you're looking for,
> the place to look is
>
> ### The Beauty Shop
> ### At Boots
>
> **(a) Lorry Drivers Blockade Ports**
>
> **(b) Ports Blockaded by Lorry Drivers**
>
> **(c) Ports Blockaded**

Figure 25.3

In the perfume advertisement students could discuss how the writer uses persuasion and engages the reader in a personal and interactive way through

- the use of the personal pronoun *you* to create an intimate and friendly style;
- the use of question and answer forms to involve the reader;
- the use of the present tense to convey a sense of universal truth – the reader is invited to collude with these propositions;
- the structural repetition giving the text a poetic quality;
- capitalisation and the use of a centred layout cutting across the normal syntactic structure – again rather like a poem;
- the use of *That Time, That Place* adding to the interactive quality and inviting readers to provide their own private associations;
- the representation of *The Beauty Shop/At Boots* orthographically as single sentences, drawing attention to this key information.

The newspaper headlines are typical. The grammar is elliptical, i.e. articles and main verbs are omitted. Although they report the same event, the differences in word order convey subtle shifts of meaning. In (a) *lorry drivers* is the subject and *ports* the object. The function of the verb *blockade* clearly makes the drivers responsible for it. They are the agents. In (b) the headline uses the passive voice. The drivers are still the main agents, but here they are relegated to the end of the sentence. One of the effects of this is to make it seem as if they are less responsible for the blockade. In (c) the agent is deleted entirely. Again we have the passive voice, but by deleting agency we have a version of events in which the drivers appear not to be in the action at all.

SOME OTHER IDEAS FOR TEACHING AND LEARNING ABOUT GRAMMAR

The ideas below give an indication of the many other ways in which learning about grammar can be made interesting and accessible to younger secondary students.

Language terms, e.g. adjective, noun

- Look at alphabet books for young children – many focus on one part of speech. Make your own alphabet book for younger children. Each word could be the same class.
- Look at the way dictionaries indicate word class (n.), (v.t.), etc. Make your own dictionary of current 'street-wise' teenage argot.
- Invent alliterative alphabetical sentences (as in Graeme Base's *Animalia*)[6] – '*Great green gorillas growing grapes in a gorgeous glass greenhouse*', using specified slots for adjective(s), noun, verb, adjective(s), noun, adverb, etc.

- Write poems to a given formula, e.g. a separate line for a noun, two adjectives, a verb, an adverbial phrase, an image including a noun, e.g. *Cat/Swift and sleek/Streams/Down the beech tree/Like a waterfall.*
- Write preposition poems where each line begins with a different preposition.
- Collect examples from jokes, advertisements and headlines where the same word is being used for different functions, e.g. *How do you make a Swiss roll . . .* or *Giant Waves Down Queen's Funnel.*
- Sharing writing – at the drafting stage, the teacher's comments should draw attention to useful terms which describe some of the writer's achievements.

Sentence structure

- Compare different versions of the same traditional story, e.g. Red Riding Hood (or new versions of Peter Rabbit with the original).

  Once upon a time there was a little girl named Elizabeth who lived with her mother in a house on the edge of a village. She was loved by all who knew her, but she was especially dear to her grandmother, who loved her more than anything in the world.

(Trina Shart Hyman)

Once upon a time a little girl lived on the edge of a forest. Her dad was a woodcutter, whose job it was to hack down trees so that all sorts of things, like houses and comics, could be made from the wood.

(Tony Ross)

- Compare the sentence structures used in some early picture books for children. Contrast these with some reading schemes. How are the authors using sentence structure to support the young reader/listener?
- Expanding sentences. Start with a short sentence, e.g. *The woman was mending her bicycle.* Ask students to expand the sentence by adding adjectives, adverbs, conjunctions, further clauses or phrases. (Not a master class in style, but an introduction to the linguistic principles of expansion and substitution.)
- Compare the same story in a range of newspapers from tabloids to 'qualities'. What are the differences in sentence length and structure?

Word formation

- Look at invented words in nonsense poetry. Discuss which look like English words and why (combinations of consonants and vowels found in English but not other languages, endings like -*ing* or -*ed*?). Write your own nonsense.
- Collect words with common prefixes and suffixes and common markers for plurals, tenses, etc.

Variation in use of grammar

Discuss how sentences are built up in different kinds of writing:

1 according to purpose and audience, e.g. by comparing, say, diaries, recipes, instructions and other text types with specific purposes;
2 according to different genres, e.g. look at the use of passives or the way verbs get turned into nouns in scientific or information books, or the way connectives are used in legal language;
3 according to different dialects, e.g. collect examples of different dialects from books (e.g. John Agard's *Go Noah Go* or Jill Paton Walsh's *Gaffer Samson's Luck*) or from transcriptions of spoken language. Discuss similarities and differences between the dialects and standard English;
4 according to whether language is spoken or written, e.g. students could tape someone telling an anecdote. They could then transcribe it exactly with conventions for pauses, false starts, hesitations, etc. Later a written

version of the anecdote could be made. Compare the way meaning is built up in the two versions. Does the spoken version use sentences as a base in the same way as written language does?

Variations in grammar over time

- Collect examples from gravestones, old newspapers or advertisements. Compare the words and structures with those used today, and then write modern 'translations'.
- Look at different versions of the same bible story. If possible find examples from the Old English or the Wycliffe Bible to compare with more recent ones.

GRAMMAR AND THE TEACHER

At this critical time for English teaching we need to know what we are teaching about grammar, why we are teaching it, and how to communicate this to others. We have to be clear about the different aspects of grammar which will help our students now in their writing, reading and speaking, and later as adult language users. At the same time we need to recognise the differing views about grammar held by those outside the classroom and the reasons for the attitudes that underlie them. We need to clarify our own knowledge of grammar and its place in English teaching and learning so that we can be confident in explaining this to pupils and their parents, to colleagues and to others concerned with education.

Getting into grammar is important for our students – as teachers, we will play a crucial role in developing the knowledge they need.

NOTES

1 Language in the National Curriculum Project (LINC): Eastern Region: *Looking Into Grammar*, Ed Print, Lawrence Court, Princes Street, Huntingdon PE18 6PA.
2 *The Usborne Book of English Grammar*, Gee and Watson, London 1983. Quoted by Bain, R., in *Reflections: Talking about Language*, Hodder and Stoughton 1991.
3 DES, *English in the National Curriculum* (2), HMSO 1990.
4 Useful glossaries occur in Crystal, D.: *Language A to Z*, Longman 1991; in 'Grammar in Action', the final section of the *LINC Materials for Professional Development*; and at the back of Hudson, R., *Teaching Grammar*, Blackwell 1992.
5 These and other useful points are included in the South Yorkshire and Humberside LINC booklet: *Grammar*.
6 These examples are quoted in the *LINC Materials for Professional Development* distributed to schools in England and Wales in 1992 and available from LINC Secretary, Dept. of English Studies, University of Nottingham, Nottingham NG7 2RO.

Part V

Research

Good teaching is a form of research, and both teaching and research are forms of a continuous learning process.

(Goodman, K.S. (1979) *Bridging the Gaps in Reading: Respect and Communication*)

As teachers we are all also learners and to engage with English teaching fully means to take part in that exploration of ideas. This part looks at the ways in which the concept of research has widened to take in action research in the classroom as well as the larger-scale research which has served to inform classroom practice.

'Girls and literature: promise and reality' began as school-based research originally part of an MA thesis. The focus is the way in which girls' identities are constructed and the role of the English teacher in this.

The LINC project, already mentioned, was one of the largest research projects undertaken in this country. The Director of the project writes here explaining the LINC perspective on language, and relates the theoretical underpinnings to classroom practice.

Lev Vygotsky's *Thought and Language* is an extremely influential piece of research. James Britton's account makes accessible a complex theory. One of the most significant findings is that speech in infancy precedes thought at a later stage; when this 'speech for oneself' becomes internalised, the child 'begins to be capable of carrying out mental operations more subtle than anything he or she can put into words'. If speech is the foundation for thought, James Britton asks, 'how can we continue to prize a silent classroom?' Theory and practice, often represented as belonging to opposing camps, the ivory tower intellectual and the down-to-earth pragmatist, are shown here to be intertwined. The work of all effective teachers is informed by a set of principles – theories – about how pupils learn, although those teachers may never have made explicit, or even recognised, the theoretical base to their teaching. The theoretical basis may not be linked in the teachers' minds to any particular writer or school of thought. Instead you might hear reference to 'years of teaching'. But what does this really mean? It means that the teacher has come to a belief about how to teach effectively, which in turn depends on a belief about how pupils learn effectively. Theory only really describes those beliefs, and writers on educational theory are different from teachers only in that they are forced to be explicit about their beliefs (and, teachers would claim, have the time to do so) and to support their positions through research. Theory is not distinct from practice. It is a description of practice. Many teachers draw from a variety of theoretical positions without necessarily recognising them as such.

The chapters in this reader are to help you to form your own theoretical basis. They explore the practice you will see during your school placements and beyond. They offer you the 'unpacked' version of the shorthand thinking teachers use daily in planning and managing their teaching. The active thinking you have been asked to undertake in reading *Teaching English* means that, by now, you will have achieved the first criterion of a good English teacher mentioned in this reader – 'knowing the subject'. It may also mean that you now hold opinions and perspectives on English teaching which will qualify you to meet the second criterion: an English teacher who is 'passionate about the work'.

Chapter 26

Girls and literature
Promise and reality

Susan Brindley

The teaching of English . . . affects the individual and social identity of us all.

(Brian Cox, Editorial, *Critical Quarterly* **32** (4), 1990)

It was this relationship between English and identity which was the central focus of my research project; specifically, following some earlier research on gender issues, I wanted to investigate the relationship between English and the ways in which identity was constructed around issues of gender.[1]

It was impossible not to notice in the readings on gender issues that the key words of ambiguity and conflict recurred when discussing girls and schooling. Sue Lees wrote:

What emerges from the transcripts is that girls' experience of school is contradictory due to the ambiguity over what education is preparing them for.[2]

Similarly, interviews with a group of 15-year-old girls where one girl observed, 'whatever we do, it's always wrong' revealed:

A real dilemma stemming from the fact that teenage girls are confronted by conflicting sets of expectations . . . characterise[d] by expectations arising from the connotations we attach to femininity and adolescence.[3]

Schools present girls with conflicting and ambiguous messages about what is required of them. My thesis was that this was not accidental, but that schools were sites where the dominant ideology of patriarchy was perpetuated. This was achieved in part through the gendered construction of girls' identity; conflicting messages about identity were part of this process. English, however, presented a problem to this argument, precisely because 'English has a special power to challenge conventions, institutions, governments . . . any established system.'[4] The construction of gender identity in girls was part of an established system; could English simultaneously both challenge and perpetuate this ideology?

The first stage in the research project was to establish whether teachers of English saw gender issues as significant. I interviewed fifteen English teachers, two Advisers and an Assistant Education Officer, all of whom worked in an outer London Borough. The replies (and the teaching I saw) indicated a positive commitment:

> I do believe passionately in equal opportunities.
>
> (Interview 7, p. 10)

> Gender issues are something I'm very committed to.
>
> (Interview 3, p. 6)

> I think it's the overridingly important issue . . . gender issues are ubiquitous . . . abuse . . . incest . . . all that stems from the gender and power issue . . . . I really feel it's the overriding issue of the time.
>
> (Interview 1, pp. 9–10)

Yet a further contradiction arose. The evidence of commitment was clear; in the classroom, however, as I knew also from my own teaching experience, gender stereotypes continued to operate. One English teacher observed:

> The boys are very sexist in their attitudes to girls . . . they'd say, 'Get me my folder, get me some paper', and I would intervene . . . but you could tell that the girls were sort of saying to me, 'Oh it doesn't matter' . . . the attitude is that's what you've got to expect.
>
> (Interview 1, p. 7)

This contradiction seemed to be encapsulated in a phrase used by Giroux when he spoke of 'the promise and reality of schooling'.[5] The promise of challenging the construction of gender identity in girls seemed to be present in both the nature of English itself and the commitment of the teachers of English interviewed; the 'reality' was evident in the classroom gender-stereotypic behaviour. It was this 'gap' that the classroom research was designed to illuminate, and it was Giroux's statement I used as the framework for this part of the project. The promise then was in the commitment. Only one teacher I interviewed when asked 'How important do you feel gender issues are?' replied in terms other than those indicating some sort of priority. She answered:

> There are other issues that are equally important . . . . Race for instance, and, in a school like this one, linguistic skills of the kids is important.
>
> (Interview 8, p. 9)

The obvious point to develop here is the paralleling of gender not so much with race – a common move, if one open to debate –[6] but with linguistic skills. The implication seems to be that gender is another 'skill' – an area needing attention for those devoid of competence in it. Yet there is a wider issue underlying this statement. I would have expected to have found from my research that most of the teachers I spoke to would shy away from gender as a skill. There was an understanding of gender as an issue of wider significance: that by constructing a gender identity for girls (and for boys), a version of reality was being structured. The teacher quoted above also had that understanding. Yet by paralleling gender issues with linguistic skills she is encapsulating the dilemma experienced by all of these teachers: exactly how do you go about teaching gender issues and undertaking the concomitant activity of constructing or deconstructing gender identity? If the 'skills' approach is not taken, what approach is?

APPROACHES

In approaching gender issues, the teachers I interviewed all avoided the 'Today we're doing work on gender' approach. For most teachers, the approach initially at least was through literature. One teacher's approach to gender issues summed it up:

> I would rather tackle the issue [using literature] so it appears to be rising naturally. Coming in and saying: 'Right now we are going to discuss gender and sexism' . . . is not the way to do it at all.
>
> (Interview 8, pp. 5–6)

There was also, however, a sensitivity towards the pupils experiencing texts as propaganda, and the dangers of a counter effect. One teacher in an all-girls school observed:

> You've got to watch . . . that you don't saturate the girls with feminist thought because it can turn them off, it can have the reverse effect.
>
> (Interview 10, p. 2)

An early attempt at teaching gender issues was described thus:

> I think you can go too far the other way, make it too much of an issue. I think I probably went through a phase when I first started teaching when I did very, very specific things and after a while I think I was pushing their noses in it, and there were more subtle ways of dealing with it.
>
> (Interview 8, p. 7)

The 'more subtle ways' were those available through literature. One interviewee observed of the significance of literature:

> language is ever so good at naturalising the distinction between men and women and literature would play a critical part in that because the construction of women in literature, and the construction of women as readers, is a very powerful weapon in the construction of female roles.
>
> (Interview 4, p. 4)

As a Head of English, Carole Gaskell[7] stated, 'Literature is, after all, the special stuff of English', and of her department, 'Members of the department feel that an approach to gender through Literature is more productive than "doing it" as a theme.' This was the approach too of the teachers I interviewed. Most teachers centred their responses to my question 'How would you go about teaching gender issues in your classroom?' around choice of texts, and central to this was the issue of presenting strong, central female characters:

> My approval is to counter all . . . gender issues through literature . . . we have got texts like *Gilly Hopkins, Caged Bird,* and *Color Purple* . . . strong female lead characters.
>
> (Interview 1, p. 7)

Another teacher described how she had, on taking up a new post, inherited texts which she found to be sexist. Her response was this:

> We threw lots of books away . . . [they] did not reflect the society in which we live . . . there were so many good books that weren't there. One of the things we've aimed to do . . . is to create a balance in terms of race and sex and we've actually now got quite a lot of readers which have females as characters and as their central character.
>
> (Interview 8, p. 4)

Choice of texts was seen as a key area. Some staff offered lists of their 'recommended texts' and many explained why they had chosen or rejected texts:

> We have things like *The Ghost of Thomas Kempe* [Penelope Lively] but that's never come off the shelf this year. I don't like it because I think it's very sexist . . . it perpetuates this stupid thing about sisters, little girls being plain and every time the girl child is mentioned it's in those terms . . . . Mother's always doing washing-up or cooking and father's always at work and if he isn't at work he's sitting on the chair, smoking his pipe and reading his newspaper.
>
> (Interview 7, p. 5)

TYKE TILER

During my research, it became clear that within the Borough a corpus of books existed as recognised, if not recommended, literature for classroom teaching. One text, mentioned by every teacher I interviewed, was *The Turbulent Term of Tyke Tiler*[8] by Gene Kemp. The story features a character, Tyke, whose adventurous exploits are recounted, with the central point of the book being reserved until the last chapter, where it is revealed that Tyke is a girl.

In '*Pour Out the Cocoa, Janet*'[9] Rosemary Stones suggests:

Read this book with the class without letting on [the sex of Tyke] and then discuss the implications of everyone's reactions to the twist at the end.

(p. 25)

This seemed to be the route most teachers took with the text. One teacher observes that she had set her class:

a trip down memory lane, on the things Tyke had done; at what points there are disputes about what a boy would have done and what a girl would have done . . . The other time I've done *Tyke*, once they knew it was a girl a lot of the boys said: 'Oh well, if she was a girl she wouldn't have done those things!' . . . . They all got very heated and upset about it. It was . . . from the girls 'Yes, they would' and 'No, they wouldn't'. Then they would concede a few points: 'Well, some girls would . . .' etc.

(What kind of things did they say '. . . girls wouldn't?')

Going down into the muddy pool! And they thought a girl wouldn't be very good at climbing into the loft to hide the money.

(Interview 2, pp. 5–6)

Another teacher recorded:

If you take *Tyke Tiler*, the first time I ever taught it was with a Year 7, and they were absolutely incensed when they found it was a girl. They felt conned.

(Interview 7, p. 11)

This last reaction seems to be most telling. *Tyke* actually reads as having a boy protagonist. The jokes at the beginning of each chapter include sexist jokes (p. 43); Tyke's very name is masculine (*Chambers Dictionary* defines tyke as a rough-mannered fellow). Sexist terms abound: the Head (notably male) is referred to as 'Chief Sir' (p. 26), the male power figure with the 'deadly deep-river voice' (p. 71) when angry. Indeed the whole structure of the school is stereotyped. A male head; a bad-tempered female deputy head ('the old ratbag', p. 34); a male form teacher for Tyke, 'Sir', against whom all others are measured, including a student teacher:

Was she going to be all right, a friend like Sir, or an enemy like Mrs Soames?

(p. 48)

Indeed the student teacher (Miss Honeywell – again a sexist name) is an extremely stereotypic character. Tyke says of her:

Looking at this one was like looking at sunshine or a shop full of sweets when you're starving . . . Sir was grinning from ear to ear . . .

(p. 46)

She is shown as reading poetry to the class (p. 80) about King Arthur and myths and legends – 'female' activities. The form master is then shown introducing reality and objectivity – male traits, as opposed to the presented subjectivity of poetry and myths:

> Sir came in . . . and said 'Of course, it wasn't really like that at all.' 'Wasn't it, Sir?' 'No. You see the real King Arthur . . . and his knights didn't have a spare moment to go around rescuing damsels in distress.'

> Miss had gone pink and just a bit cross-looking and he got off the desk and went over and ruffled her hair . . . . He was grinning. 'I don't like them to get too far from the facts.' [She demurs] 'Have a meal with me tonight and we can argue it out.'

> (pp. 83–4)

So we have the male in the position of power, the assertion of superiority through 'facts', and sexism by patronisation.

TYKE'S FAMILY

The stereotypes in school are echoed in Tyke's home: a mother who admittedly works, but at night, when her family is least likely to need her; and during the day she is never presented as sleeping. Tyke's father: an authority figure, with Tyke afraid of the school writing home to him ('What would Mum say if Dad got another letter about me?' p. 71) no doubt as head of the household. Tyke's brother is seen escaping from housework whilst Tyke and her sister have tasks. Tyke's sister Beryl, 'the bright one in the family' (p. 76), concerned only with make-up and boyfriends:

> On the way back we saw Beryl with her new boyfriend . . . she was batting her false eyelashes up and down at him . . .

> (p. 82)

Beryl is also shown as jealous of Miss Honeywell:

> Women like her shouldn't be allowed out. They should be put away in dark rooms and only exercised once a day wearing a veil and an old sack.

> (p. 90)

The examples are numerous. With characters and structures so stereotyped, it is not surprising that it is with a feeling of somehow being made fools of that readers greet the 'twist' at the end. The English Adviser made the point:

> I think *Tyke Tiler* is a cheat. I think she wrote it as a boy and then thought it would be a good idea to change it to a girl at the end. The trouble with *Tyke Tiler* is it gives a very odd message. The main character is a boy. At the end she says it is a girl but everything that she describes

about that character are actually predominantly male characteristics in our society, so in a sense it seems to under-write those values. It doesn't call them into question. There's nothing about her that says there are other qualities both boys and girls should have that are traditionally described as feminine. That's why I say that Tyke Tiler is a boy that happens to be changed into a girl in the end. It may have been a straightforward schoolboy story and she decided to give it that extra dimension. There's no point of controversy or complexity, there's no point or problem about her identity, rather like pantomime.

As Elaine Millard in 'Stories to Grow On' from *Alice in Genderland* observes of *Tyke Tiler*:

> On first reading Tyke seemed to me a potent symbol, a heroine in the feminist 'Girls are powerful' tradition [then following a comment from a girl about 'never reading books with girls in them'] I questioned the rest of this group and discovered a common assumption that both the writer (Gene) and her heroine (Tyke) were male. On first reading then, girls are denied a positive feeling of identification which I think boys are frequently offered in class. The ending is . . . a subtle cheat. Worse . . . isn't there an implied reading that girls' actions are worth attention only when they are indistinguishable from those of their brothers?
>
> (p. 60)

Tyke Tiler is, in effect, presenting non-stereotypic girls as abnormal – and as such supports the dominant ideology. So there is a real difficulty here with texts. On one hand, there is recommendation from good sources[10] for *Tyke Tiler,* and statements made by the English Adviser saying: 'I don't think there's too much of a problem picking out texts that are overtly sexist' (Interview 4, p. 4) and yet, on the other hand, *Tyke Tiler* is clearly a sexist text. Teachers here are caught by taking on a book that, superficially, is challenging sexism, but which on analysis can be shown to be reinforcing sexist roles in society. If *Tyke* could prove so misleading, it was likely other texts would also prove difficult. Were there other ways forward?

What struck me in all of this was that the girls were being presented as passive, taking on unquestioningly the messages of the text (so in *Tyke Tiler* non-stereotypic behaviour was abnormal behaviour), and constructing their identity on the basis of these gendered messages. Yet that was not the whole story. The phenomenon of resistance was also evident. (Walkerdine asserts that the adoption of the patriarchal identity of femininity is 'at best shaky and partial'.)[11] The teaching of gender issues in itself demonstrates this. So there seemed to me to be a way forward building on this resistance – the recognition that girls were not passive consumers of messages from texts.

What I wanted to argue for was a different sort of construction of identity
– one which allowed for an active role for girls. Gemma Moss in 'Rewriting
Reading'[12] states:

> Linked to the notion of powerful texts is the notion of vulnerable readers.
> As a consequence . . . . the teachers' role becomes one of regulatory
> control . . . . The view that texts . . . can fundamentally influence their
> readers, whether for good or bad, works from the assumption that
> particular textual features have fixed meanings, and that consequently the
> message any one text holds is quite easy to determine . . . by exercising
> skill and judgement . . . . But there are difficulties here.
>
> (pp. 184–5)

Tyke Tiler of course usefully demonstrated such difficulties. If, however, we
return to a comment made earlier by a teacher, that:

> the construction of women in literature, and the construction of women
> as readers, is a very powerful weapon in the construction of female roles
>
> (Interview 4, p. 4)

there is a 'way forward' here. The suggestion is that the reader (the girl)
should be positioned as the active constructor of meaning in a text (that is,
the text has more than a single authorial meaning); in the construction of
meaning in the text, she is concomitantly active in the construction of her
own gender identity. The recognition that meaning can be constructed
rather than received is in itself an act of liberation. This, as Moss points out,
frees the teacher from the role of 'polic[ing] children's reading of that text'
(p. 187). In terms of this research, it also means that English is restored to
having 'the special power to challenge . . . any established system'.[13]

I would not want to suggest that this small-scale piece of research constitutes anything other than the beginning of an enquiry into a vast and
complex area. Indeed, each time I found what seemed to be an answer, it
brought with it another half-dozen questions. But it seems to me that the
role English teaching has is critical in empowering girls to be active makers
of meaning and thereby constructors of their own gender identity, for:

> In a society disfigured by sexual and racial oppression . . . the only
> education worth the name is one that forms people capable of taking part
> in their own liberation.[14]

NOTES

1 Brindley, S. (1989) 'Gender, ideology and literature'. Unpublished MA thesis.
  University of London.
2 Lees, S. (1987) 'The structure of sexual relations in school' in Arnot, M. and
  Weiner, G. (eds) *Gender and the Politics of Schooling*, Hutchinson, London. p.
  176.
3 Hudson, B. (1984) 'Femininity and adolescence' in McRobbie, A. and Nava, M.

(eds) *Gender and Generation*, Macmillan, London. p. 31.

4 Protherough, R. and Atkinson, J. (1991) *The Making of English Teachers*, Open University Press, Milton Keynes. p. 15.

5 Giroux, H.A. (1982) *Critical Theory and Educational Practice*, Deakin University Press, Victoria. p. 114.

6 Carby, H. V. (1987) 'Black feminism and the boundaries of sisterhood', in Arno, M. and Weiner, G. (eds) *Gender and the Politics of Schooling*, Hutchinson. p. 67 (pp. 64–75).

7 Gaskell, C. (1984) 'Frills, tea sets, dolls: reflections on teaching in a girls' school' in *The English Curriculum: Gender*, The English Centre, ILEA, London. p. 117.

8 Kemp, G. (1979) *The Turbulent Term of Tyke Tiler*, Puffin, London.

9 Stones, R. (1983) *'Pour Out the Cocoa, Janet': Sexism in Children's Books*, Schools Council Programme 3, Longman, York. p. 8.

10 For example, *The English Curriculum: Gender* (p. 41) as above.

11 Walkerdine, V. (1984) 'Some day my prince will come: young girls and the preparation for adolescent sexuality' in McRobbie, A. and Nava, M. (eds) *Gender and Generation*, Macmillan, London. p. 163.

12 Moss, G. (1992) 'Rewriting Reading', in Kimberley, M. *et al.* (eds) *New Readings: Contributions to an Understanding of Literacy*, A & C Black.

13 Protherough, R. and Atkinson, J. (1991) *The Making of English Teachers*, Open University Press, Milton Keynes. p. 15.

14 Connell *et al.*, quoted in Giroux, H.A. (1982) *Critical Theory and Educational Practice*, Deakin University Press, Victoria. p. 114.

Chapter 27

Knowledge about language in the curriculum

Ronald Carter

WHAT IS LINC?

LINC stands for *Language In* the *National Curriculum*. It is a project funded by the Department of Education and Science under an ESG (Education Support Grant). The main aim of the project is to produce materials and to conduct activities to support implementation of English in the National Curriculum in England and Wales in the light of the views of language outlined in the Kingman and Cox Reports on English language teaching and English 5–16 respectively (DES 1988, 1989). The LINC Project was designed to operate from April 1989 until March 1992.

Why is KAL (*Knowledge About Language*) important to teachers?

A primary aim of the LINC Project is further to enhance teachers' understanding and knowledge about language in relation to processes of teaching and learning. The project operates with the following main assumptions:

1 Language is central to the processes of teaching and learning. Explicit knowledge about language can sharpen teachers' appreciation of children's achivements with language as well as broaden the language opportunities they provide for pupils in the classroom. It can also help teachers understand the nature of children's difficulties or partial successes with language.
2 More conscious attention to language provides tools which can enable teachers, for example, to:
   • develop their pupils' already impressive ability to talk and to comprehend spoken language;
   • help pupils to read more confidently (for example, through miscue analysis) and become autonomous readers;
   • understand how to intervene constructively at various stages in their pupils' writing – in preparation, in drafting, in final product, in commenting and evaluating;

- help pupils to develop further insights into how they use language in their day-to-day lives for many purposes;
- understand better what to make explicit and what to leave implicit in pupils' own knowledge about language.

3 KAL helps teachers to distinguish between casual reactions to ways of speaking (responses to, for example, accent, dialect or the use of forms by the speaker of a second language which show the influence of a first) and more informed professional judgements.

4 In discussing language there are certain dangers in undue abstraction and in the perception of an associated *metalanguage* as threatening or inhibiting (especially to teachers with little previous background in the study of language). LINC believes that shared frames of reference are more important than terminologies *per se* but that some selected meta-language can enable us to talk about language more precisely and economically.

5 KAL assists teachers to present achievements in language in a positive light to parents and governors; it can enable them to be better equipped to discuss such questions as standard English, 'grammar' and policies concerning marking.

6 The school is a fundamentally *social* language-using community. Deepening insights into the social functions of language and into the relationships between language and society can unlock for teachers important insights into the relationships between language and learning.

What does knowledge about language mean for pupils?

The National Curriculum for English in England and Wales includes a requirement that pupils demonstrate knowledge about language. Pupils' knowledge about language should take place within the context of reading, writing and speaking/listening development.

Members of the LINC Project believe that there are many positive benefits to supporting in pupils a fuller and more explicit knowledge about language. The team is committed to the following main principles for KAL in primary and secondary schools:

1 There can be no return to formalist, decontextualised classroom analysis of language, nor to the deficiency pedagogies on which such teaching is founded.

2 Language study should start from what children can do, from their positive achievements with language and from the remarkable resources of implicit knowledge about language which all children possess.

3 A rich experience of using language should generally *precede* conscious reflection on or analysis of language. Language study can influence use but development of the relationship between learning about language and

learning how to use it is not a linear one but rather a recursive, cyclical and mutually informing relationship.

4 Being more explicitly informed about the sources of attitudes to language, about its uses and misuses, about how language is used to manipulate and incapacitate, can *empower* pupils to see through language to the ways in which messages are mediated and ideologies encoded.

5 Metalanguage should be introduced where appropriate to facilitate talking and thinking about language but children should be allowed to come to specialist terms as needed and in context.

6 Teaching methodologies for KAL should promote experiential, exploratory and reflective encounters with language; transmissive methods are usually inappropriate for the study of language in schools.

What general assumptions about the nature of language are adopted in the LINC materials for professional development?

LINC stresses above all the richness and variety of language: the uses and functions of language over the forms of language; the description of texts in social contexts over the description of isolated decontextualised bits of language. Its main assumptions are that:

1 As humans we use language primarily for social reasons, for a variety of purposes.

2 Language is imbued with dynamism and varies from one context to another and from one set of uses to another. Language also changes over time.

3 Language is penetrated with social and cultural values and also carries meanings related to each user's unique identity.

4 Language reveals and conceals much about human relationships. There are intimate connections, for example, between language and social power, language and culture and language and gender.

5 Language is a system and is systematically organised.

6 Meanings created in and through language are often problematic; they can constrain us as well as liberate us. Language users must constantly negotiate and renegotiate meanings.

LINC strongly supports the view of language expressed by the English Working Group in paragraph 6.18 of its report (the Cox Report, DES 1989):

Language is a system of sounds, meanings and structures with which we make sense of the world around us. It functions as a tool of thought; as a means of social organisation; as the repository and means of transmission of knowledge; as the raw material of literature, and as the creator and sustainer – or destroyer – of human relationships. It changes inevitably over time and, as change is not uniform, from place to place. Because language is a fundamental part of being human, it is an important aspect of a person's sense of self; because it is a fundamental feature of any community, it is an important aspect of a person's sense of social identity.

THE LINC PROJECT: THEORETICAL PERSPECTIVES ON LANGUAGE AND EDUCATION

What specific underlying theories of language are influential in the LINC programme?

The LINC programme was designed to develop the model of language recommended in the Kingman Report (DES 1988). The Kingman model of language is a descriptive and analytical model. As such it is helpful and it certainly reflects current developments in linguistics. However, an analytical model is not a pedagogic model. The approach to language developed by LINC is true to the spirit of the Kingman model but it develops that model in order to make it pedagogically sensitive. A diagrammatic version of the Kingman model of language is given in Figure 27.1.

The LINC group noted in particular the statement in the Kingman Report that there can be no one model of the English language and that the sequence in which the parts of the Kingman model were set out should not imply pedagogic priorities. Accordingly, the LINC group has realigned the Kingman model of language in order to give special emphasis to the third and fourth 'parts' of Kingman – the development of language and language variation – with greater emphasis than in Kingman given to the variation of language in different social and cultural contexts. In fact, a principal and underlying motivation for the LINC Project is a concern with *language variation*.

A concern with social, cultural and textual variation does not preclude a concern with the *forms of language* (contained in Part 1 of the Kingman model of language). However, such forms should be examined not in and for themselves but in relation to functional variation. In educational contexts functional variation manifests itself in particular in the kinds of talk, writing and reading produced in schools and classrooms. Within the LINC model language form is systematically focused where it is judged to be relevant and enabling for teachers and pupils; but the broader social functions and parameters within which all forms are embedded operate as a constant check against decontextualised analysis of language.

The LINC approach to language is much influenced by functional theories of language. The main proponent of such theories – over a period of almost thirty years – has been Professor Michael Halliday, and the LINC model of language owes much to Halliday's work. Halliday has always placed meaning at the very centre of theories of language and LINC supports that position.

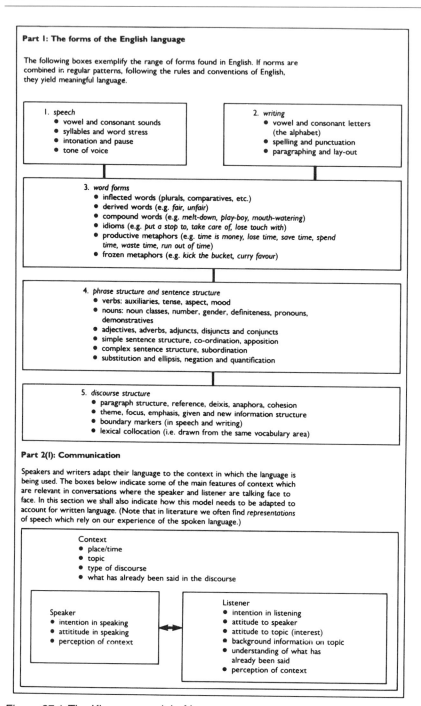

Part I: The forms of the English language

The following boxes exemplify the range of forms found in English. If norms are combined in regular patterns, following the rules and conventions of English, they yield meaningful language.

1. *speech*
 • vowel and consonant sounds
 • syllables and word stress
 • intonation and pause
 • tone of voice

2. *writing*
 • vowel and consonant letters (the alphabet)
 • spelling and punctuation
 • paragraphing and lay-out

3. *word forms*
 • inflected words (plurals, comparatives, etc.)
 • derived words (e.g. *fair, unfair*)
 • compound words (e.g. *melt-down, play-boy, mouth-watering*)
 • idioms (e.g. *put a stop to, take care of, lose touch with*)
 • productive metaphors (e.g. *time is money, lose time, save time, spend time, waste time, run out of time*)
 • frozen metaphors (e.g. *kick the bucket, curry favour*)

4. *phrase structure and sentence structure*
 • verbs: auxiliaries, tense, aspect, mood
 • nouns: noun classes, number, gender, definiteness, pronouns, demonstratives
 • adjectives, adverbs, adjuncts, disjuncts and conjuncts
 • simple sentence structure, co-ordination, apposition
 • complex sentence structure, subordination
 • substitution and ellipsis, negation and quantification

5. *discourse structure*
 • paragraph structure, reference, deixis, anaphora, cohesion
 • theme, focus, emphasis, given and new information structure
 • boundary markers (in speech and writing)
 • lexical collocation (i.e. drawn from the same vocabulary area)

Part 2(I): Communication

Speakers and writers adapt their language to the context in which the language is being used. The boxes below indicate some of the main features of context which are relevant in conversations where the speaker and listener are talking face to face. In this section we shall also indicate how this model needs to be adapted to account for written language. (Note that in literature we often find *representations* of speech which rely on our experience of the spoken language.)

Context
 • place/time
 • topic
 • type of discourse
 • what has already been said in the discourse

Speaker
 • intention in speaking
 • attitude in speaking
 • perception of context

Listener
 • intention in listening
 • attitude to speaker
 • attitude to topic (interest)
 • background information on topic
 • understanding of what has already been said
 • perception of context

Figure 27.1 The Kingman model of language

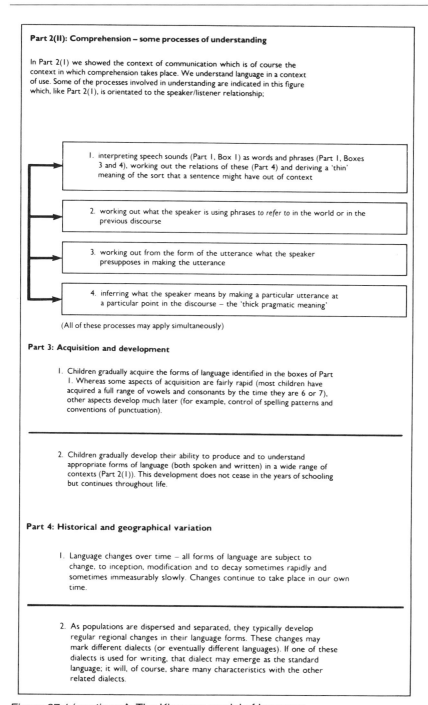

Part 2(II): Comprehension – some processes of understanding

In Part 2(I) we showed the context of communication which is of course the context in which comprehension takes place. We understand language in a context of use. Some of the processes involved in understanding are indicated in this figure which, like Part 2(I), is orientated to the speaker/listener relationship;

1. interpreting speech sounds (Part I, Box I) as words and phrases (Part I, Boxes 3 and 4), working out the relations of these (Part 4) and deriving a 'thin' meaning of the sort that a sentence might have out of context

2. working out what the speaker is using phrases *to refer to* in the world or in the previous discourse

3. working out from the form of the utterance what the speaker presupposes in making the utterance

4. inferring what the speaker means by making a particular utterance at a particular point in the discourse – the 'thick pragmatic meaning'

(All of these processes may apply simultaneously)

Part 3: Acquisition and development

1. Children gradually acquire the forms of language identified in the boxes of Part I. Whereas some aspects of acquisition are fairly rapid (most children have acquired a full range of vowels and consonants by the time they are 6 or 7), other aspects develop much later (for example, control of spelling patterns and conventions of punctuation).

2. Children gradually develop their ability to produce and to understand appropriate forms of language (both spoken and written) in a wide range of contexts (Part 2(I)). This development does not cease in the years of schooling but continues throughout life.

Part 4: Historical and geographical variation

1. Language changes over time – all forms of language are subject to change, to inception, modification and to decay sometimes rapidly and sometimes immeasurably slowly. Changes continue to take place in our own time.

2. As populations are dispersed and separated, they typically develop regular regional changes in their language forms. These changes may mark different dialects (or eventually different languages). If one of these dialects is used for writing, that dialect may emerge as the standard language; it will, of course, share many characteristics with the other related dialects.

Figure 27.1 (continued) The Kingman model of language

It is important, however, that a view of language in educational contexts should not only be systematic and detailed but should also be able to account for more than the most minute or 'lower-level' operations of language. Language studies in the 1960s and 1970s were characterised by attention to lower-level forms such as phonemes, morphemes and clauses, usually out of context. In the 1980s, however, developments in text linguistics, discourse analysis and functional grammar have provided a basis for examining higher-level patterns of language across complete texts. The LINC programme recognises the importance of this work and its relevance to education – where written and spoken texts are generated in a range of contexts and for a range of purposes.

A functional theory of language is a natural complement to influential theories of language development constructed in the 1970s by Professor James Britton and others working to similar principles. These theories make clear the centrality of context, purpose and audience in language use and the salience of this understanding for children's learning. Such theories culminated in *The Bullock Report* (DES 1975) – a very influential forerunner of the Kingman and Cox Reports – and are now central to the National Curriculum for English.

The Hallidayan diagram (Figure 27.2) illustrates the extent to which a functional model of language can be integrated with Britton's theories of language development. It illustrates the following main features of functional theory:

- The making of *meaning* is the reason for the invention, existence and development of language.
- All meanings exist within the context of culture. Cultural values and beliefs determine the purposes, audiences, settings and topics of language.
- Texts, spoken and written, are created and interpreted by making appropriate choices from the language system according to specific purposes, audiences, settings and topics.

Functional accounts of language stress the importance of the *variation* of language at all levels within this model, both from the broadest parameters of cultural variation to variations in grammatical or phonemic form. The aim is to allow constant explanation and interpretation of all layers of variation in relation to one another. The model therefore prevents generalised discussion of situations for language at the same time as it prevents decontextualised discussion of language; forms and the making of meanings are shown to be inextricably interrelated in the creation of complete texts. The LINC approach to language in education is to promote precise and systematic discussion of language in the context of established theories of language learning and development.

LINC has a special responsibility to focus on language with descriptive precision. It recognises the contribution of linguistics to our understanding

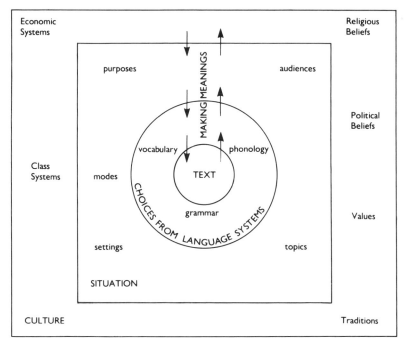

Figure 27.2 Integration of a functional model of language with Britton's theories of language development

of language, but also that of educationists, philosophers of language, socio-logists, psychologists, cultural and literary theorists, whose insights also have a continuing relevance to the central role of language in education. A functional theory of language allows us to embrace such perspectives, particularly those concerned with the making of textual meaning in social and cultural contexts.

What do we mean by variation theory?

A functional theory of language is, as we have seen, predicated on the fact that language varies. There are three main dimensions to this variation: language varies according to the uses to which it is put; it varies over time; it varies according to the language user. Variation over time is termed *dia-chronic* variation; variation according to the user is termed *dialectal* vari-ation; variation according to use is termed *diatypic* variation. In all components of variation the social context of language use is a crucial, indeed sometimes determining, factor in the nature of the variation.

For example, changes in language over time are regularly the result of socio-cultural or socio-economic changes. From the mid-seventeenth to the nineteenth century the growth of the East Midlands dialect into the standard

English dialect of Great Britain, and subsequently internationally too, can be attributed largely to the economic and political power of London and to the social attitudes which associate with such power, particularly in respect of 'non-standard' dialects with other geographical locations.

Contemporary uses of dialect forms are also often directly dependent on the social position of the user and on his or her attitudes towards it. A whole body of sociolinguistic research (e.g. Trudgill 1983) confirms that dialectal variation occurs according to a range of largely socially constructed parameters. Such work also demonstrates that dialects are not fixed entities but rather continua with users making choices along the continua according to their social status, their perception of their own and their interlocutor's social status, their assessment of the nature of the context of their language use as well as such factors as their own gender or ethnicity and their perception of their interlocutor(s) in relation to such factors. Geographical factors are also relevant and for some users a sense of belonging to a particular community will be a crucial factor in choices along the continua of dialectal variation, not least because such choices will involve expressions of their identity as individuals. A further marker of individuality resides in the *idolects* which each speaker possesses, which are particular choices of words or phrases or particular phonological characteristics which single out one user from another. Such characteristics are largely regular over time. In more senses than one, however, dialectal variation reveals who you are.

Diatypic variation is also deeply embedded in different social contexts of use. A fundamental component of this variation, particularly in educational contexts, is a continuum between spoken and written *modes*. Differences and distinctions between speech and writing result in different diatypes with different communicative functions. For example, a written report is usually different from a spoken report. We need to remember, however, that different degrees of rehearsal or planning can underlie the same function within the two modes. A planned spoken report, which can even have been written to be spoken, will contain different forms of language from an unplanned one and for this main reason poles of 'planned' and 'unplanned' may be more significant than choices in spoken and written modes, however fundamental such choices are. Also significant in this variation will be the audience and the formality of the relations between the user and the audience; and the very subject matter, as well as assumptions of familiarity with the general topic, will determine choices of mode and judgement of appropriate reception of the language. Such judgement will, of course, involve conscious or unconscious perception of the power relations which obtain in the socio-cultural context of this use of language as well as the relation of the choices of particular language forms to the ideologies, beliefs and value systems of the participants.

What is the relevance of these theories to classroom language development?

The pay-off for any applied linguistic theory of language is not its power as a theory; what counts is its relevance to classroom practice. To what extent can the above theories help teachers in their task of fostering language development? To what extent can such theories inform the kind of knowledge about language which serves pupils' understanding of language both in its own right and in generating their own more effective use of language?

In general terms it can be said that an ability to manipulate a range of styles of language is crucial to success within any curriculum. Teachers therefore need to have a quite explicit knowledge about all components of variation in order that their own practice can support such a goal of development. The more opportunities that can be provided within teacher education for teachers themselves to explore and experience language variation, to reflect on its functions and to analyse some of the forms by which such functions are realised, then the better it will be for pupils' acquisition and development of language.

As far as pupils are concerned it is a matter of judgement on the part of the teacher how far to make such things explicit, at what stages of development and in what classroom contexts. Pupils possess considerable resources of mainly implicit knowledge about the way language changes according to purpose, audience and context. They acquire such knowledge at relatively early ages and can even explore such issues in the infant class.

The Cox Report (DES 1989) provides two main rationales for knowledge about language for pupils: a *cognitive* rationale and a *social* rationale. The cognitive rationale underlines the intellectual benefits which can follow from disembedding implicit awareness of language and making it more explicit through a process of sustained reflection on the nature and functions of language; the social rationale underlines the benefits in enhanced social tolerance and understanding which can follow from greater awareness of language diversity and of the necessary variations which occur within and across languages, often for social reasons. Pupils' knowledge about language should therefore include substantial components of both dialectal, diachronic and diatypic variation – and, indeed, this is recommended in the Cox Report.

A major unanswered and unexplained question in knowledge about language for pupils concerns the relationship between knowledge about or reflection on language and a development of competence in the use of language. Such a connection is plausible, but in the absence of evidence of the kind required by extensive longitudinal studies, it cannot be demonstrated. What can be said is that pupils are likely to benefit from detailed consideration being given to the forms and function of language variation. Such is the importance of an ability to control language in all its many variations that the more angles that can be provided on those variations the better.

Most important of all is the focus for pupils on written or *diatypic variation*. Much is made of the need for pupils to extend their spoken repertoire. This will involve incorporating standard English forms for use, where appropriate. A key phrase here is *where appropriate*, for the idea of standard English being serviceable for all purposes assumes that there are no contexts where variation along dialectal continua is appropriate. There are, of course, contexts such as formal interchanges with a large or an unknown audience where standard English is applicable; but for many speakers the same dialect would be quite inapplicable in an informal context interchanging with friends on topics where the expression of ideas and feelings is intimately a part of the speaker's individuality and identity.

It should be a universal educational goal to empower pupils to use as wide a range of language varieties as competently as possible. Such a goal of language learning equips pupils to meet the linguistic demands of adult society and to work effectively within that society and, where necessary, *against* forces within that society which might operate to disempower individuals and the communities of which they are part. To this particular end competence in diatypic variation is more likely to be empowering than is competence in a range of dialects. Changes to social realities as well as to one's position within society are more likely to be brought about not by the replacement of one dialect by another, even if that dialect is standard English, but by a developed capacity to deploy and reflect on the deployment of as wide a range of varieties as possible.

Some limits to linguistic approaches to language education

This chapter supports a view that a greater degree of linguistic awareness than has been available in much teacher training can be of real benefit and value to teachers. A stronger view still is that if teachers have no formal training in linguistic awareness then they will lack categories and frameworks for thinking about and analysing crucial elements in learning and will therefore draw such categories from a common store of half-belief in which prejudice and fact combine indistinguishably.

Finally, we need to question just what it means to *know* about language. This chapter has stressed the need for conscious knowledge about language and argued for the advantages to teachers of being able to describe language explicitly. It is, of course, possible to know about language in more than one way and implicit, intuitive knowledge has an important part to play. All teachers and pupils possess considerable knowledge about language and this knowledge has to be valued, worked with, and built upon. It would also be wrong to assume that conscious knowledge operates independently of unconscious knowledge; there is a constant interplay and interaction between different modes of knowing and explicit, analytical attention to language can and should serve to deepen intuitions. There is a continuum from intuitions about language, reflection on language and analysis of language which is not linear in any simple way but rather cyclical, recursive and mutually informing. As we have already recognised, there is in the LINC programme a main emphasis, where appropriate, on explicit knowledge about language and on the contributions of linguistics to this understanding; but other emphases and other academic traditions have an important part to play in fostering the kinds of broad understanding of the nature of language which enables the full complexity and richness of language as a human resource for meaning making to be appreciated.

SUMMARY

The LINC approach to language variation in educational contexts:

1 is *functional* and Hallidayan in orientation;
2 is an educationally *relevant* model;
3 is close to the theory of language implicit in the Cox Report but sufficiently broad to subsume a *realigned* Kingman model;
4 is a broad descriptive framework which allows *systematic* analysis and *principled* pedagogic questions to be generated;
5 provides a basis for a mainly discourse-driven account of language – its functional, socio-semantic thrust ensures *ideological* issues are quite central;
6 has complete *texts* at the centre of interest;
7 is a natural complement to influential theories of language in education development in the 1970s by, for example, Britton and others – culminating in the Bullock Report – with their emphasis on categories of *audience*, *purpose* and *context*;
8 accommodates both linguistic perspectives (e.g. phonemic variation) and more holistic perspectives on language (e.g. language as cultural practice);
9 recognises that some aspects of language resist systematisation;
10 (potentially) renders distinctions between linguistics in education/ language in education passé.

Particularly in a language education perspective, we need to take a dynamic view of language in all three dimensions of its variation: *dialectal* (regional/social), *diatypic* (functional) and *diachronic* (historical). To put this in less technical terms: for any theory of language in education, it should be seen as the norm, rather than the exception, that the community of learners use a variety of codes (languages and/or dialects), that they use a variety of language functions (or registers), and that none of these ever stands still.

(Halliday 1987)

REFERENCES

DES (1975) *A Language for Life* (the Bullock Report). London: HMSO.

DES (1988) *Report of the Committee of Inquiry into the Teaching of the English Language* (the Kingman Report). London: HMSO.

DES (1989) *Report of the English Working Party 5–16* (the Cox Report). London: HMSO.

Halliday, M.A.K. (1987) 'Some Basic Concepts in Educational Linguistics', in Bickley, V. (ed.) *Languages in Education in a Bi-lingual or Multi-lingual Setting*. Hong Kong: ILE, pp. 5–17.

Trudgill, P. (1983) *On Dialect*. Oxford: Blackwell.

Chapter 28

Vygotsky's contribution to pedagogical theory

James Britton

The story of Vygotsky's influence on educational thinking in the West is a fantastic one – it reads, as they say, like a fairy story. A young Russian intellectual – in the first instance a student of literature – at the age of 38 writes a book on the relation of language to thought. Having previously worked on the ideas with colleagues for some ten years, he finishes the manuscript off in haste, a race against tuberculosis, and dies before it is published. Two years after its publication the book, *Thought and Language*, is suppressed by the Soviet authorities and remains so for twenty years though not before the substance of a magnificent last chapter, presented as a paper at an American conference, finds its way in English on to the pages of a psychological journal. A long silence is finally broken when, in 1962, twenty-eight years after its original appearance, scholars in Cambridge, Massachusetts, produce an English translation of the whole work and Bruner is on hand to write the introduction.

But that is hardly more than the beginning of the story. Perhaps as an effect of the 'cold war', recognition of the significance of Vygotsky's work is slow to develop: seminal works in language acquisition and development continue to be published with slight reference, or none, to his ideas and surprisingly enough, particularly so in the United States. Cambridge (MA), however, continued to take the lead: in 1971 MIT Press brought out an English translation of a collection of Vygotsky's early writings on literary texts under the title *The Psychology of Art* – now, unfortunately, no longer in print. And in 1978 four American editors, working with A.R. Luria, Vygotsky's close colleague, disciple and friend (and in turn his successor in Moscow), produced an edited translation of seminal work by Vygotsky and gave it the title *Mind in Society*. Finally, in 1987 there appeared a revised and re-edited translation of *Thought and Language* from MIT Press.

In his introduction to the original Russian edition of *Thought and Language*, Vygotsky had written, 'we fully realize the inevitable imperfections of this study, which is no more than a first step in a new direction'. In which direction? Vygotsky has this answer: 'Our findings point the way to a new theory of consciousness' and he goes on to indicate four aspects of the work that are *novel*, and – consequently – 'in need of further careful checking'. I have the sense here of someone embarking on an idea he knows he cannot himself carry through to a conclusion. His four discoveries, to state them as briefly as I can, are these:

1 Word meanings *evolve* during childhood: it cannot be assumed that when a child uses a word he or she means by it what we as adult speakers would mean.

2 While accepting Piaget's theory of the growth of *spontaneous concepts* – ideas arrived at by inference from (or evidenced by) our own experiences – Vygotsky adds the notion of *non-spontaneous concepts* – ideas taken over from other people (notably teachers) – taken over as problems needing solution, or as 'empty categories', so to speak, which need time to find embodiment in our own experience and ground themselves in our own knowledge base. Vygotsky sees this as a two-way movement, 'upward' of spontaneous concepts, 'downward' of non-spontaneous concepts, each mode facilitating the other – and the joint operation being characteristic of human learning.

3 Vygotsky believed that mastery of the written language – learning to read and write – had a profound effect upon the achievement of abstract thinking. The *constancy* of the written language, grafted, so to speak, upon the *immediacy* of the spoken language, enables a speaker to *reflect* upon meanings and by doing so acquire a new level of control, a critical awareness of his or her own thought processes.

4 Speech in infancy, Vygotsky claimed, is the direct antecedent of thinking at a later stage. When children discover that it is helpful to speak aloud about what they are doing, they begin to employ what Vygotsky termed 'speech for oneself'; and thereafter speech takes on a dual function and, in due course, develops differentially; conversation becomes more effective *as communication*, while monologue or 'running commentary' (speech for oneself) changes in what is virtually the opposite direction. That is to say, in conversation children extend their control of the grammatical structures of the spoken language and increase their resources of conventional word meanings. In their monologues, on the contrary, they exploit the fact that they are talking to themselves by using as it were 'note form' – skeletal or abbreviated structures that would mean little to one who did not already share the speaker's thoughts – and *personal, idiosyncratic* word meanings – pet words, inventions, portmanteau terms, rich in meaning for the originator but minimally endorsed by convention.

Vygotsky observed these changes in the speech of children from about 3 years old to about 7 – changes that set up a marked difference between their conversational mode and their use of 'speech for oneself'. On the strength of these observations he speculated that, rather than 'withering away' as Piaget had suggested, speech for oneself became internalised and continued to operate as the genesis of thought, perhaps moving through the stages of *inner speech* to *verbal thinking* and thence to the most elusive stage of all – thought itself.

By this account, then, we *think* by handling 'post-language symbols' – forms that began as speech but which have been successively freed from the constraints of the grammar of the spoken language and from the constraints of conventional, public word meanings. It is this freedom that characterises the fluidity of thought – and accounts for the necessity of *imposing organisation* upon our thoughts when we want to communicate them.

It was a brilliant insight on Vygotsky's part to realise that when speech for oneself becomes internalised it is in large part because the child, in handling the freer forms of speech that constitute that mode, begins to be capable of carrying out mental operations more subtle than anything he or she can put into words. I think we can become aware of the reciprocal process when as we listen to discussion we engender some response – a question to be asked or a comment we want to make – and have a clear sense that the process of moving from the fluid operation of thought units to the utterance of rule-governed 'public' speech using conventional word meanings is one that may demand strenuous mental effort on our part.

When *Mind in Society* appeared in 1978, a review by Stephen Toulmin in the *New York Review of Books* underlined Vygotsky's concern with consciousness. He saw Vygotsky as denying on the one hand that human consciousness can be regarded as simply an effect of the genes, of *nature*, or on the other hand as an effect of environment – of *nurture* – claiming that both influences must interact in the creation of mind in the individual. He gave his review the title 'The Mozart of Psychology' (nominating Luria in consequence as 'The Beethoven') and suggested that Western psychology urgently needed to take on the broader perspective that Vygotsky had initiated.

It is in this work that Vygotsky's central contention becomes clear – the claim that *human consciousness is achieved by the internalisation of shared social behaviour*. A series of 'temporary connections' is made by the individual within the individual life-span: each link makes possible further links, each operation begins with external *observable social behaviour* – an exposed segment, as it were, of what is to become inner behaviour. Thus is indicated, surely, a new emphasis upon the observation and study of childhood activities for the light they throw upon later behaviours not open to observation.

But social behaviour implies interaction within a group whose activities have been shaped to cultural patterns. The relationship between individual development and the evolution of society is a complex one, not a matter of mere recapitulation or parallelism. The familiar story of the psychologist Kellogg and his chimpanzee comes to mind: the chimpanzee had acted as companion to Kellogg's infant son and for a period of years both creatures developed, so to speak, in tandem – able to share each other's activities – but only up to the point where the boy learned to speak: the young Kellogg is today, I believe, himself a scientist – the chimpanzee remains – a chimpanzee! In the historical development from animal to man, the acquisition of language is a watershed: in the development of the individual child from birth to 3 or 4 years, the acquisition of language is a watershed.

Speech that begins as a shared social activity on the part of the child and becomes a principal means of the mental regulation and refinement of his individual behaviour – this is the prime example of Vygotsky's theory of internalisation to achieve consciousness. He gives us a further striking example when he claims that make-believe play in early childhood constitutes the earliest, and at that time only available, form of *imagination*. It is nearer the truth, he says, to claim that imagination in adolescence and later is 'make-believe play without action' than it is to claim that make-believe play in young children is 'imagination in action'.

The implications of these ideas for pedagogy are, of course, enormous. If speech in childhood lays the foundations for a lifetime of thinking, how can we continue to prize a silent classroom? And if shared social behaviour (of many kinds, verbal and non-verbal) is seen as the source of learning, we must revise the traditional view of the teacher's role. The teacher can no longer act as the 'middle-man' in all learning – as it becomes clear that education is *an effect of community*. Bruner, in a fairly recent book, devoted a chapter to Vygotsky's ideas, and in a later chapter makes this comment:

> Some years ago I wrote some very insistent articles about the importance of discovery learning . . . . What I am proposing here is an extension of that idea, or better, a completion. My model of the child in those days was very much in the tradition of the solo child mastering the world by representing it to himself in his own terms. In the intervening years I have come increasingly to recognize that most learning in most settings is a communal activity, a sharing of the culture. It is not just that the child must make his knowledge his own, but that he must make it his own in a community of those who share his sense of belonging to a culture. It is this that leads me to emphasize not only discovery and invention but the importance of negotiating and sharing – in a word, of joint culture creating as an object of schooling and as an appropriate step en route to becoming a member of the adult society in which one lives out one's life.
>
> (Bruner 1986: 127)

The notion that shared social behaviour is the beginning stage of learning throws responsibility upon those who interact socially with the growing child. By interacting in such a way that their awareness of approaches to skilled behaviour, their awareness of snags and obstacles to such behaviour are made available to learners, they are in fact (in Vygotsky's terms) *lending consciousness* to those learners and enabling them to perform in this relationship tasks they could not achieve if left to themselves. Again in Vygotsky's terms this is to open up for the learner 'the zone of proximal development' – an area of ability for which one's previous achievements have prepared one, but which awaits assisted performance for its realisation. That assistance may take the form of teacher/student interaction, or peer tutoring, or group activity – as well, of course, as in the give and take of social co-operation in and out of school.

Viewed thus broadly, we might add that a learner by taking part in rule-governed social behaviour may pick up the rules by means hardly distinguishable from the processes by which they were first socially derived – and by which they continue to be amended. On the other hand – along may come the traditional teacher and – with the best intentions, trying to be helpful – set out to observe the behaviour, analyse to codify the rules and teach the outcome as a recipe. Yes, this may sometimes be helpful, but as consistent pedagogy it is manifestly counter-productive.

Taking 'community' in a micro sense, it is likely that we all live in a number of communities. As teachers we are responsible for one of those – the classroom. It is clear we have a choice: we can operate so as to make that as rich an interactive learning community as we can, or we may continue to treat it as a captive audience for whatever instruction we choose to offer.

Wherever Vygotsky's voice can be heard, perhaps that choice constitutes a Zone of Proximal Development for many of us.

REFERENCES

Bruner, Jerome (1986) *Actual Minds, Possible Worlds,* Harvard University Press.
Kellogg, W. N. and L. A. (1933) *The Ape and the Child,* McGraw-Hill.
Piaget, Jean (1926) *Language and Thought of the Child,* Routledge & Kegan Paul.
Toulmin, Stephen (1978) 'The Mozart of Psychology', *New York Review of Books* Vol. XXV (14), Sept. 28.
Vygotsky, Lev (1939) 'Thought and Speech', *Psychiatry* Vol. 2, pp. 29–57.
Vygotsky, Lev (1962) *Thought and Language,* MIT Press.
Vygotsky, Lev (1971) *The Psychology of Art,* MIT Press.
Vygotsky, Lev (1978) *Mind in Society,* Harvard University Press.
Vygotsky, Lev (1987) *Thought and Language,* newly revised and edited, MIT Press.

Acknowledgements

Chapter 1 'Shaping the image of an English teacher', by R. Protherough and J. Atkinson, from *The Making of English Teachers* (1991), reproduced by permission of Open University Press.

Chapter 2 Edited version of 'Why it has happened: the "new orthodoxy"', by John Marenbon, from *English Our English* (1987), reproduced by permission of the Centre for Policy Studies.

Chapter 5 'Perspectives on oracy', by Alan Howe, from *Developing English* (1991), edited by Peter Dougill, reproduced by permission of Open University Press.

Chapter 7 'Monitoring and assessing the spoken word', by the National Oracy Project, from *Teaching Talking and and Learning in Key Stage 3* (1990), reproduced by permission of the National Curriculum Council.

Chapter 8 'Bilingualism and oracy', by Diana Cinamon, from *Talk No 1*, by the National Oracy Project, reproduced by permission of the National Curriculum Council.

Chapter 11 'Making sense of the media: from reading to culture', by D. Buckingham and J. Sefton-Green, from *English in Education* (1993), vol. 27, no. 2, reproduced by permission of the National Association for the Teaching of English and the authors.

Chapter 12 'Information Skills', by C. Harrison, from *Literacy without Frontiers: Proceedings of the 7th European and 28th United Kingdom Reading Association Annual Conference* (1991), edited by Fred Satow and Bill Gatherer, reproduced by permission of the United Kingdom Reading Association.

Chapter 15 'Out of the ghetto: teaching black literature', by Suzanne Scafe, from *The English Magazine*, no. 24, reproduced by permission of the English and Media Centre and the author.

Chapter 17 'Balancing the books', by S. Canwell and J. Ogborn, from *English in Education* (1993), vol. 27, no. 2.

Chapter 19 Edited version of Chapter 16 from *Cox on Cox: An English Curriculum for the 1990s* (1991), by Brian Cox, reproduced by permission of Hodder and Stoughton Ltd.

Chapter 24 Edited version of *Teaching Poetry in the Secondary School* (1986), by John Taylor, reproduced by permission of the Controller of Her Majesty's Stationery Office.

Chapter 27 'Differentiation in the Knowledge about Language Curriculum', by Ronald Carter, from *Knowledge about Language and the Curriculum: the LINC Reader* (1992), reproduced by permission of Hodder and Stoughton Ltd.

Chapter 28 'Vygotsky's contribution to pedagogical theory', by James Britton, from *English in Education* (1993), vol. 27, no. 2, reproduced by permission of the National Association for the Teaching of English and the authors.

Notes on sources

Chapter 1   Protherough, R. and Atkinson, J. (eds) (1991) *The Making of English Teachers*, Oxford University Press.
Chapter 2   Marenbon, J. (1987) *English Our English*, Centre for Policy Studies.
Chapter 3   Commissioned for this volume.
Chapter 4   Commissioned for this volume.
Chapter 5   (1991) *Developing English*, Open University Press.
Chapter 6   Commissioned for this volume.
Chapter 7   National Oracy Project *Teaching, Talking and Learning in Key Stage Three*, NCC.
Chapter 8   National Oracy Project Journal *Talk* 1.
Chapter 9   Commissioned for this volume.
Chapter 10   Commissioned for this volume.
Chapter 11   Buckingham, D. and Sefton-Green, J. (1993) *English in Education*, Vol. 27, No. 2.
Chapter 12   Harrison, C. (1991) *Literacy without Frontiers, Proceedings of the 7th European and 28th United Kingdom Reading Association Annual Conference, Heriot-Watt University, Edinburgh, July 1991*, ed. Freda Satow and Bill Gatherer.
Chapter 13   Commissioned for this volume.
Chapter 14   Commissioned for this volume.
Chapter 15   Scafe, S. *The English Magazine*, No. 24.
Chapter 16   Commissioned for this volume.
Chapter 17   Canwell, S. and Ogborn, J. (1993) *English in Education*, Vol. 27, No. 2.
Chapter 18   Meek, M. (1983) *Timely Voices: English Teaching in the Eighties*, ed. Roslyn Arnold, Oxford University Press.
Chapter 19   Cox, B. (1991) *Cox On Cox: An English Curriculum for the 1990s*, Hodder & Stoughton, edited version of chapter 16.
Chapter 20   Czerniewska's commentary commissioned for this volume. Landy from National Writing Project (1990) *Ways of Working*, Nelson.
Chapter 21   Commissioned for this volume.

Chapter 22   Commissioned for this volume.
Chapter 23   Commissioned for this volume.
Chapter 24   Edited version of pamphlet (1986), HMSO.
Chapter 25   Commissioned for this volume.
Chapter 26   Commissioned for this volume.
Chapter 27   Carter, R. (ed.) (1991) *Knowledge about Language and the Curriculum: The LINC Reader*, Hodder & Stoughton.
Chapter 28   Britton, J. (1988) *English in Education*, Autumn.

Index

reading and 230–2; students' writing and 227–30; teaching 28, 225, 232–4; variation in use of 233–4; variation when we write and speak 225
graphology 224
gravestones 234
group work 36, 37, 57, 59, 60, 161; discussion 69, 111; expert 38, 58; interviews 39, 61–2; sensitive groupings of children 75; use of questioning and responsiveness 39, 70; well-planned and organised 59

handwriting 177, 187
heritage version of English 127
History 183, 184
HMI (Her Majesty's Inspectorate) 50, 65, 94, 105, 106; new orthodoxy and 16, 17–18
Home Economics 184
'Home Front' work 184
'Home groups' 36, 58, 60
hot-seating 207–8

ideas 56, 57, 95, 216; Conservative 25; exploration of 235, 256; expression of 235; progressive (1960s) 27; sharing 143; trying out 58
identity: deprived of means of establishing 195; gender 244; major way in which people express 199; national 28, 128; patriarchal, of femininity 243; relationship between English and 237; relationship between language, learning and 98; speaker's individuality and 256; unique, meanings related to user's 248
ideologies 124, 127, 128, 196–7, 237–8, 254; objectionable 98
imagery 141, 214; simple, to evoke spoken language 136–7
images 139, 216; mental 161; stereotyped 73; video 161
imagination 27, 127, 202–9, 262; auditory 214–16; developing language through 208–9; feeding 141
improvisation 207
Independent, The 29
inexperienced readers 162–3
information 45, 89, 105–15, 117; collecting and shaping 173; database

as a source of 122; handling, from a wide variety of printed texts 106; key 231; literacy 89; selection, comprehension and integration of 107
information technology 90, 121
INSET (in-service training) 65
interaction 52, 53, 261
interlocutors 254

jigsawing 36, 58, 60
journalism 202
journalistic style 192
judgements 70

Key Stages 174; One 27–8, 40, 107–8, 109; Two 27–8, 40, 107, 108; Three 25, 27, 30, 41, 64, 107, 108, 140, 177; Four 41, 107, 109, 140, 177
Kingman Report (1988) 7, 27, 44–5, 79, 168, 173, 246, 249, 250–1, 252
knowledge 74; action 55; conscious/unconscious 256; control over 50; first-hand 150; intuitive 256; language 27, 29, 77, 121, 168, 175, 246–58; subject 193

labelling 112
language: ability to see through 225; ability to talk about 227; activities 97; aim to teach pupils about 18; alternative experiences 203; black literature 134–6; changes according to purpose, audience and context 255; classroom topics on 76–8; community 58, 76, 77; competence 174; content and 136; correlation between shapes on the page and 93; cross-curricular policy 178; dead 29, 30; decontextualised 248, 249, 252; difficulties of 144; discovery through 17; diversity 255; emotional reverberations of 216; emphasis given to role of 74; equality of 21; everyday, full of metaphors 215; experience of 171, 203; experiments in 177; functional model of 252–3; genre approach to 168; genres of 203; home 39, 72, 74–8, 87; how it works 224; informal 222; Kingman model of 250–1; knowledge about 27, 29, 77, 121, 168, 175, 246–58;

appropriate use of 227; attempt to reduce the importance of 20; discussing differences between dialect and 233; grammar of 21, 28, 225; importance of 22–3; incorporating forms for use, where appropriate 256; spoken 28, 29, 84–8; superiority of 23; teaching children to write and speak correctly 19; very close relationship between written language and the development of 80; written 29

standards in education 89

statement games 58

stereotypes 73, 241, 242; sexist or racist 188; social 189

stories: badly structured and boring 169; bible 234; children's awareness of structure 110; everyday 211; from oral traditions 110; implausibility of 102; interesting 169; parents etc. coming in to tell or read in class languages to all children 76; satisfying 174; tapes in community languages 76; telling 164; well-structured 169, 174

structural repetition 231

subconscious bias or prejudice 38

suffixes 233

summarising 68–9, 150

Sun 100–1, 199

syllables 214

synecdoche 213

synopsis/summary 109

syntax 224, 229, 231

talk 44, 50, 60, 74, 108; ability to 227, 246; assessment of 38, 64–71; collaborative 56; diaries 61; ephemeral nature of 56; exploratory 49; getting the climate right for 51–3; girls and boys, experiences of and attitudes to 38; opportunities which consider bilingual audiences and purpose 76; pair and small-group 57; planning for learning through 55–63; presentation 60; relationship to literacy 75; role of, in learning 72, 75; serving needs 49; tended to be squeezed out 50; well-defined ground rules for 59; what is shown through 69

tapes 58, 62, 76

tasks 205; *see also* SATs

Teacher Assessment 39–42, 64, 70

teachers 56–7; advice of, ignored by Ministers 25; appointment of 5; attitudes to poetry 213; best 195; bilingual 74; communication of interest and enthusiasm from 95; discussion and profile 52–3; good, aims of 23–4; grammar and 234; group conferences 62; intervention by 52; less experienced 28; mother tongue 74, 220; researchers and providers of appropriate reading 198; roles in the classroom 66; shaping the image of 5–15; special needs 38–9; time being wasted 27; training 6

teaching: bad 16; black literature 133–9; 'child centred' 19, 20, 23; developing new roles 37–8; as facilitating 155; grammar 28, 225; language, new ways 29; literature 213; meanings must be acknowledged in 94; personal growth model 12, 128; poetry in secondary school 210–19; pre-history of 5–7; by professionals, not by politicians 30; purpose of 130–1; reading in secondary school 154; repertoire of approaches 51; separate mother tongue 75; Shakespeare in schools 140–8; specific recommendations about methods 17; standard English writing and speaking 19; writing 167, 186–94, 229

teletext 117, 121

television 85, 92; soaps 102, 103, 197

tense forms 229

texts 93–4, 129, 252; black 133, 134; broad definition of 173; canon of 91, 127; challenging 108; choice of, for study in the classroom 28; computer 117–18; computer-related 116, 118, 119; concept must be widened 108; considerate 109; context and 133, 134, 139; creating own 120; critical readers able to place own values and experiences in relation to those of 95; deep structure of 109; device for the exclusion and separation of some from others 126; different types of